BORN IN
THE U.S.A.

BORN IN THE U.S.A.

BRUCE SPRINGSTEEN IN AMERICAN LIFE

Third Edition
Revised and Expanded

JIM CULLEN

RUTGERS UNIVERSITY PRESS

New Brunswick, Camden, and Newark, New Jersey
London and Oxford

Rutgers University Press is a department of Rutgers, The State University of New Jersey, one of the leading public research universities in the nation. By publishing worldwide, it furthers the University's mission of dedication to excellence in teaching, scholarship, research, and clinical care.

Library of Congress Cataloging-in-Publication Data
Names: Cullen, Jim, 1962- author.
Title: Born in the U.S.A.: Bruce Springsteen in American life / Jim Cullen.
Description: Third edition, fully revised and expanded. | New Brunswick:
    Rutgers University Press, 2024. | Includes bibliographical references and index.
Identifiers: LCCN 2023024819 | ISBN 9781978838062 (cloth) |
    ISBN 9781978838079 (epub) | ISBN 9781978838086 (pdf)
Subjects: LCSH: Springsteen, Bruce—Criticism and interpretation.
Classification: LCC ML420.S77 C85 2024 | DDC 782.42166092 [B]—
    dc23/eng/20230622
LC record available at https://lccn.loc.gov/2023024819

A British Cataloging-in-Publication record for this book is
available from the British Library.

References to internet websites (URLs) were accurate at the time of writing. Neither the author nor Rutgers University Press is responsible for URLs that may have expired or changed since the manuscript was prepared.

∞ The paper used in this publication meets the requirements of the American National Standard for Information Sciences—Permanence of Paper for Printed Library Materials, ANSI Z39.48-1992.

rutgersuniversitypress.org

For Gordon Anderson Sterling (1963–2015),
who listened

CONTENTS

A SPRINGSTEEN CHRONOLOGY   ix

Introduction   1

1   Republicans and republicans
Reagan and Springsteen at Center Stage   9

2   democratic Character
Springsteen and the American Artistic Tradition   31

3   Realms of Kings
Springsteen and the American Dream   59

4   Borne in the U.S.A.
Springsteen and the Weight of War   83

5   The Good Life
Springsteen's Play Ethic   109

6   Man's Job
Springsteen's Masculinity   133

7   God and Bruce Springsteen   169

Conclusion   203

ACKNOWLEDGMENTS   207

NOTES   209

INDEX   227

A SPRINGSTEEN CHRONOLOGY

1949

Bruce Frederick Springsteen is born on September 23 in Freehold, New Jersey, to Douglas Springsteen and Adele Zerilli Springsteen. He will be joined by sisters Virginia (1950) and Pamela (1962).

1965

Springsteen joins the Castiles, a local rock band. It is the first of a number of bands he will lead, join, or form over the next five years, including Steel Mill, Child, and Dr. Zoom and the Sonic Boom.

1969

Springsteen's parents and younger sister Virginia relocate to San Mateo, California. He stays behind in New Jersey, moving to nearby Asbury Park.

1971

After playing in ensembles that include future E Street Band drummer Vini Lopez, organist Danny Federici, pianist David Sancious, saxophonist Clarence Clemons, and guitarist Steve Van Zandt, Springsteen decides to pursue a solo career as a singer/songwriter.

1972

Springsteen signs a management contract with independent producers Mike Appel and Jim Crecetos (Appel later buys out his partner's interest). Springsteen auditions for John Hammond of Columbia Records. Label president Clive Davis agrees to sign Springsteen to the label.

1973

Greetings from Asbury Park, NJ is released in January. Sales are poor.
The Wild, the Innocent & the E Street Shuffle is released in November. Sales are better, but still tepid.

1974

Springsteen's performing and recording ensemble is now officially known as the E Street Band, after the address just south of Asbury Park in Belmar where pianist David Sancious lives with his mother. E Street intersects with Tenth Avenue (as in "Tenth Avenue Freezeout").

Rolling Stone record-reviews editor Jon Landau attends a Springsteen show at the Harvard Square Theater in Cambridge, Massachusetts, in May. "I saw rock and roll future, and its name is Bruce Springsteen," he writes in a review for Boston's *Real Paper*.

1975

In August, Springsteen makes a series of acclaimed performances at New York's fabled Bottom Line nightclub (one show is broadcast live on a Manhattan radio station). A review by critic John Rockwell appears on page one of the *New York Times*.

In September, *Born to Run* is released. In October, Springsteen makes the covers of *Time* and *Newsweek* simultaneously.

1976

Amid growing tensions, Appel and Springsteen file suits against each other in July. Appel wins an injunction preventing Springsteen from producing an album with Landau.

1977

Springsteen and Appel settle their differences out of court in May. Landau is now officially Springsteen's manager and producer.

1978

Darkness on the Edge of Town is released in July.

1979

Springsteen performs for the Musicians United for Safe Energy (MUSE) concerts at Madison Square Garden in September. He later appears in the documentary film about the event.

1980

The River, a double album, is released in October. It becomes his first in a string of number-one albums on the *Billboard* chart. The album's first single, "Hungry Heart," lands in the top ten on the *Billboard* pop chart.

1981

Springsteen organizes a benefit concert for the Vietnam Veterans of America in Los Angeles in September, an expression of concern for veterans' affairs that will culminate in *Born in the U.S.A.*

1982

Nebraska, a solo record of largely acoustic songs, is released in September.

1984

Born in the U.S.A. is released in June. It will become one of the bestselling albums of all time (in excess of 30 million copies) and will spawn seven top-ten singles.

At a campaign stop in New Jersey while running for reelection to the presidency, Ronald Reagan cites "the message of hope in songs of a man so many young Americans admire—New Jersey's own Bruce Springsteen."

1985

Springsteen performs a duet with Stevie Wonder in "We Are the World," a single and album of the same name—to which he also contributes a rendition of the Jimmy Cliff song "Trapped"—as part of the "USA for Africa" efforts to help victims of the Ethiopian famine. He also works with Steve Van Zandt on *Sun City*, a benefit song and album to combat apartheid in South Africa.

Springsteen marries model/actress Julianne Phillips in May.

1986

Bruce Springsteen Live 1975–85, a forty-song, multi-disk set, is released in November.

1987

Tunnel of Love is released in September.

1988

Springsteen headlines a six-week global Amnesty International tour with Sting, Peter Gabriel, Tracy Chapman, and Youssou N'Dour.

1989

Springsteen and Phillips divorce.

Springsteen dissolves the E Street Band, though he will continue to play with assorted members on an ad-hoc basis and will reconstitute the ensemble periodically over the course of ensuing decades.

1990

A son, Evan James, is born to Springsteen and E Street Band member Patti Scialfa.

1991

Springsteen and Scialfa marry in June. A daughter, Jessica Rae, is born in December.

1992

Human Touch and *Lucky Town* are released simultaneously in April.

1993

Springsteen writes and performs "Streets of Philadelphia" for the Jonathan Demme film *Philadelphia*. It will win an Academy Award for Best Original Song the following winter.

1994

A son, Sam Ryan, is born in July.

1995

Greatest Hits is released in January. Springsteen reunites the E Street Band for a club performance filmed by Demme and broadcast on MTV.

The Ghost of Tom Joad is released in November.

1998

Douglas Springsteen dies in April.

Tracks, a four-CD, sixty-six–song compilation including many previously unreleased recordings, is issued in November.

Songs, a book of Springsteen lyrics with commentary, is published. It will be reissued in an expanded edition in 2003.

1999

Springsteen is inducted into the Rock & Roll Hall of Fame.

Springsteen begins an international tour with the reconstituted E Street Band.

2001

Bruce Springsteen and the E Street Band / Live in New York City is released in March. One song, "American Skin (41 Shots)," generates controversy for perceived anti-police sentiment.

Springsteen performs "My City of Ruins" as part of a relief telethon in the aftermath of 9/11.

2002

The Rising, a response to 9/11, is released in July. It is Springsteen's first studio album with the E Street Band since *Born in the U.S.A.*

2004

Springsteen endorses and performs for Democratic presidential candidate John Kerry.

2005

Devils and Dust is released in March.

2006

We Shall Overcome, a collection of folk songs honoring Pete Seeger, is released in April.

2007

Live in Dublin, an album performed with a Preservation Hall-style jazz band that mixes folk songs and Springsteen compositions, is released in June.

Magic, an album with the E Street Band, is released in September.

2008

Springsteen campaigns for Democratic presidential candidate Barack Obama. He will perform at the Lincoln Memorial during Obama's inauguration the following January.

2009

Working on a Dream is released in January.

2012

Wrecking Ball is released in March.

2014

High Hopes is released in January.
The E Street Band is inducted into the Rock & Roll Hall of Fame.

2016

Born to Run, a memoir, is published in September.
Springsteen is awarded the Presidential Medal of Freedom by President Obama in November.

2017

Springsteen on Broadway opens in New York. It will run into 2018 and will be revived in 2021.

2019

Western Stars is released in June.

2020

Letter to You is released in October.

2021

Renegades: Born in the U.S.A., a coffee-table compendium including transcripts of a Spotify podcast of the same name with Barack Obama in early 2021, is published in October.
Springsteen sells the rights to his recordings and publication of his songs to Sony Music, parent company to Columbia Records, where he has spent his entire career. The deal, estimated at $550 million, is believed to be the largest transaction of its kind to date.

2022

Springsteen's first grandchild, Lily Harper Springsteen, is born to son Sam in July.

Only the Strong Survive, the first in a series of planned albums of cover songs, is released in November.

BORN IN
THE U.S.A.

GROWIN' UP

FIGURE I.1. Still from a live performance of Bruce Springsteen performing "Spirit in the Night" at the Ahmanson Theatre in Los Angeles on May 1, 1973. For many of us, whether we have seen him live or not, Springsteen has been a lifelong companion. (Source: ABC-TV)

Introduction

I N THE DRAMA OF OUR INDIVIDUAL LIVES, each of us has a large
cast of supporting players. Some stay with us over a course of many
decades. With others, our dialogue may be relatively brief but intense.
Still others periodically wander on or off our stages, characters we
find amusing, bemusing, or irritating when we encounter them in
short scenes of lesser or greater personal significance. Such are the
means by which our stories are scripted.

There's another set of people in our lives worth noting here: people
we've never met but with whom we may nevertheless have a meaningful relationship. Some of these figures are long since dead—ancestors,
literal or figurative, whose legacies affect the way we live in the present.
Others may come into our lives more indirectly, like distant bosses for
whom we work or celebrities who happen to be our generational peers.
We may not be able to address such people directly, but we nevertheless
engage with them in ways that are no less meaningful, even if silently.

For tens of millions of Americans, Bruce Springsteen is one of
those people (figure I.1). We began listening to him at different points
and in different walks of life, with greater or lesser degrees of intensity. For many of us, this relationship has been lifelong. One reason
it's often been intense is because Springsteen himself has shown a
high degree of consciousness about his audience, as revealed in things
he's said and choices he's made, in a career that's now spanned more

than a half-century. The fact that you're reading this book is evidence of that bond—and evidence of a longing to be part of a larger community. In an important sense, it's that community—one that extends back long before any of us were born and will live on long after we are gone—that's the main reason for this book: to stake our place in a grand saga. I'd like to take a moment to explain why and how I tried to write it, in the hope that we can understand our time, our place, and our roles in that saga a little better.

———

I think of myself as a second-generation Springsteen fan. The first generation—people I've read about and listened to for many years—witnessed the immaculate conception of the Springsteen legend. They were there on the Jersey Shore, in the clubs, and at record stores for *Greetings from Asbury Park* and *The Wild, the Innocent and the E Street Shuffle*. The first apostles who evangelized for Springsteen—those right there in Asbury Park, like Robert Santelli, followed by the national rock critics of the 1970s whose careers coincided with a golden age of music journalism—were people who rubbed elbows backstage with him, relating what they heard from firsthand experience and direct conversation. There was nevertheless a sense of awe about their encounters, reflected as early as 1973, when Peter Knobler and Greg Mitchell wrote "Who Is Bruce Springsteen, and Why Are We Saying All These Wonderful Things about Him?" for the early rock magazine *Crawdaddy*. The "rock critic establishment," a term coined by *Village Voice* writer Robert Christgau, consisted of figures like Lester Bangs, Jon Landau, and, a little later, Dave Marsh, all of whom lionized the young Springsteen. (Landau became his producer and manager, Marsh his biographer).[1]

I was a child when all this happened. I had older, savvier cousins, and that's how I happened to see the covers of albums like *Born to Run* and *Darkness on the Edge of Town* as an early adolescent, but they didn't mean much to me. It was only with the release of *The River* in 1980 and Springsteen's first hit single, "Hungry Heart," that I snapped to attention. And I haven't stopped listening since.

I was an ordinary specimen in the Springsteen demographic: young, White, and suburban (I would once have included "male" as well, but

I long ago learned that Springsteen's female audience is also considerable).[2] Also, like many such people, I was upwardly mobile—and inclined to romanticize the working-class roots I was leaving behind. Born at the tail end of the Baby Boom, I was late to the party in any number of ways, among them for Springsteenmania. A student journalist with inchoate literary ambitions, I lacked the experience, imagination, and worldliness of that first generation of Springsteen enthusiasts. But I was nevertheless sufficiently obsessed to spend my senior year of college writing a thesis on Springsteen. I look back with affectionate gratitude for my adviser, the distinguished ethnomusicologist Jeff Todd Titon, who patiently endured my song-by-song reading of Springsteen's catalog, an effort more notable for its enthusiasm than its insight.

However, I did go on to acquire one thing that the previous generation of Springsteen writers did not: a PhD. I completed a doctorate in American Studies with the hope that it would teach me how to write books. And that's what I did, beginning with a dissertation on how the Civil War has been portrayed in twentieth-century popular culture, and a second book tracing the rise of the mass media from the colonial period to the present. Then, while holding a junior teaching post at Harvard, I circled back to my adolescent obsession and began work on the first iteration of this book.

It was clear from the outset what I could *not* do: produce an insider or biographical account of Springsteen's life and work. What I thought I *could* do was to situate him historically in what my editor told me to make the subtitle of the book: "the American Tradition." I didn't like the phrase—in an age of multiculturalism I was rightly uneasy about that definite article. But like a lot of ambitious people, I made compromises. I couldn't be an apostle, but there was still room to be St. Paul: the outsider who codified and spread the Word to the gentiles in the groves of academe.

The fact that Mr. Springsteen had not been crucified, much less resurrected, was only the first in a series of problems with this conceit. Another was my callowness and relative youth, in which I failed to see the degree to which my work would be seen—and in fact was—a "clip job" in which I depended heavily on existing sources that I didn't always interpret in compelling (or sufficiently well contextualized) ways. But if my lack of self-doubt wasn't exactly a saving grace, it did endow me with enough doggedness to pursue and achieve publication. I distinctly remember a night on an Amtrak train ride commuting between Boston and New York in the winter of 1997, a few months before the book's release, when I suspended my usual caution and allowed myself to believe I was on the cusp of becoming rich and famous.

An equally vivid memory—the realization that this wouldn't happen—occurred while on tour to support the book, in a hotel room in West Long Branch, New Jersey, overlooking the boardwalk that ran through Springsteen's beloved Asbury Park. My life would take a somewhat ironic turn: within a few years I would leave Harvard to become a high-school teacher, while simultaneously embarking on a quarter-century of writing academic books for university presses, moving away from the musical obsessions that had been central to my work up to that point.

There was a lot of uncertainty amid this struggle to find my level, but one thing remained clear: I was done with Springsteen for the foreseeable future. The idea of successfully staking a claim to such territory seemed not only unlikely but pathetic, and in the years that followed I wrote about a variety of subjects, among them the American Dream, Roman Catholicism, the U.S. presidency, television, and film history, even making a foray into fiction. I continued to follow Springsteen's career, of course, and watched as a steady stream— perhaps more accurately, a flood—of books entered the publishing bloodstream, among them works by Springsteen himself. I reviewed a couple and wrote an occasional essay, but had no intention of going back to my subject in any substantial way.

In 2018, I was approached to write a piece for *Long Walk Home*, a collection of essays organized to commemorate Springsteen's seventieth birthday the following year.[3] I was honored to be included among a set of authors that included the great rock critic Greil Marcus, the novelist Richard Russo, and Peter Ames Carlin, author of a bestselling Springsteen biography, as well as a host of younger scholars who were taking Springsteen scholarship in entirely new directions. Because the editor of that volume, with whom I was eager to work again, specialized in the regional history of the New York metropolitan era, I pitched an idea comparing the careers of two native sons: Billy Joel of Long Island (a subject about which I had started a manuscript, later dropped) and his geographic counterpart in Bruce Springsteen of New Jersey. The project, *Bridge and Tunnel Boys*, was slated for publication in time for the two men's seventy-fifth birthdays.

Having now reimmersed myself in Springsteeniana, I decided I wanted to return to this project. And, finally, just possibly, to get it right—or, at any rate, make it a little better. That's how we ended up here together on this page.

––––––

When I wrote *Born in the U.S.A.* in the mid-1990s, my goal was to situate Springsteen in the larger landscape of American history through a series of chapters that engaged aspects of our national experience: its democratic cultural traditions, its fabled work ethic, the American Dream. I've long felt that the second half of the book worked better than the first half, which I felt strained a little too hard to place him on the side of the angels. My goal in this revision will be to temper the occasional stridency of the original while enriching the text with another generation of historical experience.

The book begins with "Republicans and republicans," revisiting a notorious chapter in Springsteen's life: Ronald Reagan's appropriation of "Born in the U.S.A." while running for re-election in 1984. Springsteen partisans at the time considered this to be a cynical ploy that belied Springsteen's cherished liberal values. There is much truth to this, but it's not the whole story. "Born in the U.S.A." is, among other things, a celebration of American resilience, and Reagan's handlers shrewdly identified a vein of conservatism in Springsteen's artistic vision, something that has continued to course through his work even as he has moved more avowedly toward the progressive left in the decades since.

Chapter 2, "democratic Character," in effect flips the script and looks at the way Springsteen also embodies a contending national tradition that emphasizes equality rather than mobility. I still think it makes sense to position Springsteen in a heritage first articulated by

Ralph Waldo Emerson, embodied by Walt Whitman, and carried forward by a cavalcade of successors that include Mark Twain and John Steinbeck.

Chapter 3, "Realms of Kings," stakes out two poles of the American Dream—those of Elvis Presley and Martin Luther King, Jr.—and situates Springsteen between them. Presley represents the Dream in its most lavish, as well as most tragic, materialism, while King appealed to the nation's yearning for its better self. Though Presley is the more obvious lodestar of Springsteen's career, he has continued to demonstrate a consistently integrationist vision associated with MLK long after it was fashionable to do so.

Chapter 4, "Borne in the U.S.A.," remains the book's keystone chapter, tracing the origins of what is arguably Springsteen's most famous song and contextualizing it in the American experience of armed conflict. The subject of "Born in the U.S.A." is the Vietnam War, a crucible experience for Springsteen's generation. In the decades since, that conflict has receded in the national collective imagination, but Springsteen's engagement with war and the challenges it poses in a democratic society has remained strong, as reflected in the songs from his 9/11 album *The Rising* (2002) as well as *Devils and Dust* (2005).

Chapter 5, "The Good Life," inverts the mythology of the American work ethic in favor of something I call "the play ethic"—an impulse to make play a form of joyful exertion—drawing on the work of scholars such as Hannah Arendt, Johann Huizinga, and Jackson Lears. The play ethic is evidenced most fully in Springsteen's legendary live shows but is apparent in many of his individual songs as well. As he and his audience have aged, the challenge of sustaining that ethic while has come into focus, as have, perhaps, the limits of productive play as a goal.

Chapter 6, "Man's Job," was perhaps the most vexing to revisit, having dated the most quickly. The model of masculinity that Springsteen crystallized in his heyday reflected traditional notions of manhood inherited from his father, the currents of feminism he absorbed as a young man, and an emerging queer consciousness that he embraced at century's end. The question now is what components of this synthesis remain viable in a time when notions of sex and gender are as contested as they have been in many decades.

The final chapter of the book, "God and Bruce Springsteen," explores Springsteen's religious vision. A lapsed Catholic who emphatically embraced apostasy, Springsteen gradually returned to the fold as he moved into middle age—a process that has intensified in the decades since. In a time of receding religious engagement, his ongoing commitment to his faith, however uneasy and contested, is worth exploring for what it says about him, and, perhaps more importantly, about an evolving nation.

Bruce Springsteen's peak of notoriety in the 1980s coincided with a time when American life seemed to have a broad and stable center, reflected in a broadcast-media culture, a huge record-buying public, and a strong sense of national identity that was revitalized in the Reagan era. By the 1990s, however, this equilibrium was dissipating amid a globalizing economy, rapid technological change, and the rising moral force of minority identities. *Born in the U.S.A.* was written against this backdrop and implicitly suggested that Springsteen represented what was best in a receding synthesis. This new edition, notwithstanding the significant amount of rewriting and updating that it represents, still reflects its genetic origins in the nineties. By the 2020s, that synthesis had become a historical artifact to which many Americans wished a gleeful good riddance. That's understandable and even necessary. But as our society continues to splinter, it remains worthwhile to consider what has held it together for so long. This has been the central preoccupation of Bruce Springsteen's career. That career merits ongoing reconsideration.

—*Jim Cullen*
November 2023

UPSTAGING THE BOSS

FIGURE 1.1. Ronald Reagan at a campaign rally in Hammonton, New Jersey, September 19, 1984. "America's future rests in a thousand dreams in our hearts," he told the crowd that day. "It rests in the message of hope so many young people admire: New Jersey's own Bruce Springsteen." Some Springsteen fans reacted with outrage over Reagan's cooptation of Springsteen's appeal, but it reflected a shrewd and not entirely inaccurate recognition of Springsteen's embodiment of core American values. (Source: Reagan Library)

CHAPTER 1

Republicans and republicans

Reagan and Springsteen at Center Stage

B RUCE SPRINGSTEEN'S LIFE STORY is well known to many of his fans, and over the course of the last half-century a series of anecdotes and incidents—termed "Bruce stories" by ethnomusicologist Daniel Cavicchi—have taken on the quality of folklore.[1] There's his troubled relationship with his father, for example, which Springsteen himself mythologized in many songs and to which many of his listeners relate. There are testimonials, described in near-religious awe, about his legendary string of shows at New York's Bottom Line nightclub in 1975, when he dazzled an audience of industry insiders and clubgoers as he was poised on the brink of stardom.[2] But no episode is more widely known among those who were alive at the time than President Ronald Reagan's invocation of Springsteen at a campaign rally in New Jersey when Reagan was running for reelection in 1984 (figure 1.1).

Nowadays, pop stars are common figures in presidential campaigns, and Springsteen himself would eventually form a buddy relationship with Barack Obama. But back then it was pretty unusual. (Frank Sinatra had been close to John F. Kennedy before he was president, but Kennedy's advisers told him to create some distance between the two after he was elected, largely because of Sinatra's mob ties.)[3] Even to casual observers at the time, Reagan's citation of Springsteen was widely considered clueless, cynical, or both—the tactic of a venal politician seeking to tap the magic of a generational icon for electoral advantage.

There is, of course, considerable validity in this interpretation of the event. But it's also the case that the people who made it happen knew exactly what they were doing in orchestrating this campaign set piece. And what they were doing, beyond exploiting Springsteen's name for Reagan's benefit, was intuitively recognizing an important truth: that Reagan was a Republican, and Springsteen was a republican, and that there was bona fide overlap in the two terms despite the meaningful difference in capitalization. More than that: both were also conservatives.[4] Admittedly, not in the same way—Reagan's conservatism was political and Springsteen's cultural; Reagan sought a restoration of pre-New Deal laissez-faire capitalism, while Springsteen sought to preserve the legacy of the 1960s—but these very real and important differences jostled alongside powerful temperamental commitments to a patriotic idiom, one that would later form the basis of Springsteen's friendship with Obama.[5] Only by recognizing this facet of Springsteen's life and work can we truly understand just how fully he inhabited the spirit of his times, as well as the legacy he would bequeath to musical history. Reagan, in that sometimes exasperating, seemingly obtuse way of his, was onto something about Springsteen. We need to understand what it was if we're going to understand the resonant place of both in American life.

Right Turns

His attention elicited from me two responses. The first was . . .
"Fucker!" The second was, "The president said my name!" Or maybe it was the other way around.

—Springsteen on Ronald Reagan's
mention of him on the campaign trail, 1984

Before getting into the details, it's worth taking time to reconstruct the moment in which the Reagan-Springsteen affair unfolded. It took place in September of 1984, when Reagan was in the final stretch of his reelection campaign against Democratic candidate Walter Mondale, who had been the nation's vice president four years earlier. In the 1980 election, Reagan had run against the incumbent Jimmy Carter, and for a long time there were many who regarded Reagan as "an amiable dunce," in the words of longtime Democratic political operative Clark Clifford.[6] The sixty-nine-year-old Reagan was considered too old, and insufficiently informed, to become president. But amid a weak, inflation-riddled economy and the humiliating spectacle of the Iran hostage crisis, Reagan won a surprisingly decisive victory. He garnered additional goodwill after surviving an assassination attempt two months after his inauguration. Doubts about Reagan's competency—and the decency of his economic policies—nevertheless intensified during the severe economic downturn of 1981–1982, the worst the nation had experienced since the Great Depression. But in 1983 the economy began to recover, and Reagan's sunny optimism began to synch with the rising spirit of the times. His campaign slogan in 1984 was "Morning in America," and a brightening national mood made him an increasingly prohibitive favorite in the election. Indeed, he would go on to win forty-nine of fifty states (losing only Mondale's native Minnesota) in one of the most crushing victories in American political history.

September of 1984 was also a bright moment in the history of popular music. The record business had undergone a sharp downturn at the end of the seventies, losing ground to video games and home taping on cassettes. But the industry was revitalized by the advent of the compact disc and the arrival of the music video, including the launch of the MTV network in 1981. As summer gave way to fall in 1984, the premier pop stars of the eighties were riding high. Michael Jackson's *Thriller*, released almost two years earlier, was still spawning hits, and Prince, Madonna, Cyndi Lauper, and a revitalized Tina Turner were jostling on the radio. It was, by many reckonings, a golden age.

This was also a high point in the career of Bruce Springsteen. He had developed a fervent following a decade earlier, even if his early records had underperformed relative to expectations. The release of *Born to Run* brought him national recognition in 1975, but in the years that followed Springsteen was still more of a critical darling than a bona fide star. The release of *The River* in 1980 gave him his first number-one album and generated his first hit single with "Hungry Heart." But *Nebraska*, released in the fall of 1982, was a stark, mostly acoustic record that arrived in the depths of economic recession, whose mood it matched. The ensuing album, *Born in the U.S.A.*, was built on a foundation of tracks laid down at the time of *Nebraska* and reflected some of its downbeat themes. But it was a much brighter record musically, with polished production values that reflected the shifting currents of the culture. Springsteen and his label, Columbia Records, made an all-out commercial push, and the album became a smash, generating seven hit singles and ultimately selling tens of millions of copies. Embarking on an international tour in 1984, Springsteen was on the top of the world pretty much at the same time Reagan was.

That said, the figurative worlds the two inhabited were largely self-contained, with little in the way of obvious contact between them. The sequence of events through which their careers would converge was triggered by Becky Weinberg, a high-school history teacher in New Jersey who was married to Springsteen's drummer.[7] Weinberg was a fan of *This Week with David Brinkley*, a Sunday-morning news program in which the famed anchorman hosted a series of regulars and guests to discuss current events. A fixture of the show was the conservative writer George Will, the former editor of the *National Review* who had moved on to become a syndicated columnist for the *Washington Post*, a job he holds to this day. Weinberg wondered if Will and ABC reporter Sam Donaldson would like to see a Springsteen show when the E Street Band came to Washington in late August of 1984. She and her husband asked a mutual friend to contact Will, who agreed to attend. The forty-three-year-old columnist, known for his formal diction and signature bow ties, was excited by the prospect of attending his first rock concert. "He called me up and asked 'What should I dress like?'" Becky remembered. "So he came in his bow tie, of course, but he wore a sport jacket and slacks rather than a suit."[8]

Will liked what he heard, despite packing cotton in his ears and leaving early. "I have not got a clue about Springsteen's politics, if any, but flags get waved at his concerts while he sings songs about hard times," he wrote in a column that was syndicated nationally on September 13. "He is no whiner, and the recitation of closed factories and other problems always seems punctuated by a grand, cheerful affirmation: 'Born in the U.S.A.!'"[9]

"Grand" and "cheerful" would not likely be among the first words a Springsteen fan would associate with the title track of Springsteen's latest album. Springsteen's biographer Dave Marsh described the column as "such a perversion of what Springsteen was trying to communicate that it constituted an obscenity." Others, however, were intrigued by Will's remarks. Among them were members of the Reagan communications team with whom Will was in contact. Reagan would be campaigning the following week in New Jersey; perhaps Springsteen would be willing to appear with him there. His agent politely declined. (John Mellencamp and Billy Joel had already rejected similar overtures.)[10]

Reagan proceeded with the trip—and proceeded to cite Springsteen. "America's future rests in a thousand dreams in our hearts," he told a large crowd in the suburban town of Hammonton, New Jersey, on the afternoon of September 19. "It rests in the message of hope so many young people admire: New Jersey's own Bruce Springsteen." (The crowd roared its approval.) "And helping those dreams come true is what this job of mine is all about."[11]

It's not hard to see why Reagan's campaign regarded Springsteen as a useful political asset. The White working class, vividly celebrated in Springsteen's songs, was a pillar of Reagan's emerging constituency, a crucial bloc which, along with evangelical Christians and free-market libertarians, was forming a governing coalition that would dominate American politics straight through the 1980s and beyond. So laying claim to Springsteen's appeal was more than political window dressing; it reflected a broader strategy in a major electoral realignment. Among other tactics, this strategy involved stoking the resentments of those uneasy about Black gains since the civil rights movement and capitalizing on the ill will generated by elite liberals who had regarded the working class with suspicion, if not outright hostility, since the late 1960s.[12] This strategy also involved championing religious and patriotic causes that the American left had largely abandoned in the wake of the Vietnam War.

Although he was still relatively apathetic and ignorant about politics in these years, Springsteen instinctively rejected key components of the Reagan political synthesis. "I don't know if he's a bad man," he told Kurt Loder of *Rolling Stone* a few months later. "But I think there's a large group of people in this country whose dreams don't mean that much to him, that just get indiscriminately swept aside."[13] Springsteen was largely correct. But before explaining how and why, it may be worth taking a little time to unpack the distinctive political consciousness he had absorbed by that point in his life, a consciousness he inherited from a long line of literal and figurative ancestors whose traits unconsciously surfaced in his work like ideological DNA.

Natural Aristocrats

We may define a republic to be, or at least may bestow that name on, a government which derives all its powers directly or indirectly from the great body of the people, and is administered by persons holding their offices during pleasure, for a limited period, or during good behavior.

—James Madison, *The Federalist* (#39), 1788

Many of us know that, strictly speaking, the United States is not a democracy. Democracies are societies in which all citizens have a say in lawmaking, with ancient Athens as the classic example. Even there, participation was actually tightly circumscribed, as the ambit of citizenship did not include women or slaves, among other inhabitants. This nation, by contrast, is a republic—a society in which representatives make decisions in the name of the people. Those representatives are elected by citizens (again, a term with many exclusions). This is why, most precisely, the United States is a democratic republic ("democratic" being in this case a modifier of its republican essence, distinguishing this country from, say, oligarchic republics led by a ruling class). Though we often speak of the United States in a shorthand way as a democracy, in so doing we obscure the limits of the term and the struggles it would take to widen its meaning, not to mention the fact that the Founders, fearful of mob rule, actually regarded pure democracy with skepticism and even alarm.

It may seem odd to belabor the point about the United States not being a democracy, but it's important to emphasize that, for the Founders, the concept of a republic had primacy.[14] The immediate point of comparison for their cherished republicanism was not democracy but rather the alternative posed by the British empire: a constitutional monarchy. As monarchies went, the British variety was not, even in the eighteenth century, the most tyrannical, given that there was a long-standing agreement—then as now, the British constitution was unwritten—that there were limits on what a king could do, going back to the Magna Carta of 1215. But Great Britain was still a political entity with a king as the head of state and a deeply rooted aristocracy. In such a society, opportunity and privilege were, to put it in the most elemental of terms, a matter of who your daddy was.

The Founders—very few of whom, relative privilege notwithstanding, came from the top tier of society—were after something different. Here, as in so many other contexts, it was Thomas Jefferson who defined that alternative vision most succinctly, in an 1813 letter to John Adams: "There is a natural aristocracy among men. The grounds of this are virtue and talents."[15] But while Jefferson considered such an aristocracy a more legitimate foundation for governance than a traditional—which is to say *un*natural—aristocracy, he was aware that there was nevertheless an elitism in his own formulation that needed to be hedged. Like many of his contemporaries, Jefferson had a deep belief in what was called "the moral sense," an ability to grasp right and wrong that was inherently egalitarian. He also believed that the legitimacy of a natural aristocracy rested on its willingness and ability to act on behalf of—as James Madison put it, to "administer"— the common good. This is something Jefferson explained to his nephew Peter Carr in a letter of 1787: "State a moral case to a ploughman and a professor. The former will decide it as well, and often better than the latter, because he has not been led astray by artificial rules."[16]

The professor—a term Jefferson was using metaphorically—had both expertise and an ability to grasp the elemental in ways that fostered both virtue and competency, and then to act on behalf of the plowmen, who were wise enough to recognize, and choose, good governance. The political coalition over which Jefferson and his successors (including Madison and James Monroe) presided was formally known as the Democratic-Republicans. The name itself implies Jefferson's concept of the ideal mutual relationship between privilege and equality, though in common parlance its members were called simply "Republicans." In contrast, the faction led by Alexander Hamilton, the Federalists, were more frank about their elitism, even if Hamilton—"a bastard son of a Scotch pedlar," in the contemptuous words of John Adams—was about as natural a natural aristocrat who ever lived.[17]

John Adams was less sanguine about the self-evident appeal of natural aristocracy than Jefferson, and he was far more clear about the way slavery undermined the clarity and legitimacy of Jefferson's formulation. While he shared with Jefferson a belief in the existence of a natural aristocracy, he also noted that, human nature being what it is, old habits had a way of worming their way into new traditions. "Birth and Wealth are conferred on Some Men, as imperiously by Nature, as Genius, Strength or Beauty," he told Jefferson a couple of weeks after his "natural aristocracy" letter. Good looks and money tended to go together, whether or not the person who enjoyed them was smart or virtuous, he noted.[18] As in so many other ways, Adams was less confident than Jefferson that beautiful ideas would become benevolent realities.

Such skepticism notwithstanding, the ghosts of the Jeffersonian formula infuse one of the more powerful ideological constructs of our time: meritocracy. In its purest formulation, meritocracy is a system that identifies talent and develops it, without regard to birth, so that the best and brightest can serve society as a whole. It's a notion that in fact has done a lot of good in the world. But modern meritocracy, like the idea of natural aristocracy on which it's based, has always generated opposition. One early manifestation was Shays Rebellion of 1786, when a Massachusetts Revolutionary War veteran took up arms against the state over onerous economic policies that were widely regarded as elitist. It was at its core a democratic rebellion. An alarmed James Madison convinced George Washington to throw his support behind reforming the infant nation's government so as to provide more authority and accountability, which is how we got the U.S. Constitution: a new blueprint that centralized authority and circumscribed the aspirational ideals of the Declaration of Independence. (Adams may have been a skeptic about dreamy Jeffersonian ideals, but it was Madison, the Constitution's architect, who actually checked them and kept Jefferson grounded.)

In some important respects, Bruce Springsteen is an heir to the Jeffersonian ideal. It's telling in this regard to note that he was born in Freehold, New Jersey, a town where his ancestors had deep roots. Freehold's origins extend back to the late seventeenth century, and the town is a case where the place-name reflected the tenor of its population. A "freeholder" was a person who owned a relatively small piece of land outright ("in fee simple") and typically farmed it for family use. Such people lived in marked contrast to plantation owners, who controlled vast estates; to urban or rural workers, who were tenants; and to slaves, who did not control their own labor. For Jefferson, freeholders were, in his famous description, "the chosen people of God, if ever he had a chosen people, whose breasts he has made his peculiar deposit for substantial and genuine virtue."[19] The Springsteen family of the mid-twentieth century was not exactly what Jefferson had in mind: though Bruce's forebear Joosten Springsteen did fight in the American Revolution, his own father was a wage-earning factory worker, and Springsteen's heritage has lots of lowly Irish and Italian immigration thrown in. Still, Springsteen came from a long line of economically middling sorts in Freehold who, despite enduring periods of economic struggle, were homeowners and relatively self-reliant.[20]

It was in such soil that the mighty oak of Springsteen's talent took root. But his genius, unlike that of the Founders, was artistic rather than political. Few people could write and perform songs as thrillingly powerful as even the young Springsteen. But like the truest of natural aristocrats, he harnessed his powers into expressing and honoring the deepest yearnings of the people from whose ranks he sprang. He has been happy to reap the rewards of his talents in terms of fame and fortune, and indeed has spent most of his life at a perch of privilege where he has rubbed elbows with those at the very top of American society. But his legitimacy, both in his own eyes and those of his audience, has always rested on his fundamentally republican psyche and his fidelity to the egalitarian accents in his origins. It can be a wobbly perch at times (as when he has caught flak for excessively high ticket prices),[21] but it has proven to be a durable one.

Casting Springsteen as a twenty-first-century natural aristocrat, and positioning him in terms of culture rather than politics, point to the way that echoes of eighteenth-century republicanism have persisted in American culture long after the concept has gone largely underground. The Whigs—who laid the foundation for the Republican Party of the 1850s—as well as the Progressives of the twentieth and twenty-first centuries, tended to skew high in terms of income, education, and cultural aspirations, all markers that fall under the umbrella of "class." Franklin Delano Roosevelt, who was as blue-blooded as they come in America, and who presided over a cabinet known as the Brain Trust, is an example of the way a natural aristocracy can cross party lines. All these people saw themselves as acting on behalf of the great body of the people—and, in advocating on behalf of slaves, women, and immigrants, often extending the definition of "the people"—even as their style and manner reflected patrician language, values, or mores.

The post-eighteenth-century opponents of the natural aristocrats are also a mixed lot. Perhaps the best umbrella term to describe them is "populist," a concept that often combines features of the left and the right.[22] The heirs of Daniel Shays are discernible in the Jacksonian Democrats of the second quarter of the nineteenth century, the Populists of the last quarter of that century, supporters of Joseph McCarthy's anticommunism in the twentieth century, and the Make America Great Again (MAGA) crowd of the twenty-first. At their best, populists have been able to puncture the pretensions of natural aristocrats, exposing the indifference, disdain, or contempt beneath

their professed democratic spirit. At their worst, populists have nurtured grievances and resentments that corrode faith in government
and demean those they consider different from themselves. (One can
also see populist tendencies coursing through the popular music of
recent decades: outlaw country, punk rock, and gangsta rap all have
traces of populist sentiment running through their veins.)

What I'm describing here are of course broad tendencies, and the
lines between natural aristocrats and populists are not always hard
and fast. Franklin Roosevelt would occasionally invoke the vernacular of populism when it suited him politically, as when he described
his plutocratic opponents as "unanimous in their hatred for me—and
I welcome their hatred" in his famous renomination acceptance
speech at the 1936 Democratic National Convention.[23] Donald
Trump, a Manhattan real-estate baron whose celebration of conspicuous consumption appalled elite New Yorkers, who regarded him as
an outer-borough arriviste, became the great champion of the pickup-
truck class. ("I love the poorly educated," he famously said in 2016.)[24]
It's the hallmark of effective politicians to be able to use language
selectively to blur lines and establish coalitions, even if the overall
nature and appeal of their identities remain clear enough to those
who are most passionate about them.

This crossover appeal was the secret of Ronald Reagan's success. He
was the son of an alcoholic shoe salesman in Tampico, Illinois, and
there was little about his early life that suggested a future member of
the natural aristocracy in the making. But Reagan was capable of par-
laying good social skills, some acting talent, and an ability to distill and
succinctly express ideological convictions in ways that added up to a
package of increasingly evident political mastery. Never a populist, he
nevertheless spent the first half of his life as a Democrat, and indeed
served as the head of a labor union, the Screen Actors Guild, in the
1940s (while remaining a committed anti-communist). But over time,
his growing affluence and association with conservative business interests led him to move to the right politically, where his new allies—
wealthy and powerful businessmen—recognized and supported his
political ambitions because he advocated elite goals in homespun lan-

guage, with a self-effacing sense of humor. But his new orientation also reflected a larger political climate in which the White working class was growing weary of the expertise-driven promises of liberalism and the anti-establishment values of the countercultural young. Opposition to both these tendencies on the left fostered a populism of a decidedly conservative sort on the right, and Reagan tapped it.

He also tapped a conservative ideological offshoot sometimes called "producerism": the notion that it's those who labor—not financial speculators, government bureaucrats, or social reformers—who actually create wealth and who thus should have a preeminent place in society. Producerism was a loose ideological construct that could be seen in various unionization movements of the nineteenth century, notably the Knights of Labor. In his speech at Hammonton, Reagan made a producerist gesture when, in describing "proud Italians and hard-working farmers," he said, "You are what America is all about. You didn't come here asking for welfare or seeking special treatment. You came for freedom and opportunity." It was in this stretch of his speech that he went on to praise Springsteen.[25]

There was, however, some rhetorical sleight of hand in these remarks. In praising those who "didn't seek welfare or special treatment," Reagan was implicitly suggesting, in an indication of the harder edges of producerist-style populism, that those who did so were unworthy. (Similarly, in 2012 the GOP presidential candidate Mitt Romney would note that 47 percent of the electorate would vote Democratic because they were dependent on government aid—a category that included disabled veterans, stay-at-home mothers, and any number of other worthy people whose very real contributions to society were not necessarily a matter of wage labor.)[26] Perhaps more importantly, Reagan's remarks dovetailed with the interests of anti-tax libertarians who were hostile to fiscal policies that threatened their profit margins. These were the people, more than any others, who were benefiting from the neoconservative economics of the 1980s. Though Reagan may have been a natural aristocrat, he ultimately served the interests of those who were in the business of cementing a new American aristocracy, one where, more and more, it really *did* matter who your daddy—and mommy—were. One key strategy in doing so was using populist rhetoric and citing heroes like Springsteen, thereby providing plutocrats with ideological cover.

Given the sophistication of Reagan's campaign apparatus, it's not surprising that his operatives sensed that Springsteen would be a useful asset—and that Springsteen himself, a political novice, would be caught flat-footed. But not for long.

This Land Is *Your* Land

My idea in the early and mid-1980's was to put forth an alternate vision of the America that was being put forth by the Reagan-era Republicans. They basically tried to co-opt every image that was American, including me. I wanted to stake my own claim to those images, and put forth my own ideas about them.

—Bruce Springsteen, 1995

Springsteen had just finished a four-night run in Philadelphia, about forty miles southeast of Hammonton, on the day of Reagan's campaign swing into New Jersey. He made no immediate reply to Reagan's speech. Springsteen had always been diffident about taking public political positions. In 1972, as a favor to a friend, he had played a benefit show for Democratic presidential candidate George McGovern—and immediately regretted it. In 1979, during the Musicians United for Safe Energy (MUSE) benefit shows, he was skittish about making a public statement against the use of nuclear power, declining to sign the statement endorsed by other performers in the concert program. His song "Roulette," which he played at the shows, depicted a family's imagined flight from the nuclear accident at Three Mile Island in 1979. But he dropped it from his album *The River* the following year, apparently because he considered it too pointed.[27]

As news of the Reagan speech spread, however, speculation about Springsteen's reaction intensified. As the *Christian Science Monitor* reported, Springsteen had become "the first popular singer to be recruited by the President of the United States as a character reference."[28] Fans and observers alike wondered what his response might reveal about him or his music.

The night after Hammonton, Springsteen played in Pittsburgh. He had still made no comment. But when he learned that the president of Local 1397 of the United Steelworkers of America, of Homestead, Pennsylvania, was seeking a meeting with him, Springsteen agreed.

The fact that Springsteen would meet with a union official from Homestead in the aftermath of Reagan's speech is rich with historical irony. The term "homestead," like "freehold," evokes a Jeffersonian vision of yeomen tilling the land; indeed, Abraham Lincoln had signed the Homestead Act of 1862 with the explicit idea of extending Jefferson's legacy. Within a generation, however, Lincoln's Republican successors, increasingly attuned to free-market capitalism, had presided over the emergence of a Darwinian industrial order that turned Homestead into a factory town inhabited by industrial workers producing steel at the behest of, and with enormous profits for, the vastly wealthy Andrew Carnegie.

Carnegie considered himself a latter-day embodiment of Jefferson's natural aristocrat. Born in a Scottish weaving village, he came to the United States as a child and entered the railroad business before switching to steel. Although he was an industrialist rather than a farmer, Carnegie was fully invested in the Jeffersonian notion that the elite should lead on behalf of the masses. In "Wealth," his 1889 manifesto celebrating the individual capitalist, Carnegie described an ideal state "in which the surplus wealth of the few will become, in the best sense, the property of the many, because it's administered for the common good; and this wealth, passing through the hands of the few, can be made a much more potent force for the elevation of our race than if distributed in small sums to the people themselves."[29]

Jefferson himself would no doubt have been troubled by the amassing of power by an industrialist who he would have considered frighteningly Hamiltonian. But Carnegie took his role of natural aristocrat seriously and, at least some of the time, played it in good faith. You can still see his handiwork in the thousands of town libraries he built all across the country (Carnegie paid for the buildings, but expected local governments to staff and maintain them). He also started the Teacher's Insurance and Annuity Association pension fund (now TIAA-CREF), designed to offer financial security to educators, a group of people not particularly known for their financial acumen. But Carnegie could also be ferocious about maintaining control of prerogatives that he regarded as solely his, as at his Homestead steelworks in 1892.

By the late 1880s, many workers at Carnegie's company belonged to the Amalgamated Iron, Steel, and Tin Workers, the largest and most powerful union in the American Federation of Laborers (AFL). The union won a strike in 1889 that resulted in higher pay for skilled workers than those in neighboring mills, and wages for unskilled workers, many of them immigrants from southern and eastern Europe, were pegged to those of craftsmen. Carnegie considered this unacceptable. After three years of labor tension, he took a vacation in Scotland and designated his lieutenant, Henry Clay Frick, to announce a twenty-percent wage cut and the company's unwillingness to negotiate with the union. Knowing the workers would reject such terms, Frick simultaneously prepared for a strike by ordering the construction of a wooden stockade with holes for rifles and barbed wire on top. Local government refused to assign police to work on management's behalf, so Frick brought in a private security force. When that security force tried to reach the factory under cover of darkness, it was met with gunfire by striking workers, and the subsequent battle resulted in the deaths of ten strikers and three security guards (figure 1.2). The governor of Pennsylvania called in 8,000 National Guardsmen to restore order. Salary cuts went into effect and union leaders were blacklisted; the Amalgamated union was broken not only at Carnegie's Homestead works but at every major steel company in the nation.[30] It would be more than forty years before the Wagner Act, part of Franklin Roosevelt's New Deal, required corporations to recognize the rights of workers to organize unions in order to seek better pay and working conditions.

As president of Local 1397 of the United Steelworkers in Homestead in 1984, Ron Weisen was one of the union's dissident voices, opposing concessions to management that were regarded as inevitable by other union leaders. Local 1397 had formed a successful food bank that had

THE HOMESTEAD RIOT.—Drawn by W. P. Snyder after a Photograph by Dabbs, Pittsburg.—[See Page 676.]
THE PINKERTON MEN LEAVING THE BARGES AFTER THE SURRENDER.

FIGURE 1.2. "The Homestead Riot," drawn by W. P. Snyder for *Harper's Weekly* magazine, July 16, 1892. This tense Pennsylvania labor confrontation was one of a series of struggles between labor and capital at the time. Nearly a century later, Bruce Springsteen would meet a union official from Homestead as he sought to respond to President Ronald Reagan's appropriation of his image when running for reelection in 1984. (Source: Library of Congress) helped hundreds of laid-off workers. And at their meeting he impressed Springsteen, who made a large donation to the food bank.

Three nights after Reagan's speech, on September 22, 1984, Springsteen played his third concert in Pittsburgh. In the middle of his first set, he paused to address the audience. "The President was mentioning my name the other day, and I kinda got to wondering what his favorite album musta been. I don't think it was the *Nebraska* album," he said, referring to his collection of songs in the vein of the populist folksinger Woody Guthrie. "I don't think he's been listening to this one." With that, Springsteen surged into performing "Johnny 99." (Later in the concert, he would throw a few sarcastic bars of "Hail to the Chief" into "Rosalita [Come Out Tonight].")[31]

"Johnny 99" is a stark piece of music, rendered in minimalist form on *Nebraska*. He begins the piece by yodeling—an eerie, melancholy wail conjuring up the ghost of Jimmie Rodgers, the beloved "Singing Brakeman" of Mississippi who became one of the founding fathers of country music. Even before saying a word, Springsteen was thus invoking a great working-class tradition.

The story he goes on to tell is rendered with sparse clarity. The shuttering of a Ford automotive plant in Mahwah, New Jersey—it had been one of the largest in the country before it was shut down over labor and quality-control problems in 1980[32]—throws the song's protagonist, Ralph, out of work. He drinks too much, shoots a clerk, and subsequently acquires the nickname of the song's title. The basic plot elements here—unemployment, alcoholism, easy access to guns, and the fatal results of combining them—are all too recognizable and could have come together as easily in the Homestead, Pennsylvania, of the 1880s as in the Mahwah, New Jersey, of the 1980s.

As in crime novels, however, the murder is only the beginning. In a part of town where "if you hit a red light you don't stop," a crazed Johnny threatens to kill himself. "When an off-duty cop snuck up on him from behind / Out in front of the Club Tip Top they slapped the cuffs on Johnny 99." Seemingly offhand details—like the implicit instability of "Tip Top"—give the story its resonance. And although it seems incidental, it's quite revealing that an *off-duty* policeman finally intervenes at the scene, suggesting a sense of responsibility that is more than official or contractual.

Subsequent verses depict the grimly mechanical nature of the legal process. In the space of a verse, Johnny is tried, convicted, and sentenced to 99 years in jail. There's little order in the courtroom where this summary judgment is handed down: a fistfight breaks out, Johnny's girlfriend must be dragged away, and his mother makes a fruitless plea for mercy.

But Johnny does get a chance to make a final statement, and he makes the most of it. He says he has "debts no honest man can pay" and notes that his home has been repossessed. "Now I ain't sayin' that makes me an innocent man," he states. "But it was more 'n all this that put that gun in my hand." He then goes on to ask for his execution, because he believes he's better off dead. We don't learn whether the judge honors his request—a hauntingly incomplete end to a story that's meant to leave us unsettled.

Johnny takes responsibility for his crime. But he also implicates the CEO of the auto company, its board, the bank, and state and federal regulators who contributed to a situation in which people are saddled with debts they cannot honestly repay: the ghost of Daniel Shays hovers. The exploitative company stores of the post–Civil War South; the misleading railroad-company brochures luring homesteaders onto the arid plains; the unenforced civil rights laws in the wake of hundreds of lynchings—this is an old story in American life, and one more common than the Ronald Reagans of the world would care to admit.

There are a number of ways to understand "Johnny 99." One could characterize it as a populist fable, but it's probably best seen as a depiction of what happens when natural aristocracy breaks down, when privilege without accountability leads to tears in the social fabric. "Johnny 99" questions the system but makes no systematic or even rational attempt to try to overthrow it.

However, there are times when Springsteen *does* edge toward suggesting the legitimacy of more radical action. In "Seeds" (released on his *Live 1975–85* album) he depicts a displaced oil worker talking to an executive who drives by: "Well, big limousine, long shiny and black, /

You don't look ahead, you don't look back." An ominous air of impending reckoning hovers over the song, as it does over "Death to My Hometown" and a number of other brooding tracks on his 2012 album *Wrecking Ball*.

For the most part, though, Springsteen's work is less about imagining new worlds than about trying to preserve what's valuable in old ones. This is what makes him temperamentally conservative—a truth that Reagan's handlers slyly exploited for their own purposes, implicitly aligning themselves with his patriotism and resilience. But in 1984 the two men were trying to conserve markedly different things. Reagan's conservatism was about bolstering privileges rooted in race and class, while speaking with an egalitarian accent. Springsteen's was about sustaining the legacies of the class mobility and racial equality that shaped his youth—about keeping an old promise alive. Decades later, this struggle continues.

Choosing the Boss

I appropriate to myself very little of the demonstrations of respect with which I have been greeted. I think little should be given to any man, but that it should be a manifestation of adherence to the Union and the Constitution.
—President-elect Abraham Lincoln, Trenton, New Jersey, February 21, 1861

In 1834, the twenty-five-year-old Abraham Lincoln launched his second race for the Illinois state legislature (he had lost his first two years earlier). Lincoln was running as a Whig, which meant that he was opposed to the policies of the highly popular president, Andrew Jackson, and was firmly committed to the "American System" of government-sponsored projects such as roads, canals, and railways championed by his hero, Senator Henry Clay, from Lincoln's birthplace, Kentucky—father of the phrase "self-made man."[33] Such positions were hard to hold in highly Jacksonian Illinois, with its wariness about big-government projects. (Populistic Jacksonian Democrats would dominate the state until Lincoln's election to the presidency in

1860.) But even people skeptical of Lincoln's politics seemed to like him; in his first losing effort, he won 277 out of 300 votes cast in his hometown of New Salem.[34]

This time out, Lincoln decided to campaign more directly, eschewing speeches and statements of principle in favor of a more personal approach. On one excursion, he made a pitch to about thirty men who were harvesting a field. When some grumbled that they would never support a man who was ignorant of field work, he reputedly responded, "Boys, if that is all, I am sure of your votes." Taking a farming implement and handling it with ease, he led the harvesters on one full round in the field. "The boys was satisfied," a later observer said, "and I don't think he lost a vote in the crowd."[35] Lincoln won a seat in the legislature handily and went on to serve four consecutive terms.

This story suggests how, in the most literal Jeffersonian sense of the term, Lincoln staked his appeal to voters on his bona fides as a plowman, but one who would become our greatest professor of democracy. Yet even as Jefferson himself was formulating his maxim, the terms of that maxim had been changing. Lincoln would leave the countryside for the towns and cities of Illinois. And if Andrew Jackson, the dominant political figure of Lincoln's youth, was effectively a plowman with little interest in becoming a professor—indeed, that very lack of interest was a source of his political power—Lincoln's own successors would be professors with diminishing contact with plowmen, neither the literal ones who still ranged across the nation's interior nor the figurative ones who sowed the seeds of the nation's industrial growth.

As this gap began to widen, a new word was introduced to describe those who increasingly controlled the nation's economy: "boss." The term, of Dutch origin (Springsteen's own Dutch ancestry is reflected in his surname), had racial as well as class overtones. Journeyman apprentices had been supervised by a figure known as a master workman, but "master" was increasingly perceived as too closely associated with Black slaves, against whom White workers measured themselves in a time of rising racial consciousness. "Boss," meanwhile, simply emphasized the authority of the man in charge—though perhaps the less meritocratic basis of that authority, now more commonly earned through being appointed by a banker or manager than through moving up the ranks from apprentice.[36]

Despite the material realities implied in such linguistic changes, however, memory of—and belief in—the original republican vision has survived. To this day, and with varying degrees of plausibility and success, candidates seek to demonstrate their common touch to voters. This happens across party lines, not only because both Democrats and Republicans include men and women of modest origins, but also because a successful politician in a republic *should* have the common touch. Of course, by the time they run for office, few are actually humble folk; Lincoln, who desperately needed a salary when he campaigned for office in 1834, was a wealthy railroad lawyer by the time he ran for president a quarter of a century later. Nevertheless, one's rise from humble origins often serves as an important credential in achieving leadership stature.

Such plowman-like qualities are relevant in a more broadly cultural sense as well. Indeed, they can explain a seemingly strange aspect of Bruce Springsteen's career: why this champion of the working class was tagged with the honorific "the Boss." It's, moreover, a tag that Springsteen long loathed (though he seems to have made his peace with it in recent years).[37] "I hate being called Boss," he has said, and during a 1985 rendition of "Rosalita" he went so far as to change the lyrics: "You can call me lieutenant, honey, but don't ever call me boss."[38] He rarely resisted the name actively, however—except to insist that his newborn granddaughter could refer to him by any number of names except that one.[39]

The fact is that Springsteen for the past half-century really *has* been a boss, providing a livelihood for what is now a large organization as well as stage-managing his own shows. But he's a natural aristocrat, which is to say a good boss, the kind we accept because we believe he truly represents those in whose name he acts. As such, he embodies the republican values woven into his constitution. In a living version of the Jeffersonian maxim, Springsteen represents what a boss should be: One of us. But better.

FIGURE 2.1. Steel engraving of Walt Whitman in 1854, on the eve of publication of the first edition of *Leaves of Grass*. Whitman's romantic celebration of ordinary American lives laid the foundations for a truly democratic artistic tradition of which Bruce Springsteen is a direct inheritor. "Will you give me yourself? Will you come travel with me?" Whitman wrote in "Song of the Open Road." A century later, in "Born to Run," Springsteen asked, with a similar sense of urgency, "Will you walk with me out on the wire?" (Source: Wikimedia Commons)

democratic Character

Springsteen and the American Artistic Tradition

B Y FEBRUARY OF 1842, when he arrived in New York to deliver a series of lectures on "The Times" at the New York Society Library, thirty-eight-year-old Ralph Waldo Emerson was well on his way to becoming the preeminent man of letters in American history. In essays like "Nature," "The American Scholar," and "Self-Reliance," he outlined a vigorous, pragmatic philosophy suited for a democratic society. "Books are for a scholar's idle times," he famously told audiences in a line typical of his inversion of conventional wisdom. "A foolish consistency is the hobgoblin of little minds," he said. "A man is a god in ruins."[1] Emerson's devoted followers obsessively decrypted his essays in the nineteenth century the way Bob Dylan fans decrypted his lyrics in the twentieth.

The descendant of a long line of Boston ministers, Emerson had been one himself before he left the pulpit to gain literary fame. So by breeding and accomplishment he was well-connected socially, and on this New York trip he had the pleasure of meeting with some of the most important figures of his day: editor and poet William Cullen Bryant, editor and future presidential candidate Horace Greeley, and Henry James, Sr., father to the novelist Henry James and the philosopher/psychologist William James (who, as the future founder of an Emerson-influenced American school of pragmatism, met the Sage of Concord as a two-month-old infant).

On March 5, Emerson gave a lecture titled "The Poet," a version of which would be published two years later and would become one of his most celebrated works. The topic was a familiar one. For over fifty years, American intellectuals had looked to the day when a distinctively national culture would emerge. The United States had achieved its *political* independence, but its *artistic* independence was proving more elusive. For thinkers like Emerson, the nation's culture seemed polarized between an infatuation with European writers like Sir Walter Scott on the one hand, and vulgar American dreck such as the dime novel *Confessions of a Free-Love Sister* on the other.

In "The Poet," however, Emerson told his audience that art is less about formal technique than about the ability of the artist, in strong, clear language, to reveal beauty in the most unlikely of places. "Readers of poetry see the factory-village and the railway, and fancy that the poetry of the landscape is broken up by these; for these works are not yet consecrated in their reading," he explained. Later, he flatly stated that "I look in vain for the poet I describe."[2]

That poet was in the audience—not that Emerson could have been expected to know that. His name was Walter Whitman, and he was a twenty-three-year-old journalist reviewing the lecture for *The Aurora*, a New York newspaper he edited (figure 2.1). Young Whitman, still over a decade away from publishing his first book of poems, liked what he heard. "The lecture was one of the richest and most beautiful compositions, both in its manner and style, we have ever heard anywhere, at any time," he wrote.[3]

It's not surprising that the newspaperman and fledgling writer of free verse would find Emerson's pronouncements attractive. Far more than Emerson himself, Whitman was intimately familiar with the rhythms of the factory village and the railway. A Long Island farmboy who had come to the big city, he spent countless hours walking the streets of New York, talking to—and, more importantly, listening to—the shipbuilders, firemen, and even gang members who roamed the city (as well as Brooklyn, his hometown across the East River). When, thirteen years later, Whitman finally published the first edition of *Leaves of Grass*, he described a world Emerson only theorized about:

> The clean-hair'd Yankee girl works with her sewing-machine or
>   in the factory or mill,
> The paving-man leans on his two-handed rammer, the report-
>   er's lead flies swiftly over the note-book, the sign-painter is
>   lettering with blue and gold,
> The canal boy trots on the tow-path, the book-keeper counts at
>   his desk, the shoemaker waxes his thread,
> The conductor beats time for the band and all the performers
>   follow him,
> The child is baptized, the convert is making his first
>   professions,
> The regatta is spread on the bay, the race is begun, (how the
>   white sails sparkle!)
> . . . And of these one and all I weave a song of myself.[4]

In the most literal of terms, Walt Whitman was a democrat, depicting ordinary people in ordinary language while finding the music, drama, and beauty ("sparkle!") of their lives. His identification with them was total.

Bruce Springsteen is the direct inheritor of this democratic artistic tradition. When, in "Growin' Up," he sings "I found the key to the universe in the engine of an old parked car," he unwittingly fulfills Emerson's prescription for finding transcendental meaning in the stuff of everyday life. When, in "Jungleland," he sings, "We'll meet beneath this giant Exxon sign / That brings this fair city light," he carries forth the Whitmanic tradition of working-class romanticism that endows—"consecrates," to use Emerson's term—ordinary life with grandeur. But Emerson and Whitman are not the only forebears one hears in Springsteen's music. They belong to a broad, varied—and coherent—democratic tradition.

Simple Gifts

The messages of great poets to each man and woman are, Come to us
on equal terms, only then can you understand us, We are no better than
you, What we enclose you enclose, What we enjoy you may enjoy.
           —Walt Whitman, Preface to the 1855 edition of *Leaves of Grass*

"Thunder Road," which opens *Born to Run,* is one of Springsteen's
"monologue" songs.[5] While "Johnny 99," with its cast of characters
and omniscient narrator, unfolds like a short story, "Thunder Road"
is largely an outpouring of emotion by one character to another, as in
a play: "Roy Orbison singing for the lonely / Hey that's me and I want
you only."

The only instruments preceding and accompanying these words
are harmonica and piano, which help set the scene (the harmonica in
particular lends an air of yearning comparable to that of the lyrics).
It's notable that Springsteen opens an unabashedly rock album like
Born to Run with acoustic instruments. This strategy, combined with
the domestic imagery (the screen door, the porch, the dress waving in
the breeze), gives the song a timeless quality, as if the scene could be
unfolding in the 1920s—"like a vision she dances across the porch as
the radio plays"—as easily as the 1970s.

The sole detail that anchors this opening tableau in a particular
historical moment is the reference to Roy Orbison (whose "Only the
Lonely" reached number two on the *Billboard* chart in June of 1960).
"Only the lonely know the way I feel tonight," Orbison begins, conjuring a community of the emotionally disenfranchised. Springsteen's "only"/"lonely" rhyme reinforces the narrator's identification
with the song—and Springsteen's debt to Orbison.

But perhaps the most salient quality of the song's lyrics is their simplicity. To make the point in a reductive but useful way: virtually every
word in the opening verse is two syllables or less. By using only the
most basic diction and active verbs—"the screen door *slams,*" "Mary's
dress *waves,*" "she *dances* across the porch"—Springsteen conjures up
a vivid, resonant picture of a relationship in motion. At the same time,

this sense of motion is coupled with a lack of resolution, hinted at through the repetition of the word "again"—"Don't turn me home again / I just can't face myself alone again"—to indicate that these people have been here before. This time, however, our narrator intends for things to turn out differently: "Don't run back inside, / Darling, you know just what I'm here for."

Such words point toward a corollary to the simplicity of "Thunder Road": frankness. "You ain't a beauty, but hey you're alright," our suitor sings. The potential brutality of his honesty is offset by his vulnerability—he has, after all, been "turned home" by her at least once. And yet his command to "Show a little faith" is delivered with the power of a Baptist preacher.

The simplicity and frankness of "Thunder Road" place it squarely in the democratic tradition. The components of that tradition were perhaps first hinted at by the American Revolutionary Royall Tyler in his 1787 play *The Contrast*, which pitted foreign pretense against native simplicity.[6] The former was represented by the pretentious, Anglophile New Yorker Dimple and his valet, Jessamy, while the latter was embodied by the pointedly named Colonel Manly and his servant Jonathan. As befitting the nation's republican foundations, the hero of the play was Col. Manly. But in an important sense, the future belonged to the democratic Jonathan, whose unpretentiousness, skill, and decency would persist as the virtues of popular-culture icons ranging from Natty Bumppo to Davy Crockett to John Wayne, all of whom would add independence to that list of salient traits. Springsteen himself, in his frequent use of words like "Mister" and "Sir" in his lyrics (such as "Mister, I ain't a boy" in "The Promised Land"), carries forward the plainspoken themes and language articulated by Tyler.

This quest for a native idiom that "we may fairly call our own" became the central preoccupation for American intellectuals of Emerson's generation. In fact, there was a group of journalists known collectively as "Young America" in the 1840s whose work was premised on rejecting the claim of John Quincy Adams and other writers for elite publications that "literature, in its nature, must be aristocratic."[7] Whitman, himself part of the Young America movement, described its goals: "The art of art, the glory of expression and the sunshine of the light of letters is simplicity," he explained in his first preface to *Leaves of Grass*. "Nothing is better than simplicity."[8]

Whitman viewed simplicity as the core of American art because he viewed it as the core of American life. So did other observers. "In America, where privileges of birth never existed and where riches confer no particular rights on their possessors, men unacquainted with one another are very ready to frequent the same places and find neither peril nor advantage in the free interchange of their thoughts," Alexis de Tocqueville noted in *Democracy in America*, his classic study of nineteenth-century American society. "If they meet by accident, they neither seek nor avoid intercourse; their manner is therefore natural, frank, and open; it's easy to see that they hardly expect to learn anything from one another, and that they do not care to display any more than conceal their position in the world."[9]

It was this stylistic as well as material reality of equality in American life (that is, among White Americans—though, as we'll see, it shaped Black American culture too) that suffused the literary aesthetics of writers like Tyler, Emerson, and Whitman. They recognized a living tradition of simplicity in the society they inhabited, and it was one they tried to sustain and extend. If that reality receded amid the excesses of the Gilded Age in the late nineteenth century (or, for that matter, the glitzy materialism of the late twentieth century), their values survived nonetheless.

The main avenue for transmission of these values to Springsteen was not poetry or theater, however, but vernacular music in the century preceding the arrival of rock and roll in the 1950s. Springsteen's most obvious ancestor is Stephen Foster, whose often lively songs about the American scene, such as "Camptown Races" and "Oh! Susannah," won him enormous popularity in the decades before the Civil War. But there can be no mistaking its emotional power for millions of listeners, as the very title of the rough-hewn but evocative "Hard Times Come Again No More" attests. "While we seek mirth and beauty / and music light and gay / There are frail forms fainting at the door," Foster wrote in lines that indicate his class-conscious edge. In the aftermath of the Great Recession in 2009–2010, Springsteen would incorporate "Hard Times Come Again No More" into his live shows.

Foster, of course, is one of the founding fathers of a cultural tradition known as minstrelsy. This racist art form emerged mid-century; its most obvious visual feature was the way men (initially White, but later African American as well) "blacked up" their faces and hands with burnt cork to embody exaggerated versions of enslaved men and women in ways that both explicitly and implicitly ridiculed them through stereotypes like Sambo (the dumb slave), Jim Dandy (who put on fashionable airs), Zip Coon (a sly, manipulative figure), and Aunt Jemima (a mammy archetype). Minstrelsy rapidly evolved into a specific theatrical format that involved an opening routine featuring comic banter between a White "interlocutor" and a minstrel ensemble—you can draw a reasonably straight line between this and what became the standard opening segment of late-night comedy talk shows—followed by a middle dramatic section known as the "olio," and a climactic third act that could often feature plenty of whoopie cushions, thrown pies, and other kinds of slapstick. The comedy was interspersed with songs, such as Dan Emmett's famed "Dixie," sung from the point of view of runaway slaves expressing a sense of nostalgia or loss for the good old days of bondage ("I wish I was in the land of cotton / Old times there are not forgotten"). "Dixie" became the unofficial national anthem of the Confederacy. Springsteen would explicitly connect his work with the minstrel musical tradition when he recorded Emmett's playful "Old Dan Tucker" on his *Live from Dublin* album in 2007.[10]

Viewed from a modern perspective, minstrelsy can be overpoweringly offensive—as indeed it was to many at the time. But there were important countercurrents lurking in it. At the most obvious level, the contempt expressed for African Americans jostled with a deep fascination with slave culture, and minstrels often prided themselves, however misguidedly, on their studied intimacy with Black folkways, whose power would become an important foundation for a distinctively American culture. Moreover, minstrelsy's obvious racial dimension could sometimes obscure the degree to which class conflict was also central to the form, and indeed offending elite sensibilities was in some cases as much the point as affirming White supremacy. (This dynamic has remained with us and was an important source of political power for Donald Trump, for example, as well as in various idioms of popular music, like gangsta rap.) And there were times when class solidarity could foster genuine interracial solidarity.

One could see this in Foster's melodies, which were extraordinary in their catchiness and elasticity across time and place.[11] A good deal of his music's power drew on his familiarity with Black musical traditions—traditions which, more than any other, have made American music American. The cornerstone of that idiom has also been simplicity. This is not to say that African American music lacks complexity, as any listener to jazz will quickly learn. But great jazz artists from Louis Armstrong to Duke Ellington to Wynton Marsalis and their heirs built such work on foundations laid by generations of nameless enslaved musicians who made music communally and without the benefit of a formal training. As such, their music was designed to be easily appreciated even as it remained the repository of more subtle artistry.

Sometimes such complexities are a matter of making virtuosic performance seem easy, like the phrasing of a Billie Holiday song. At other times it's a matter of veiled meanings residing in seemingly innocuous words or delivery. Take, for example, "Blue-Tail Fly," popularized by Emmett and written in Black dialect:

> Ole Massa gone, now let him rest
> Dey say all t'ings am for the best
> I nebber forget till the day I die
> Ole Massa and dat blue-tail fly

Many of us know this song from its chorus: "Jimmy crack corn and I don't care . . . Massa's gone away." What we may not have realized is that "Blue-Tail Fly" is sung from the point of view of a slave celebrating the death of his master. In such a context, the clichéd condolence that things are for the best takes on an ironic sting as deadly as that of a disease-carrying insect.

It would be foolish to suggest that the textured simplicity of such art can be attributed to the democratic theorizing of Emerson or even Whitman. The point here is precisely the opposite—that the Black and White cultural streams from which Springsteen later drew were broadly consonant with democratic aesthetics because pivotal figures like Whitman, a devotee of popular music, were attuned *to* them and thus influenced *by* them. Effortlessly and unconsciously.[12]

These are the broadest, loosest outlines of Springsteen's cultural heritage. But one can make direct connections as well. Woody Guthrie, for example, fused Whitman's democratic poetics with Foster's folk sensibility and became a major influence on Bob Dylan. Dylan, in turn, influenced Springsteen in the most obvious of ways. Compare, for example, "Once upon a time you looked so fine / Threw the bums a dime in your prime" in Dylan's 1965 hit "Like a Rolling Stone," with "Madman drummers bummers and Indians in the summer / with a teenage diplomat" in Springsteen's "Blinded by the Light," from his debut album of 1973. Despite the obvious contrast in tone— Dylan is caustic while Springsteen is jubilant—there's clear continuity in the way both use simple words, romanticize the ordinary, and play with the inherent musicality of language.

These are precisely the same tendencies Whitman exhibited in "Song of Myself":

> Echoes, ripples, buzz'd whispers, love-root, silk-thread, crotch
>   and vine
> My respiration and inspiration, the beating of my heart, the
>   passing of blood and air through my lungs . . . [13]

The differences here are clear, the most obvious being the lack of a rhyme scheme (Whitman considered rhyme a stultifying convention—except, in a case like "inspiration and respiration," when it represented a kind of syncopated freedom within a line, as one sometimes sees in contemporary hip-hop). But one can see the same exuberant cataloging at work, the same musicality, the same density achieved by piling on images. Above all, the language is similarly simple and arrestingly accessible.

By the time of "Thunder Road," however, Springsteen had begun moving away from such dense simplicity to a more streamlined form. In so doing, he achieved a different kind of density, one attained not by clusters of words but by highly compressed phrases. A very good example is furnished by "Hungry Heart," his first hit single: "I met her in a Kingstown bar / We fell in love, I knew it had to end." Like "Blue-Tail Fly," "Hungry Heart" has such a catchy, buoyant tune that it's easy to overlook the complexities lurking within it. "We fell in love, I knew it had to end" encapsulates not only an entire relationship but the fatalism of the man who entered it (but can't quite leave it behind, either). Moreover, it does so with sixteen monosyllabic words (plus the place name of Kingstown), none more than four letters long. Economy of expression was never Whitman's strong suit. But within a few years of releasing his first album, Springsteen had mastered it.

Simplicity, whatever its nuances, is obviously not a uniquely American value. Leo Tolstoy embraced it in his short stories about Russian peasants, for instance, and it's central to the poetic tradition of haiku in Japan. But nowhere has simplicity informed a living social and political tradition to the degree it has in the United States. Here, simplicity was not only a matter of style, a philosophical school, or a religious aspiration. It was also a material reality.

Moving Aspirations

Camerado! I give you my hand!
I give you my love more precious than money,
I give you myself before preaching or law;
Will you give me yourself? will you come travel with me?
Shall we stick by each other as long as we live?
                              —Walt Whitman, "Song of the Open Road"

"Thunder Road" is a typical Springsteen song not only in its simplicity. It also showcases one of his favorite images and symbols: cars. "Roll down the window and let the wind blow back your hair," he tells

Mary. "These two lanes will take us anywhere." There are two romances here: one between these two people, and the other between these people and the open road.

In a healthy democracy, there are no free rides. ("You pay your money and you play your part," Springsteen sings in "Hungry Heart," another song about inner restlessness.) But hard bargains are nevertheless there to be struck. Americans were hitting the road long before there were cars—and for that matter, long before there were roads. Happiness, Jefferson said, must be *pursued*.

Moving—for a buck, for a dream, or simply for the sake of moving—has been one of the great themes of American art. Here again, that's because it has been one of the great realities of American life, not only for heroic figures like Daniel Boone or Lewis and Clark but for ordinary citizens as well. De Tocqueville noted this, too. "In the United States a man builds a house in which to spend his old age, and he sells it before the roof is on; he plants a garden and lets it just as the trees are coming into bearing; he brings a field into tillage and leaves other men to gather the crops; he embraces a profession and gives it up; he settles in a place which he leaves to carry his changeable longings elsewhere," he wrote in 1840.[14] The "changeable longings" is a nice touch, it's as if de Tocqueville thinks desires are an item that metaphorically gets packed in American luggage. In our national romances with travel, people move not as a result of forces like social chaos or famine, such as drove emigration from China or Ireland in the nineteenth-century, but rather out of an inner compulsion: however logical or irrational, it often simply feels better to be on the move. One of the tragedies of slavery was its imposition of immobility, and in that regard it's telling that one of the first things many emancipated people did after the Civil War was to roam. It's perhaps a sign of our growing collective brittleness that such mobility has become less common in the twenty-first century.[15]

In art and life, the means of transportation have varied widely, from covered wagons to the internet (once breathlessly dubbed "the information superhighway"). Natty Bumppo, the hero of James

Fenimore Cooper's Leatherstocking saga, traversed Indian trails from upstate New York to the Great Plains. Herman Melville's characters wandered the globe in navy vessels and whaling ships. The Beats went west in any old jalopy they could find, crossing the continent for no apparent reason other than that it was there.

Huck Finn hopped on a raft to get away from his unhappy home life, while also helping his friend Jim escape from slavery. But rafting's appeal for Huck was also more primal, something that becomes evident especially after a stay with the hospitable yet murderously rivalrous Grangerford clan: "I never felt easy till the raft was two mile below there and out in the middle of the Mississippi. Then we hung up our signal lantern, and judged that we was free and safe once more. . . . We said there warn't no home like a raft, after all. Other places do seem so cramped up and smothery, but a raft don't. You feel mighty free and comfortable on a raft."[16]

For Huck, the journey matters far more than the destination. His creator agreed. "When I was a boy, there was but one permanent ambition among my comrades in our village on the west bank of the Mississippi. That was, to be a steamboatman," Mark Twain wrote in 1875.[17] His permanent ambition, in other words, was permanent impermanence. A century later, Springsteen would express a similar idea in "Growin' Up," when he sang of finding the key to the universe in an old parked car. For Springsteen's alter egos no less than Twain's, the essence of freedom is movement.

And yet movement is more often than not accompanied by an air of uncertainty, even anxiety. Cooper's Leatherstocking can never get far enough away from encroaching civilization. For Huck and—especially—Jim, staying still is not simply disquieting but dangerous, which pushes them to keep moving, pressing onward. In Jack Kerouac's *On the Road*, one suspects that Neal Cassady and company could not stop moving even if they wanted to; the amphetamines they pop seem less the source of their anxious energy than a reflection of it. These characters are always anxious to leave where they've been, but never really know where they're going. Even the ebullient Whitman displays not-so-quiet desperation. He ends his paean to travel, "Song of the Open Road," on a note of uncertainty, assertions giving rise to questions ("Shall we stick together as long as we live?").

It's revealing to compare Whitman's finale with that of Springsteen's own song of the open road, "Born to Run." "Will you walk with me out on the wire?" his narrator asks Wendy, her name an allusion to the Peter Pan saga.[18] He professes to cleave to her with all the madness in his soul, and yet expresses uncertainty about what love really is. "Can you show me?" he asks.

Love is a universal experience, but "Born to Run" is truly an American love song. The assertion that one *will* walk in the sun in the face of doubt; the assumption that one can make this happen through sheer force of will; the insistence on movement, be it horse, raft, rail, or motorcycle—these are sentiments the first Pilgrim or the most recent immigrant would recognize. In this sense one can speak of "Born to Run," like "Thunder Road," as a democratic love song.

Great Defeats

Have you heard that it is good to gain the day?
I also say it is good to fall, battles are lost in the same spirit in which
they are won.

—Walt Whitman, "Song of Myself"

Five years after "Thunder Road," Bruce Springsteen released "The River," in which a man tells a story about himself and his wife—who also happens to be named Mary. The two met in high school, when she was seventeen, and consummated their romance.

Things go downhill from there. The man gets Mary pregnant. He gets a job with a construction company but loses it during a recession. The love he and Mary share dries up like the river in which they used to swim during their courting days. "All them things that seemed so important / Well, mister, they vanished right into the air," he explains. "Now I act like I don't remember / Mary acts like she don't care." But they *do* remember and care. That's why the song is so sad.

"The River" is a song about the way poor judgment, personal failure, and bad luck ruin individual lives. It's not an overtly a political
statement, but democratic values nevertheless animate the song. A
good democrat looks at a situation like the one described by "The
River" and asks whether there's anything that can or should be
done—whether the problems of these individuals might actually
be systemic. Conversely, a good democrat avoids labeling people with
abstractions ("the poor") and instead sees them as individuals with
rich private lives—a habit of thought which, if practiced assiduously,
is likely to have ramifications in terms of ideas that get political support with the public at large. The best democratic artists are those
who connect particular lives with a larger community; to use the language of Emerson, they pierce "rotten diction and fasten words again
to visible things." So, for example, when Mark Twain critiqued slavery in *The Adventures of Huckleberry Finn,* he did so not through the
use of abstract symbols or tightly reasoned argument, but rather
through depicting the anguish of a young boy caught between the
immoral legal code by which he was raised and loyalty to his fugitive
friend. "All right then, I'll *go* to hell," he concludes, casting his lot
with Jim.

Whitman adopted a similar strategy. In his first edition of *Leaves of
Grass* in 1855, he describes a scene that is both profoundly personal
and political:

> The runaway slave came to my house and stopt outside,
> I heard his motions crackling the twigs of the woodpile,
> Through the swung half-door of the kitchen I saw him limpsy
>   and weak,
> And went where he sat on a log and led him in and assured him,
> And brought water and fill'd a tub for his sweated body and
>   bruis'd feet . . .

For this narrator no less than for Huck Finn, aiding a fugitive slave is
a federal offense. While the scene described here is somewhat archetypal, even generic, specific details like the crackling twigs and the

half-door of the kitchen give it particularity and immediacy. Later in the same poem, Whitman goes even farther in representing a fugitive:

> I am the hounded slave, I wince at the bite of the dogs,
> Hell and despair are upon me, crack and again crack the
>   marks-men,
> I clutch the rails of the fence, my gore dribs, thinn'd with the
>   ooze of my skin,
> I fall on the weeds and stones . . .

Upon hearing Whitman's poetry read aloud for the first time, the formerly enslaved abolitionist lecturer Sojourner Truth asked who wrote it, but then added, "Never mind the man's name—it was God who wrote it, he chose the man—to give his message."[19]

Springsteen's own embrace of this facet of the democratic tradition was largely instinctive, relying less on the conscious emulation of older models (most of which came to him through movies and records) than on careful observation of the world in which he grew up. But by the late seventies and early eighties—the years when "The River" and "Hungry Heart" were being written—he did begin seeking out kindred spirits.

Perhaps the most important was Dylan's hero, Woody Guthrie (figure 2.2). As much as any artist in American history, Guthrie bridged the cultural and political strands of democracy, fusing populist themes with vernacular language. The most celebrated example is "This Land Is Your Land," his love song to America. Generations of schoolchildren have sung this virtual national anthem unaware that it was penned by a Communist sympathizer, or that Guthrie wrote it as a response to what he perceived as the smug piety of Irving Berlin's "God Bless America." Along with lyrics celebrating the redwood forest and Gulf Stream waters, Guthrie also included lyrics about people on relief lines, and high walls with "private property" signs. Far from an innocuous folk song, "This Land Is Your Land" was written as a pointed statement about who the fruits of this nation really belonged to: everyone.

INSTRUMENT OF DEMOCRACY

FIGURE 2.2. Woody Guthrie performs on a guitar with a "This machine kills fascists" sticker, 1943. Guthrie's 1940 song "Tom Joad" furnished the inspiration for Springsteen's modern-day sequel, "The Ghost of Tom Joad," fifty-five years later. (Source: *New York World-Telegram and The Sun* newspaper. Photograph Collection, Library of Congress)

Guthrie first came to the mature Springsteen's attention on November 5, 1980, the day after Ronald Reagan had been elected to the presidency. He was given a copy of the acclaimed journalist Joe Klein's biography of Guthrie, where he learned about the history of "This Land Is Your Land," and he soon incorporated it into his repertoire (one rendition appears on *Live 1975–85*). Springsteen later recorded "I Ain't Got No Home," Guthrie's mournful meditation on vagrancy, and "Vigilante Man," his attack on mob justice, for *A Vision Shared*, a 1988 tribute album to Guthrie and Leadbelly organized by the Smithsonian.

More importantly, Guthrie informed Springsteen's own work. Nowhere is this influence more obvious than on *Nebraska*, whose stark acoustic songs evoke Guthrie's Dust Bowl ballads. Just as Guthrie's "Pretty Boy Floyd," his ballad of a populist bank robber, depicts a topsy-turvy world in which poverty is a form of crime, Springsteen songs like "Johnny 99" and "Highway Patrolman" (in which a policeman allows his brother to escape the law) protest a country that imposes debts on its poor that no honest man can pay. While not all these figures are blameless—the narrator of "Nebraska" is a mass murderer—most are forced to shoulder the burden of sins not of their own making. The motorist narrator of "State Trooper" speaks for many when he says, "License, registration, I ain't got none / But I got a clear conscience about the things that I done."

Yet what's most surprising about so many of these people is not their sense of anger or disillusionment, but rather the tenaciousness with which they hold on to their dreams. "Everything dies, baby, that's a fact / But maybe everything that dies someday comes back," asserts the narrator of "Atlantic City," a sentiment particularly striking in the context of the civic corruption described in the song. On "Reason to Believe," the song that closes *Nebraska*, Springsteen catalogs a series of deaths and abandonments experienced by ordinary people, who respond by simply getting on with their lives. Their reasons for believing have a religious character, but they have a political one as well. A democratic republic does not depend on perfection, but it does depend on the possibility—and, sooner or later, the reality—of improvement. Americans' faith in their social contract, though severely stretched, has never been broken—even when, in the eyes of some, it should have been.

Tom Joad's Children

The nonchalance of boys who are sure of a dinner, and would disdain as much as a lord to say aught to conciliate one, is the healthy attitude of human nature.

—Ralph Waldo Emerson, "Self-Reliance"

I'll be in the way kids laugh when they're hungry and they know supper's ready.

—Tom Joad, protagonist of John Steinbeck's (and John Ford's) *The Grapes of Wrath*

On March 3, 1940, Woody Guthrie appeared at New York's Forrest Theater in a benefit performance for what was billed as "The John Steinbeck Committee for Agricultural Workers."[20] Steinbeck's novel *The Grapes of Wrath* (figure 2.3) chronicling the mass migration of displaced farm workers from Guthrie's beloved Oklahoma, had been published the previous spring and was still a major bestseller. The film version of the novel, directed by John Ford, had premiered in New York with great fanfare six weeks before.

It was a great night for Guthrie. Explaining that he was pleased to perform in a "Rapes of Graft" show, he amused and moved the audience, which included Alan Lomax, the budding ethnomusicologist who would go on to lasting fame by recording Guthrie's work and that of other folk musicians. Shortly after the benefit, Lomax persuaded Victor Records to release an album of Guthrie's Dust Bowl ballads. "The Victor people want me to write a song about *The Grapes of Wrath*," Guthrie told his friend Pete Seeger, asking him if he knew where he could find a typewriter. Seeger directed him to the apartment of a friend, where, with a half-gallon of wine, Guthrie sat down to work. The song that resulted, "Tom Joad," was a seventeen-verse ballad that tracked the plot of the book and the movie. It should be noted that there are significant differences between the two versions. This is not only because a movie must necessarily condense a novel, but also because director Ford softened some of the novel's more

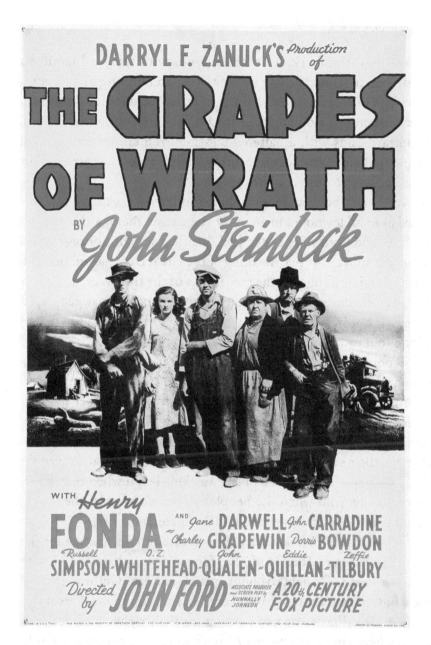

FIGURE 2.3. Poster for the 1940 film version of John Steinbeck's novel *The Grapes of Wrath*. This germinal work proved to be an inspiration for John Ford and Woody Guthrie before it was for Bruce Springsteen, who absorbed it primarily through the performance of Henry Fonda (center), who played the pivotal character of Tom Joad. (Source: Wikimedia Commons)

radical edges. Steinbeck, for example, ends with the Joad family in very desperate straits, fleeing a rising flood and finding only temporary refuge in an abandoned barn (where, in a scene that underlines the importance of women, Rose Joad nurses a starving man). Ford, by contrast, ends with a battered-but-stabilized family on the road again, and Ma Joad commenting on the endurance of the people—not on the necessity for change in the system.[21]

Nevertheless, book and movie share fundamental values. As historian Alan Brinkley noted in an essay comparing them, as far as both Steinbeck and Ford were concerned, "neither despair nor rage could adequately convey the real meaning of the Great Depression. Instead, the novel and film suggest, the true lesson of the time was the importance of community: not community defined in traditional, geographical terms; not in the community of a neighborhood or a town, or a region—but in a community of the human spirit."[22]

This point is made in Tom Joad's pivotal parting words to his mother, which are similar in book and film (the following comes from the latter because it's shorter and uncluttered with reference to other characters in the story): "I'll be all around in the dark. I'll be everywhere. Wherever there's a fight so hungry people can eat, I'll be there. Wherever there's a cop beatin' a guy, I'll be there. I'll be in the way guys yell when they're mad; I'll be in the way kids laugh when they know supper's ready. And when the people are eatin' the stuff they raise, and livin' in the houses they build, I'll be there, too."[23]

Woody Guthrie's version adapted the core of this passage for the climax of his song "Tom Joad." So, for example, where the movie's character speaks of "a fight so hungry people can eat," Guthrie writes of little children who are hungry and cry. He sums up the various struggles Joad describes as people fighting for their rights, and declares, "That's where I'm gonna be, ma / That's where I'm gonna be." Guthrie's lyrics lack the crisp clarity of the language in the book or the film, but their essential musicality is unmistakable even on the page. Taken together, the three texts (to which I'd add Henry Fonda's beautifully understated performance in the film) converged to create a

Tom Joad who remains one of the most vivid characters in the American cultural gallery.

However urgent and moving the work of Steinbeck, Ford, and Guthrie, however, all were in some sense being outpaced by history. By the time Guthrie appeared at the Steinbeck benefit, many of the displaced Okies he sang about were finding jobs in California defense plants gearing up for World War II. That war, and the energies it unleashed, transformed the United States in the four years between the time Guthrie wrote the first draft of his response to "God Bless America" in February 1940 and his first recording of the song as "This Land Is Your Land" in the spring of 1944.[24] Twenty years later, starving migrants were hosting backyard cookouts, and the defining voice of California life—itself increasingly the defining voice of American life—was not Woody Guthrie but the Beach Boys. Springsteen's own parents would migrate to California at decade's end in search of a better life.

Of course, poverty did not disappear in California or anywhere else in America. And other struggles, most notably the civil rights movement, were only beginning. But with the exception of the early years of that movement, there was a steady ebbing of the egalitarian spirit—a spirit suffusing Whitman when he wrote "Song of Myself"—that had animated the artists of the thirties. Even on the left, the tenor of the newer art was less an affirmation of egalitarianism than an embrace of self-actualization, which is not quite the same thing.

Springsteen's discovery of Woody Guthrie in 1980 coincided with the advent of an era of accelerating economic inequality in the United States, a development he chronicled on *Nebraska* and subsequent records. But by the end of the decade even Springsteen had retreated from his concern with social injustice. Records like *Tunnel of Love, Human Touch,* and *Lucky Town,* while hardly rejecting the political stance of his earlier records, lacked the sense of active engagement that had characterized his music in the early eighties. But during a sleepless night in early 1995, while trying to write new songs, Springsteen picked up *Journey to Nowhere,* a book on the new American underclass written by Dale Maharidge with photographs by Michael

Williamson. (They would go on to share a Pulitzer Prize in 1990 for *And Their Children after Them,* which traced the subsequent history of Alabama sharecropping families first chronicled in James Agee's classic 1940 study *Let Us Now Praise Famous Men.*) *Journey to Nowhere* had originally been published in 1985, which is when Springsteen bought it, but only a decade later was he actually reading the book. Maharidge and Williamson's depictions of the decaying industrial city of Youngstown, Ohio, and their portraits of contemporary boxcar hoboes were the direct inspiration for two new songs, "Youngstown" and "The New Timer." "What Springsteen is trying to do is something so incredible," Maharidge said in 1996, when *Journey to Nowhere* was reissued (with a new introduction by Springsteen). "He's a musical Steinbeck."[25]

Springsteen made this political and artistic connection clear in his decision to title the ensuing album after the song that opens it: *The Ghost of Tom Joad.* His primary tie to the character, as he has made clear in interviews and in the source notes that accompany the album, is the John Ford version. Whatever the lineage, though, it's apparent that Springsteen sought to put his own imprint on the material.

He does this in a number of ways. One is the use of contemporary details that anchor the songs in the present even as they resonate with the past. So, for example, "The Ghost of Tom Joad" opens with men walking along railroad tracks—and highway patrol choppers coming over a ridge. Steinbeck/Ford/Guthrie focus on poor White Southerners; Springsteen's locus is the Southwest, and many of his characters are non-White (this was true of some of Steinbeck's other fiction). While the original Tom Joad sought to navigate the shoals of the Great Depression, Springsteen's narrator, observing a line of people waiting for shelter, dryly welcomes "the new world order" proclaimed by George H. W. Bush in 1990. Indeed, there's a bitterness in "The Ghost of Tom Joad" that may even exceed that of Steinbeck. "The highway's alive tonight," begins the chorus on a hopeful note—only to continue with an acerbic "But nobody's kiddin' nobody about where it goes." Thunder Road, it would seem, is a dead end. Despite this apparent despair, however, Springsteen's Tom Joad casts his lot with the others, echoing the spirit—and in some lines even the letter—of the original: "Wherever there's somebody strugglin' to be free / Look in their eyes, Ma, you'll see me."

But the obvious similarities between this Tom Joad and his predecessors may be less important than a more fundamental affinity. While this jaded narrator knows "nobody's kiddin' nobody," he keeps searching for—and at the end of the song claims to be "sittin' here in the campfire light with"—the ghost of Tom Joad. Springsteen's militance would be reborn a generation later when he re-recorded "The Ghost of Tom Joad" on his 2014 album *High Hopes*, featuring the supple yet fierce guitar playing of Tom Morello, the founder of Rage Against the Machine, who joined the E Street Band for a stretch of the 2010s.

"We're the people that live," Ma Joad says to her husband and son as they drive through California at the end of the film version of *The Grapes of Wrath*. "They can't wipe us out. They can't lick us. We'll go on forever, Pa, because we're the people that live." Almost a half century later, also in California, Springsteen introduced another song from *The Ghost of Tom Joad*, "Across the Border," by saying, "This song's about the mystery of human nature, human spirit. How people just keep going, keep going. . . . We've been beat up pretty bad, but we keep going."[26] The ensuing song—think of it as "Thunder Road" with a female character named Maria—captures the essence not only of the Joad ethos but also their dream. "For what are we without hope in our hearts?" this migrant asks. "I know that love and fortune will be mine / Somewhere across the border."

Simplicity, mobility, hope: this is the art of democracy.

Blues States

Through stories about ordinary people, to Vietnam veterans to steel workers, his songs capture the pain and the promise of the American experience.

—From the citation awarding Springsteen the Presidential Medal of Freedom at the White House, November 22, 2016

In the twenty-first century, Springsteen's work continued in the deeply democratic vein he established early in his career. It also continued in another vein, alternating between songs whose democratic values inhered more in the way he dramatized and dignified ordinary life and those which can be said to have a more overtly political dimension (though no Springsteen song has ever made a direct partisan statement, even as his politics have moved more decisively and self-consciously to the left).

Perhaps the purest expression of the ongoing Whitmanesque tradition in Springsteen's work surfaced in "Land of Hope and Dreams," a 1999 song that has become a staple of his stage shows, and which has appeared on a number of records, anchored by its debut on *Live in New York City* and bookended by a studio version on *Wrecking Ball* in 2012. The song's most obvious lineage derives from soul artist Curtis Mayfield's 1965 hit "People Get Ready," which became something of a civil rights anthem in the sixties and seventies. It also contains echoes of "This Train Is Bound for Glory," a gospel song commonly associated with Sister Rosetta Tharpe—and also recorded by Woody Guthrie.[27] But, however unconsciously, it's Whitman's all-embracing vision of America that suffuses this ten-minute epic, with its incantatory repetition of "this train" that will carry saints and sinners, losers and winners, thieves and sweet souls departed. "Dreams will not be thwarted!" Springsteen shouts with the fervor of a Baptist preacher. It would not be a stretch to dub this a democratic hymn.

More typical of Springsteen's recent body of work are more sharply etched intimate portraits, now of characters who are older and (generally, but not always) wiser than their counterparts in "Thunder Road," "Born to Run," and "Hungry Heart." Among the most moving of these are the firefighters of "Into the Fire" and the title track of his 2002 album *The Rising*. These are people with rich personal lives who sacrifice all they hold dear in keeping the faith with their civic commitments—democracy as a vocation fused with a religious devotion (the two never that far apart in any democracy that can sustain itself). They also include those who grieve those people, as well as a gallery of passing characters, like the waitress Shaniqua of "Girls in

Their Summer Clothes" from *Magic* (2007), who populate towns like the Freehold of "Long Walk Home" from that same album, where a flag flies over the courthouse of a community "that just wraps its arms around you."

But in the twenty-first century Springsteen's work occasionally has taken an overtly ideological turn, this time with a historical consciousness that now extends more widely than Joe Klein's Woody Guthrie biography. In the decades since reading that book, he had become something of an amateur ethnomusicologist, one with a particular affinity for American roots music. This was most obvious in *We Shall Overcome: The Seeger Sessions* (2006), Springsteen's first album of covers, all of them associated with Pete Seeger, as well as *Live in Dublin* the following year, which mixed songs from Springsteen's own catalog with a series of class-conscious folk classics including the nineteenth-century sea shanty "Pay Me My Money Down," the 1905 Thomas Allen song "Erie Canal," and Blind Alfred Reed's 1929 Depression-era anthem "How Can a Poor Man Stand These Times and Live?" To these he added a new composition of his own in that vein, "American Land," which adopted the point of view of late—nineteenth- and early-twentieth-century immigrants, with a distinctly puckish streets-paved-with-gold irony: "There's diamonds in the sidewalk, the gutters lined in song / Dear, I hear that beer flows through the faucets all night long." But the final verse of "American Land" pays tribute to immigrants—"the McNicholas, the Posalskis, the Smiths, Zerillis too / The Blacks, the Irish, Italians, the Germans and the Jews"—laboring in the nation's fields and factories. And the song climaxes with a pointed contemporary message: "They died to get here a hundred years ago, they're still dying now / The hands that built the country we're always trying to keep out."

Such statements notwithstanding, Springsteen had long avoided partisan party politics. But in 2004 he publicly supported and performed for Democratic presidential candidate John Kerry, writing an op-ed piece endorsing his candidacy in the *New York Times*.[28] In his song "Last to Die" (a clear reference to Kerry's famous line during his 1971 testimony as the leader of Vietnam Veterans against the War:

"How do you ask a man to be the last man to die for a mistake?"),
Springsteen came closer than he ever has to a partisan statement. The
song appeared on *Magic*, whose title track is a thinly veiled critique of
the political legerdemain of GOP figures like Secretary of Defense
Donald Rumsfeld, who manipulated the nation into war in 2003.
"*Magic* was my state-of-the-nation dissent over the Iraq War and the
Bush years," Springsteen explained a decade later in his memoir. And
yet he insisted that he wanted to avoid a straightforward polemic:
"You can listen to the whole thing without ever thinking of the politics of the day or you can hear them ticking deadly through the internal thread of the music."[29]

Since the Kerry campaign, Springsteen has been associated with
the Democratic party of Obama—whom he befriended—as well as
Hillary Clinton and Joe Biden. This has cost him in the eyes of some
of his fans, not only because many never shared his politics, but also
because the Democrats have become noticeably less populist in the
twenty-first century, their progressive cultural values now often
accompanied by an increasing indifference, if not hostility, toward
working-class people who they regard as misguided at best. But
Springsteen's music of the 2010s and 2020s has generally tacked back
toward less overtly political themes. The title track of his 2009 album
Working on a Dream has a sentimental quality despite its working-
class patois ("Rain pourin' down, I swing my hammer / My hands are
rough from working on a dream" goes a line from the title track),
while "Queen of the Supermarket" is an awkward valentine to the
checkout worker who bags the protagonist's groceries. Such an
approach continues straight through *Western Stars* in 2019, which is
populated with laconic characters of modest hope and demeanor,
including the title character, a faded movie-star barfly remembering
an encounter with John Wayne. The title of Springsteen's 2020 song
"Rainmaker" refers to slick lawyers, though the real focus of the
song is the desperate farmers living through the drought of debt.

The great exception to all of this, and what is likely to be Springsteen's final populist statement, is his 2012 album *Wrecking Ball*, an
extended commentary on the financial crisis of 2007–2009 that left

durable scars on the nation's working classes. The most harrowing of these songs, "Jack of All Trades," begins with a casual laborer talking about mowing lawns and clearing gutters but ends with a sudden and violent declaration: "If I had me a gun, I'd find the bastards and shoot 'em on sight." (The album's militant edge is sharpened by Morello, on hand to play guitar on this song and others on *Wrecking Ball*.)

But even at his darkest, Springsteen resolutely insists on dignity and hope. *Wrecking Ball* concludes with "We Are Alive," narrated from the point of view of a series of ghosts: a rail worker killed in the Great Strike of 1877, a child murdered in the Birmingham church bombing of 1963, a contemporary Latin migrant who perished making a crossing. "Our souls will rise," goes the chorus. "To carry the fire and light the spark / To stand shoulder to shoulder and heart to heart." Simplicity, mobility, and hope: the art of democracy indeed—generation after generation.

FIGURE 3.1. The entrance to Elvis Presley's famed Graceland estate. A trespassing Bruce Springsteen was escorted from the grounds after a concert in Memphis a few months before Presley's death in 1977. "The guard who stopped me at the door did me the biggest favor of my life," he later remembered. "It was innocent, and I was having a ball, but it wasn't right. In the end, you cannot live inside that dream." (Source: Library of Congress)

CHAPTER 3

Realms of Kings

Springsteen and the American Dream

IN THE EARLY-MORNING HOURS of April 30, 1977, Bruce Springsteen finished a live show in Memphis, hailed a taxi, and asked the cabdriver to take him, his publicist, and E Street Band member Steve Van Zandt to a quiet restaurant. The driver, suspecting his customers were out-of-town VIPs, suggested they drop by Elvis Presley's house. Springsteen enthusiastically agreed. He had never met Presley but had just written a song, "Fire," expressly for him. Now he was headed to Graceland.

Springsteen and his entourage arrived at the gates of the mansion around 3 A.M. No one was visible, but the house lights were on. Acting on impulse, Springsteen scaled the gate and started up the long driveway (figure 3.1). He had just about reached the front door when he was accosted by a security guard. Springsteen asked if Presley was home and was told he was not. "Well, now I'm pullin' out all the cheap shots I can think of—you know, I was on [the cover of] *Time,* I play guitar, Elvis is my hero, all the things I never say to anybody," he later recalled of his encounter with the guard. "Because I figure I gotta get a message through. But he just said, 'Yeah, sure. Why don't you let me walk you through the gate. You gotta get out of here.' He thought I was just another crazy fan—which I was."[1]

Few observers would have regarded Springsteen as "just another crazy fan," except perhaps Presley himself, who since the time of the

Beatles had been largely indifferent about, if not dismissive of, the rock artists who had followed him.[2] On the other hand, there were many who thought Presley himself could only be taken seriously by, well, a crazy fan.

Yet even some of these people could not forget the young Presley, who had transformed generations of musical traditions into a vehicle for expressing the excitement, even joy, of the American Century as it crested. That transformation had touched Springsteen as a child in the late fifties when he first saw Presley on the *Ed Sullivan Show* (figure 3.2). "Man, when I was nine, I couldn't imagine not wanting to be Elvis Presley," he later remembered. (He later devoted an entire chapter of his memoir to Elvis, which he titled "The Big Bang.")[3] While later influences, notably Bob Dylan, were more obvious, to this day Presley remains a touchstone for Springsteen.

The reasons for Presley's appeal are musical but also mythic. The simple outlines of Presley's life—of a poor, insecure boy who rose to fame and fortune through sheer force of talent—represented in many minds the very definition of the American Dream that Springsteen himself would live out. Springsteen saw himself as the inheritor of that Dream, and one imagines that, walking up the driveway that night in Memphis, he fantasized about being recognized as the King's heir.

A little over three months later Presley was dead, the victim of a drug overdose. By the end of his life, he was hardly a role model for anyone, an addict who in 1969 had successfully lobbied Richard Nixon to deputize him as a narcotics officer (the photo-op picture of the two men in the Oval Office has become a camp classic). Elvis jokes went on to become a staple of popular culture and a point of reference for others with larger-than-life appetites, including President Bill Clinton, whose Secret Service code name was Elvis.

But if Presley's later life and death were the stuff of farce, they were also a tragedy. To commemorate them, Springsteen began performing a new song, "Johnny Bye Bye," in the early eighties. The style, lyrics, and even title of "Johnny Bye Bye" are patterned on the work of Chuck Berry, whose "Bye Bye Johnny" (1960) even shares the same opening lines: "Leaving Memphis with a guitar in his hand / with a one-way

SHOOTING STAR

FIGURE 3.2. Elvis Presley, still from *Jailhouse Rock*, 1957. "Man, when I was nine, I couldn't imagine not wanting to be Elvis Presley," Springsteen later remembered. ("Jailhouse Rock" was the first record he ever bought.) Presley personified a dream came true—and the painful realities that accompanied it. (Source: MGM Studios)

ticket to the promised land."[4] But while Berry's song is a paean to the joy and power of rock and roll, Springsteen's is a eulogy to lost hope: "They found him slumped up against the drain / With a whole lot of nothin' runnin' in his veins." "Johnny Bye Bye" is a relatively obscure song in the Springsteen canon. But Presley remained an important figure for him, whether as a cautionary example he would discuss in interviews or as an inspiration for songs like "Fire," which became a hit for the Pointer Sisters in 1978–79 and for Springsteen himself in 1987.

Springsteen's most explicit form of homage, however, was his decision to begin singing Presley's "Follow That Dream" in his live shows of the eighties (it would occasionally also surface in later decades). The song from the 1962 film of the same name was released as Presley's cultural preeminence was beginning to ebb. Its very title is emblematic of who Elvis Presley was to himself and the tens of millions of fans who adored him: a person who had indeed followed— and realized—a dream of success on an almost unimaginable scale.

Springsteen's admiration for Presley was not quite that simple, however, and his tribute did not take the form of mere imitation. Though he would sing with Presleyesque ardor that he would follow his dreams wherever those dreams might lead (among other places, to true love), Springsteen broadened the song's fairly generic meaning by adding an original verse in which he celebrates an individual's "right to the chance to give what he has to give" and "to fight for the things he believes." Describing freedom as the right to give, or dreams as products of fights, was not exactly standard fare in Presley's musical diet. But by then, Springsteen's understanding of following the American Dream had become more complex, and more challenging, than living like a rock-and-roll king.

The Bars of Graceland

We [the E Street Band] wanted to play because we wanted to meet girls, we wanted to make a ton of dough, and we wanted to change the world a little bit, you know?

—Bruce Springsteen, 1984

In our day, the term "American Dream" has become a cliché, most commonly invoked by real-estate agents and Hollywood screenwriters. The former use it in a tireless effort to sell home ownership, the most concrete version of the Dream. The latter use it to sell a vision of wealth, fame, and power all the more alluring for its seeming effortlessness.

It may be logical, then, that these two versions of the American Dream converge at Presley's baronial home. Here he took care of his beloved mama, and here he fed his bottomless appetites (sustained via income from his movies). Its very name, Graceland, testifies to its almost totemic power as the supreme expression of the Dream: heavenly grace in earthly form.

But however potent a symbol, Graceland cannot wholly represent the American Dream in its many dimensions.[5] The Dream has gone by different names: "the American Creed," "the American Way of Life," or, simply, "the American Way." All are united by a common underlying faith that runs through the many versions of the Dream. This faith is rarely articulated explicitly, and it has never been formally codified. Nor has it ever been universally accepted. But it can be summed up in the following assertion:

Anything Is Possible If You Want It Badly Enough.

Americans have historically invested so heavily in this Dream because America itself is a product of it. Its earliest formulation was perhaps best expressed by John Winthrop, the first governor of the Massachusetts Bay Colony, in a lay sermon he delivered to the Puritans in 1630 while still crossing the Atlantic. "We shall find that the God of Israel is among us, when ten of us shall be able to resist a thousand of our enemies; when he shall make us a praise and glory that men shall say of succeeding plantations, 'the Lord make it like that of New England,'" he reputedly said. "For we must consider that we shall be as a city upon a hill."[6] A city of God—a state of salvation.

The heart of the Puritans' American Dream was what they called their "covenant," an implicit pact that God would provide for them spiritually if they formed a community to honor him according to his precepts as they understood them. As time passed, however, the individualism at the heart of the Puritan vision—rooted in a person's ability to discern the will of God directly from the Bible rather than via corrupt crypto-Catholic clergy—increasingly asserted itself. And the original energy persisted, even as it diffused across the country at large, most obviously in the form of an increasingly secular work ethic that had once served as a signpost to spiritual grace (more on this in chapter 5).

By the end of the eighteenth century, another version of the Dream, this one more political than religious, was articulated by the signers of the Declaration of Independence. Thomas Jefferson's assertions to the contrary, it was by no means "self-evident," then or now, that "all men are created equal, that they are endowed by their Creator with certain inalienable rights," and that these rights can be summed up as "life, liberty, and the pursuit of happiness." But such were the appeal, will, and good fortune of the Founders that they did achieve political autonomy from Britain, and they bequeathed to us a vision of possibility that we have honored—if all too imperfectly realized—ever since. And so it was that the promised land became a land of promise.

There were a number of American Dreams in the nineteenth century. Some, like the Transcendentalists' quest for self-realization, were relatively modest in scope. "I have learned this, at least, from my experiment: that if one advances confidently in the direction of his dreams, and endeavors to live the life he has imagined, he will meet with a success unexpected in common hours," wrote Henry David Thoreau after his sojourn in the woods of Walden.[7] Other versions, like the so-called Manifest Destiny, were far more collective, though not especially communitarian. Coined by journalist John L. Sullivan, the term referred to the drive for a continental empire that stretched to the Pacific—the American Dream as imperial conquest.

In the decades following the Civil War, with capitalism ascendant and technology triumphant, the primary expression of the Dream was economic. In its most powerful and durable formulation, it was a hope that one's children would enjoy a higher standard of living than oneself, a hope embraced with particular intensity by a rising tide of immigrants. A variation on this Dream was expressed in the fictional characters of novelist Horatio Alger, whose poor boys made good because they *were* good (and lucky). Still others, like Andrew Carnegie, tried to couch this American Dream in terms of progress that would allow those of modest means to achieve happiness no less than the millionaire. "Material prosperity is helping to make the national character more unselfish, more Christlike," wrote Reverend William Wallace, Episcopal bishop of Massachusetts, in 1901 in one such formulation of this gospel of wealth.[8]

The maturation of American industrial capitalism in the early twentieth century led to yet another reorientation in the American Dream. Now it was less about religion, politics, empire, or money—though each continued to have its adherents—than about personal freedom and pleasure. Athletes like Babe Ruth and movie-star couples like Mary Pickford and Douglas Fairbanks were enviable not simply because they were rich and powerful but because they always seemed to be having a good time. This vision was expressed most perfectly not in real life but in another fictional character: James Gatz, an ordinary boy from small-town Minnesota, who transformed himself into the fabulous Jay Gatsby to win the heart of the beautiful Daisy Buchanan in F. Scott Fitzgerald's *The Great Gatsby* (1925).

Fitzgerald had a sophisticated grasp of the American Dream. Gatsby, of course, fails to attain his; the woman on whom he pins his hopes is not really worthy of him. Not that Gatsby is necessarily so great, either; in the end, he seems little more than a pathetic man who confuses appearances with reality. But even the clear-eyed narrator, Nick Carraway, cannot help but be moved by the intensity of the man's vision, a vision comparable to that of a European explorer who encountered a continent "commensurate with his capacity for wonder."[9]

Ten years after the publication of *The Great Gatsby,* Elvis Aaron Presley was born in Tupelo, Mississippi. In an important sense, Presley was the opposite of Gatsby, because he really did achieve his Dream. That Dream has been vividly described by Greil Marcus in his now classic essay "Presliad," whose very title suggests the degree to which Presley's life evokes a myth of origin. Marcus's point of entry is the way in which Presley was nurtured by—and broke from—country music. Marcus argues that while the Protestant work ethic in the North "set men free by making them strangers," Southerners, Black and White, emphasized community, bound together through rituals like music, which could provide solace for the lonely and consolation for rebels whose cause was lost. To be sure, there was plenty of hell-raising and good times to be had on Saturday night. But that's as far as it went. Come Sunday morning, there was a service to attend, and on Monday morning everyone returned to work. What made Presley and his fellow rock and rollers special, Marcus says, was their attempt to make Saturday night last forever. "You had to be young and a bit insulated to pull it off," he concedes. But the promise of the idea was irresistible: "Reality would catch up sooner or later—a pregnant girlfriend and a fast marriage, the farm you had to take over when your daddy died, a dull and pointless job that drained your desires until you could barely remember them—but why deal with reality before you had to? And what if there was a chance, just a chance, that you *didn't* have to deal with it?" Presley himself put it more succinctly: "When I was a boy, I was the hero in comic books and movies. I grew up believing in a dream. Now I've lived it out. That's all a man can ask for."[10]

As Presley learned, however, stardom *too* could be a "dull and pointless job." He became a latter-day King Midas; by 1956, any song his voice touched went gold, and simply appearing before the cameras guaranteed a handsome payday. Lacking an essential curiosity or even simple business acumen about his future, he left most of the crucial decisions shaping his career to the rapacious "Colonel" Tom Parker, who committed Presley to projects that were beneath him.[11] Before long, his work was a profitable joke, and by the late sixties it wasn't even so profitable anymore.

Presley's career was not simply a tale of steady decline. All through this period, he showed flashes of commitment; and when it became unmistakably clear to him that he'd lost his touch, he turned Colonel

Parker's plans for a 1968 Christmas special into an astonishing display of resiliency and the springboard for his celebrated comeback. He recorded some of his best work in this period, went back on the road for the first time in a decade, and conquered America all over again. But after his first few appearances in Las Vegas, Presley acted like (in the words of Marcus) a man with "talent so vast it would be demeaning to apply it."[12] Presley himself had said that becoming a hero "was all a man could ask for," and after attaining this goal in the fifties, losing it in the sixties, and recapturing it as the seventies approached, he apparently had no idea what else to do except to take refuge in the dreamless sleep of narcotics. And so Presley's American Dream became his prison and, ultimately, his tomb.

Reflecting on Presley's life and death a decade after his death (and a decade after his own pilgrimage to Graceland), Springsteen called Presley's dream "a cult of personality" in which fame and wealth were the only objectives. By now Springsteen was a superstar in his own right, featured as the lead interview in the twentieth-anniversary issue of *Rolling Stone*. The magazine, once the voice, and even the conscience, of the counterculture, was now itself devoted to cults of personality, attaining its commercial preeminence in the closing decades of the century by stoking sleek, updated versions of Presleyesque fantasies.

But if Springsteen was in this world, he was not quite *of* it. "When I jumped over that wall to meet Elvis that night, I didn't know who I was gonna meet," he reflected in that interview. "And the guard who stopped me at the door did me the biggest favor of my life. I had misunderstood. It was innocent, and I was having a ball, but it wasn't right. In the end, you cannot live inside that dream."[13]

Integrating Dreams

If you desire negro citizenship, if you desire to allow them to come into the state and settle with the White man, if you desire them to vote on an equality with yourselves, and to make them eligible to office, to serve

on juries, and to adjudge your rights, then support Mr. Lincoln and the
Black Republican party.

—Senator Stephen A. Douglas, first Lincoln-Douglas Debate,

Ottawa, Illinois, August 21, 1858

On March 21, 1956, the number-one song on the *Billboard* pop chart
in the United States was "Heartbreak Hotel," by twenty-one-year-old
Elvis Presley. It sounded like nothing else on the airwaves. Tapping
the wellspring of musical traditions in the Mississippi Delta, Presley
had given them a new spin, haunting yet oddly assured, that sounded
like the voice of modernity itself. It was the start of a great career.

That same day, the *New York Times* published one of its "Man in the
News" profiles on a young preacher named Martin Luther King, Jr.
(figure 3.3), whose recent arrest in Montgomery, Alabama, had made
national headlines. Blending philosophical principles that included
those of Henry David Thoreau as well as Mohandas Gandhi, King
represented a new generation of African Americans engaged in an
epic struggle for freedom. "He can build toward his climax of impas-
sioned pulpit-pounding that overwhelms the listener," the reporter
wrote of King, in language that could have described Presley's impact
on his own listeners.[14] Here was the start of another great career.

Presley and King were two Southern men shaped by Black religious traditions: Presley's musical and King's theological. Each in his
way was an agent of integration—Presley on the cultural plane, King
on the social and political. The differences between them, in life and
in death, are important, even as they remain comparable. Presley
changed the nation's tune; King changed the nation's moral vision.

King did it with a dream of his own, one he called "deeply rooted"
in the American Dream. He described it most memorably in 1963 at
the Lincoln Memorial, in a melodious address that electrified the
world, describing a dream that his children would someday live in a
country where they would be judged "not by the color of their skin
but by the content of their character."[15] King wasn't alone in his quest
to realize this redefined American Dream, of course. But more than
any other figure, he articulated it in ways that most Americans could

FIGURE 3.3. Martin Luther King, Jr., preaching at Washington Temple Church in Brooklyn, 1962. King's life and work are a reminder that the American Dream was never solely, or even primarily, about secular economic gain, embodying a powerful alternative Dream of collective aspiration with a spiritual cast. Bruce Springsteen was raised on this integrationist vision, and it has been reflected in his work for his entire career—even after integration ceased to be an ideal in progressive circles. (Source: O. Fernandez, *New York World-Telegram*)

understand, and in logic they could follow, however reluctantly. At the core of that logic was a demand that the nation live up to the principles it had first enshrined in the Declaration of Independence—the de facto charter of the American Dream, which most Americans professed to honor and in which most Americans liked to believe. If you say you're for life, liberty, and the pursuit of happiness; if you say you believe in rule by law; if you say you believe that the Constitution really does guarantee everyone the same rights—well, then, you can't in good conscience discriminate, lynch, or, as a practical matter, segregate. And if you do—as television cameras have repeatedly shown that you do—then you have to change your words or change your actions. When push came to shove on King's watch, we chose—in terms of our laws, anyway—the latter.

King's more radical critics, such as Malcolm X, accused him of having a misplaced confidence in the American legal system and its capacity for reform from within. Malcolm and other Black Power advocates like H. Rap Brown and Stokely Carmichael also believed King had far too much faith in a Dream that not only wasn't a reality but was in fact a fraudulent lie. In his famous "The Ballot or the Bullet" speech of 1964, Malcolm put the matter plainly: "I don't see any American dream; I see an American nightmare."[16] The contrast with King was clear.

But King was not alone in his faith in the American Dream. Frederick Douglass, one of the great integrationists in American history, shared it as well. Despite his hatred for slavery, which he knew firsthand, Douglass never rejected his claim on—or desire for—the promise of American life. "I am not indifferent, but profoundly solicitous for the character, growth and destiny of this American republic, which but for slavery would be the best governed country of the world," Douglass told a crowd in Rochester, New York, after the outbreak of the Civil War. "All that I have and am, are bound up in the destiny of this country."[17] Despite numerous disappointments before, during, and after the war, Douglass never surrendered this faith. And, more than coincidentally, he was a steadfast advocate on another frontier of the Dream—women's suffrage—throughout his life.

King is a direct inheritor of this durable strand of Dream language, which repeatedly surfaces in his own work—and is often a justification for it. It was apparent, for example, in a *New York Times* piece he wrote about the Greensboro lunch-counter sit-ins of 1961. These student protesters were not fighting simply for themselves, he explained: they were saving the soul of their country. "They are taking the whole nation back to those great wells of democracy which were dug deep by the Founding Fathers in the formulation of the Constitution and the Declaration of Independence," he wrote. "In sitting down at lunch counters, they are in reality standing up for the best of the American Dream." King would repeat similar words throughout his life, most notably on the night before he died.[18]

And what did young Bruce Springsteen, who was 19 years old when King died, think about all this? Well, you could infer. Which was a bit of a problem.

Dream Flight

Northern men, northern mothers, northern Christians, have something more to do than denounce their brethren in the South; they have to look at the evil among themselves.

—Harriet Beecher Stowe, *Uncle Tom's Cabin* (1851)

Musically speaking, racial integration has always been important to Bruce Springsteen. Its importance can be seen in the personnel of the E Street Band, including David Sancious (a pianist who would go on to have a distinguished jazz career), Ernest "Boom" Carter (a drummer who would leave to join Sancious), and Springsteen's longtime saxophonist Clarence Clemons. It can also be measured in terms of the artists whose work he has performed, among them Chuck Berry, Little Richard, and Gary U. S. Bonds. After encountering Bonds toiling as a lounge act in 1978, Springsteen wrote, played, sang, and produced songs on two albums for him, including Bonds's first hit single in almost twenty years ("This Little Girl" in 1981).

More decisively, African American musical traditions are the cornerstone of Springsteen's own music. His music has always drawn heavily on the percussive, rhythmic, and improvisatory elements central to the African American musical idiom. And while some of his recent work has relied on folk and country music, even many of Springsteen's White influences—among them Woody Guthrie, Hank Williams, Bob Dylan, and Van Morrison—themselves drew on Black music to give their own work its uniquely expressive power.

All this said, race as an explicit *theme* in Springsteen's work was another matter. For a long time, he had almost nothing to say on the subject. Given Springsteen's acknowledged influences, it comes as something of a surprise to realize how little a role race played in his lyrics in the first half of his career. There's nothing particularly biased in his songs, and the fact that a number of African Americans have recorded them, among them Donna Summer and the Pointer Sisters, suggests at least some racial elasticity. On the other hand, it's a little hard to picture a Black protagonist bewailing his lack of personal autonomy in songs like "The Promised Land" or "Badlands." In some sense, these songs reflect the obsessions of a relatively naive White boy who is shocked to learn that the world is not his oyster.

There was a time when one might have plausibly said that Springsteen's songs were not overtly racial because he cultivated a genuinely color-blind sensibility. A more likely explanation, though, is that, like many White people in the 1970s and '80s, Springsteen avoided the topic of race because it seemed too incendiary. Many White audiences simply did not want to listen to stories about Black people, and many Blacks would find unconscious racism even in Whites' best-intentioned gestures. Of course, it was impossible to sidestep the issue. Since the nineteenth century, virtually all White popular musicians, even those who were avowed racists, had been too dependent on Black culture to reject it completely. And silences can speak volumes.

Until the mid-eighties, only once did Springsteen directly discuss race in his music: "My Hometown," a single from *Born in the U.S.A.* that became a top-ten hit in 1985. The song is rendered from the point of view of a man who has lived his entire life in a small town and is now witnessing its decline. His dismay takes on added poignance in that he is now a father and is trying—but not completely able—to give his son the same sense of security his own father gave him. That security is symbolized by the two generations of sons who sit in their fathers' laps behind the steering wheels of their cars and navigate the local streets.

Characteristically, "My Hometown" deals with social issues—in this case, economic deterioration, racial tension, and the connection between them—in a highly personal way. "In '65 tension was running high in my high school," he sings in what is clearly an autobiographical vein. "There was a lot of fights between the black and white / There was nothing you could do." He then goes on to relate an incident about a gunfight: "Troubled times had come to my hometown." Everything about "My Hometown"—the earnest voice of the singer; the gentle, melancholy lilt of the music; the familiar yet still disheartening tenor of the story he tells—invites identification. "Yes," some may think on hearing this song, "It's too bad these things happen. A real shame."

The situation this man describes does, in fact, have historical resonance. Working-class Whites, unable to segregate themselves to the extent middle-class and upper-class Whites did, coexisted uneasily with Blacks throughout the postwar period, and such eruptions— often followed by the white flight that the family of the song finally prepares to undertake—were all too common. From this angle, the supposed victims of the song are perpetrators in their own right.

Such a view may be too severe; economic forces like the closing of factories have at least as much to do with the narrator's motives for departure as racial ones. But the real problem with this picture is that there's something airless, even antiseptic, about it. No one is actually creating or fomenting the racial tension: it's just there. So are the "words." And the "shotgun blast." A dismaying passivity character- izes the singer (and Springsteen himself). Perhaps even more than overt hostility, *this* was the attitude that Martin Luther King gave his life to combat: the idea that racism was inevitable, even natural. Springsteen seems to have realized this, and he changed.

Redeeming Dreams?

What I've come to learn is that the world is never saved in grand
messianic gestures, but in the simple accumulation of gentle, soft,
almost invisible acts of compassion.

—Chris Abani, 2008

Since the time of *Born in the U.S.A.*, Springsteen's experiences have
been less those of a man chasing a runaway American Dream than
those of one who has attained it—posing, at least theoretically, a
problem for a man whose work was originally premised on the
Dream's pursuit. Whatever else may have impelled the albums that
followed, one senses in *Tunnel of Love, Human Touch,* and *Lucky Town*
a kind of moral scruple about pretending to be something he is not.
So, for example, the very first words out of Springsteen's mouth in
Tunnel of Love, from "Ain't Got You," are "I got the fortunes of heaven
in diamonds and gold." On *Human Touch,* Springsteen begins his
satire of television, "57 Channels (and Nothin' On)," with the line
"I bought a bourgeois house in the Hollywood Hills." While most of
his more recent songs are not so quick to issue these virtual apologias,
and his music does not really focus on conspicuous consumption,
Springsteen seems to have been careful not to overreach himself in
the worlds he depicts in his work. That went for his depictions of race
as well, where there continued to be conspicuous silence.

This context is what makes his 1995 album *The Ghost of Tom Joad*
such a surprising, risky record. The degree of Springsteen's narrative
inventiveness is documented in the brief bibliography included in
the album's CD booklet. These sources describe milieus—the drug
trade, Ku Klux Klan activity, and, of course, the Okie migration to
California—a world apart from any he has ever known. Springsteen
had begun a reassessment.

The geographic locus of *Tom Joad* is the American Southwest,
especially Texas and California. But this is not the Texas of *Darkness
on the Edge of Town* or the California of *Human Touch* or *Lucky Town.*
Instead, it's the Southwest of an underclass even more impoverished

REALMS OF KINGS 75

than that of *Nebraska*. Once again, a socioeconomic lens is key. But the specific reason for the impoverishment of these people—and on this count the album as a whole is quite clear—is race. "Sinaloa Cowboys," for example, illustrates the way in which illegal Mexican immigrants in central California participate in the methamphetamine trade, and the disastrous end for two brothers who embarked on it because they could make as much in one day in the drug trade as they could in one year as migrant farmers. We know many other characters on the album are also Latino because of their names (e.g., Bobby Ramirez of "The Line") or because of the settings and language (the boy prostitute of San Diego's "Balboa Park" grew up in the "Zona Norte" and buys jeans "like the Gavachos wear"). Even as *Tom Joad* pays nuanced attention to the particulars of racial identity, however, it also points toward broader resonances. The underlying dynamics of the brothers' situation in "Sinaloa Cowboys" were basically the same dynamics as those driving the crack business among African Americans in a northeastern city or the crimes of an Asian drug cartel in the Pacific Northwest. Similarly, it would be very easy to imagine a Black man as the edgy, ambivalent ex-con of "Straight Time" (who could be a character out of a Richard Wright story), the murdered boxcar mentor of "The New Timer," or even the irritated spouse of "My Best Was Never Good Enough." None of these situations are inherently racial, but the burden of history—from the bonds of slavery to broken treaties—makes such circumstances disproportionately common in minority communities. What we're hearing is not racial appropriation but rather racial imagination.

Most commonly, the racism that enmeshes the non-White characters of *Tom Joad* is systemic. The border guard who narrates "The Line," for example, is not really a bad man; he's just doing his job in patrolling a boundary (though surrendering to a sexual pull he doesn't quite understand by letting a woman named Louisa through). The situation here is similar to "My Hometown" in that it depicts racism as an inescapable fog that cannot be fought and can only sometimes be escaped. But it also demonstrates Springsteen's increasingly sophisticated understanding of the ways in which oppression depends on silence, ignorance, and facelessness at least as much as it does on overt ill will.

Ill will, however, remains a big part of the equation, and it's confronted directly on "Galveston Bay." This song—more like a short story set to minimal music—was inspired by *A Season for Justice*, the memoir of the Alabama civil-rights activist Morris Dees, who founded the Southern Poverty Law Center in 1979 to combat hate crimes.[19] Springsteen adapted a story Dees told about a former officer in the South Vietnamese army who settles on the Gulf Coast of Texas into the fictionalized tale of Le Bin Son, a soldier who comes to the United States with his wife and daughter after the fall of Saigon. The family relocates in the East Texas town of Seabrook and buys a shrimp boat with his cousin. Grateful for what he has received and attained, he pauses to kiss his daughter before he heads off to work each day.

Meanwhile, another character, Billy Sutter, also lives in Seabrook. Billy, a Vietnam veteran injured in combat, returned home in 1968 and entered the family's fishing business to support his own wife and son (whom he also kisses before leaving for work each day). Like many of his friends who see Vietnamese refugees settling near Galveston Bay, Billy is uneasy and resentful. Although the narrator doesn't explicitly say so, he may be one of three Klan members who attempt to burn Le Bin Son's boat. When Le shoots and kills two of the men, and then is cleared by a jury on the grounds of self-defense, Billy vows vengeance. "My friend, you're a dead man," he says with chilling irony.

Just as the hopeful Mary of "Thunder Road" reappears as the hopeless wife and mother of "The River," Billy Sutter can be viewed as a later incarnation of the Vietnam-vet protagonist of "Born in the U.S.A.," his passion and defiance curdled into cynicism and hatred. By this point in his career, Springsteen had shown an almost frightening familiarity with evil, a familiarity that surfaces, for example, in his accounts of the murderous bank robber of "Highway 29" and the seductive temptations of "Straight Time." At the climax of "Galveston Bay," Billy Sutter is on the verge of acting out a bloodthirsty dream of vengeance: "Billy stood in the shadows / His Ka-Bar knife in his hand." And yet, at the crucial moment, he relents and lets Le pass. Our final view of Billy has him drinking a glass of water, kissing his sleeping wife, and heading back to cast his net into Galveston Bay. From such actions, we can infer that his decision not to murder Le is rooted in his unexpected recognition of a shared humanity and a glimpse of a different, better American Dream. Rather than remain in a spiritual wilderness, a fallen son goes home.

Not all Springsteen's racial stories end on a hopeful note. Four years after "Galveston Bay," he unveiled his starkest statement on race relations—more specifically, Black/White relations—with "American Skin (41 Shots)." This is a rare case of Springsteen commenting directly on an actual event: the police murder of an unarmed twenty-three-year-old Guinean immigrant, Amadou Diallo, in the vestibule of his Bronx apartment building. In February of 1999, plainclothes police were on patrol seeking a rapist reportedly wandering in the neighborhood and called out to Diallo. He responded to the officers' call the way he had been trained in his native land—by putting his hand into his pocket to produce identification—which was interpreted by the officers as reaching for a gun. They fired 41 shots, with 19 hitting him.[20] The eight-minute song that resulted, a brooding counterpart to "Land of Hope and Dreams," which was written around the same time, is similarly incantatory. But instead of offering hope, it proffers a stark warning: "You can get killed just for living in your American skin." That risk, the song makes clear, is much greater if that skin happens to be dark, which is why a mother in the song gravely teaches her son to make sure his hands are always visible in any encounters with the police—standard instructions in many Black families, of which many White ones are likely to be oblivious.

Springsteen debuted the song at a live show in Atlanta in June of 2000. By the time he featured it as part of a two-and-a-half-week stand at New York's Madison Square Garden later that month, word of mouth had circulated—and distorted—its message. Police officials criticized the song, with the leader of the New Fraternal Order of Police calling Springsteen "a floating fag."[21] There were apparently lots of boos, but they were hard to sort out from the chant "Bruuuce" that had been a longstanding staple of Springsteen concerts, though

at least one attendee stood at the foot of the stage and gave Springsteen the finger.[22]

"It wasn't a diatribe," Springsteen said, reflecting on the brouhaha
two decades later in a podcast with former president Barack Obama.
("You're kneeling over his body in the vestibule, praying for his life,"
goes one line, apparently the thoughts of an anguished police officer
taking stock of what he's done.) "It wasn't a finger-pointing song. It
just tried to tally up the human cost of those kinds of killing and mur-
ders that go on day after day."[23] Amadou Diallo's American Dream
died with him. That doesn't necessarily mean the Dream itself is dead.
But it's never something we can take for granted, either.

Common Sense

As Americans, we are all descendants of George Washington—and
his slaves.

—Michael Lind, *The Next American Nation* (1995)

"I would not be understood as advocating intermarriage between the
races," Frederick Douglass once wrote, addressing the deepest fear of
many Whites in the late nineteenth century, and one that, through
most of the following century, many Southerners in particular swore
would never be allowed to happen. But Douglass's remark was not
meant to reassure such people. "I do not say that what I say *should*
come to pass, but what I think is likely to come to pass, and what is
inevitable," he explained.[24]

This was not intended to be an incendiary statement. "I am not a pro-
pagandist but a prophet," Douglass asserted.[25] Unlike many of his fellow Americans, however, he was not at all troubled by his prediction. It
was part of a patient, hopeful expectation that his country was in a tran-
sitional stage to a truly blended America in which the contributions of
all would be recognized and woven into the fabric of American life.

Not that this would be easy. Attitudes are more difficult to change
than circumstances—so difficult, in fact, that many are skeptical of
even trying. "You can't legislate morality," went one of the truisms of

the 1950s, usually spoken by Whites resistant to ending segregation. To such people, King had an answer: "It may be true that morality cannot be legislated, but behavior can be regulated. The law may not change the heart, but it can restrain the heartless."[26]

In King's most famous address, he envisioned a world in which the sons of slaves and former slaveholders broke bread together at a table of brotherhood. But the core of King's dream was not simply that this would be possible but that it would become an ordinary event. This greatest American Dream, appropriately enough, continues to challenge us in its very simplicity.

Bruce Springsteen, of course, has had neither the experiences nor the vision of people like Frederick Douglass and Martin Luther King. Relative to them, his achievements are small, even ordinary. But it's a measure of *their* achievements that he has so thoroughly assimilated their commonsense dream and that its significance for him has only grown. In an important sense, he is their son, a product of the same cultural intermarriage that produced Elvis Presley, and one who instinctively makes room for other outsiders at the national table.

Into the 2020s, Springsteen remained rich and famous, a cultural icon who had succeeded in living out the American Dream on a scale comparable to that of his hero Elvis Presley. But the heart of his dream is less fame and money than the ability to make his life's work— music—a way of life. And what this has meant, in practice, is an ongoing dialogue with the musical traditions that nurtured him. In 2022, he released *Only the Strong Survive*, a set of cover versions of soul music he has loved, ranging from the obscure 1965 discarded Motown classic "Do I Love You? (Indeed I Do)" to "Nightshift," the loving tribute to Marvin Gaye and Jackie Wilson that became a major hit for the post–Lionel Richie Commodores in 1985.

Few White pop musicians today would try—or get away with— making an album that could plausibly be charged with cultural appropriation. But it's unlikely that most of those who monitor such offenses will care. Like Eric Clapton (who was also a major innovator of the blues idiom on which he built his career) or Van Morrison (who seamlessly fused African American and Celtic strains into a unique synthesis that was an important influence on the young Springsteen), he is too deeply immersed, and too reverent of his sources, to be effectively accused of glib exploitation.

Actually, that's a bit of a problem. *Only the Strong Survive* is a beautiful record. The strings—in profusion here—are honeyed; the production gleams. The background vocalists, who in his live performances seem no less curated by gender and race, are impeccable. The musicians, and in particular the drummer/producer Ron Aniello, are worthy of Elvis Presley's TCB ensembles of the seventies, which propped him up amid his descent into self-destruction. Unlike Presley, however, Springsteen remains an active and engaged student. The album is actually a means for him to work on his voice—much as his 1992 album *Human Touch* was a vehicle for him to work on his guitar playing—and he sings with more careful diction than he does on his own songs. His live and video performances feature movement and gestures that come straight out of the Diana Ross playbook. Really: it's uncanny. But it's also unclear what he's adding to these songs by recording them.

Ironically, the most potent message that comes out of this record is an implicitly political one. In absorbing this music, recording it, and actively striving to keep it in circulation in his now narrower ambit, Springsteen is affirming the power of racial integration as the core of a meaningful life. It's not Black music or White music, he seems to be saying—it's *American* music. We should recognize and savor it. This is not currently a fashionable stance in progressive circles eager to protect the integrity of particularistic identities. But Springsteen, who has long considered himself a man of the left, remains committed to sustaining the dreams of once and future Kings of America.

FIGURE 4.1. Still of Springsteen in Jonathan Demme's "Born in the U.S.A." video, 1984. A vehement opponent of the Vietnam War, Springsteen nevertheless developed a deep interest in veterans' experiences, one he continued to cultivate in songs of wartime experience in *The Rising* (2002) and *Devils and Dust* (2005). (Source: Columbia Records)

CHAPTER 4

Borne in the U.S.A.

Springsteen and the Weight of War

ON JANUARY 3, 1982, Bruce Springsteen made a tape with demo versions of a number of songs for his next album. He recorded them in his living room, accompanied only on an acoustic guitar, intending them as a kind of note-keeping for further reference. Eventually, these demos would form the core of *Nebraska*. One song from this very first group was called "Born in the U.S.A." This particular version had a faster pace than what came later, and it had a different melody. But the lyrics were the same. "It was a real odd thing, and it was not like anything else on the *Nebraska* album," producer Jon Landau later recalled. "And it was not like any other thing I've ever heard from Bruce—it sounded alien. It just didn't sound like it fit." Springsteen put the song aside.

His next step was to present the new material to the E Street Band. The group endured two weeks of frustration while Springsteen tried to shoehorn the songs into band arrangements that he and Landau felt distorted them. (He would ultimately release *Nebraska* with the tracks largely as he recorded them on that demo tape.) Concluding that they were getting nowhere, and with valuable studio time already booked, Springsteen—to the surprise of Landau and others—turned to "Born in the U.S.A." "To me, it was a dead song," Landau said. But Springsteen thought the very thing that was hampering the *Nebraska* material would help "Born in the U.S.A."—what Landau called "that turbulence and that scale" of a full-fledged rock song.[1]

So Springsteen ran through it, and taught keyboardist Roy Bittan the riff that would become its dominant motif. He told drummer Max Weinberg to keep going after he finished the verses and then asked the band as a whole to play it in its entirety. Landau recalls that it was the second complete take that ended up on *Born in the U.S.A.*, an album dominated by live (as opposed to studio-constructed) tracks. With some hyperbole, the producer-manager described the recording of "Born in the U.S.A." as "the most exciting thing that ever happened in a recording studio."[2] The excitement one hears in this recording is palpable, but difficult to describe. It opens with Bittan's synthesizer and Weinberg's snare drum, both of which seem as if they're being played in a cavernous space. Bittan's six-note phrase has a vaguely martial air to it; Weinberg's snare sounds like a shotgun. Without anything that actually resembles one, the song evokes a march: energetic yet precise.

The lyrics are another story. "Born down in a dead man's town / First kick I took was when I hit the ground," they begin. The narrator compares himself to a beaten dog who spends "half his life coverin' up." Considered alone, these words sound like they could be sung by a mournful Mississippi Delta bluesman. But—and this is crucial to the power of the song—Springsteen does not sing them that way. His voice is raspy yet focused; he sounds positively ferocious. Weinberg punctuates the words "hit the ground" with his bass drum, underlining what's being described but adding even more energy to the song—as if an engine is being jump-started.

Then, before Springsteen begins the next verse, a prominent rhythm guitar enters the mix, churning the song forward. "Got in a little hometown jam / So they put a rifle in my hand," he sings. "So they sent me off to a foreign land / To go and kill the yellow man." In their terse, assonant style—"jam," "hand," "land," "man"—these lyrics establish a somewhat different argument about the Vietnam War than that of much popular culture, which often depicts a sense of betrayal, so powerful because the victims of the war had held the nation's ideals in such high esteem. Here, however, betrayal has taken place as soon as this man "hit the ground," long before he was ever sent abroad.

While this veteran is hardly blameless—as he admits, he got *himself* in a "hometown jam"—the very fact that he's sent abroad is a by-product of misguided, if not cynical, social policy. In many communities in his era, judges dealing with youthful delinquents offered the armed forces as a substitute for jail time, in the hope that both the army and the youth would benefit from the experience. Very often, neither did. "We tried to persuade ourselves that all we needed was better leadership to bring the delinquents around," Colin Powell, who was an officer in Vietnam before he became chairman of the Joint Chiefs of Staff and later Secretary of State, recalled of such soldiers he encountered in the 1950s and '60s. "Meanwhile, good troops saw the bad ones get away with murder, a situation destructive of morale overall."[3]

If the army was not a happy experience for our protagonist, neither was returning home. He finds little in the way of the opportunity that Americans endlessly invoke: "Come back home to the refinery / Hiring man says, 'Son, if it was up to me . . .'" The folks back home mean well but they lack credibility; in a metaphorical sense, they can't finish what they start. The veteran, by contrast, represents himself and others in concrete, vivid language, even when describing an absence: "Had a brother at Khe Sahn / Fighting off the Viet Cong / They're still there / He's all gone." He notes that his brother had a Vietnamese lover and that he keeps a photograph of them together. His remembrance of a lost, shattered world goes to the very heart of what "Born in the U.S.A." is about: making us know, and care, about losers. In that regard, it's crucial that the narrator does unto others what he implicitly asks that we do unto him.

But he never asks for our pity, and that too is crucial to the power of the song. In the last verse, he stands in the shadows of a local penitentiary and refinery with nowhere to run. But his chant of "Born in the U.S.A." is less a lament than an assertion of pride. Pride not in the hope for, or fulfillment of, American Dreams, but rather in the will to survive them. That's why this man makes the improbable declaration, "I'm a cool rocking daddy in the U.S.A." at the end of the song: he's recasting the very definition of what it means to be a success in America.

A will to survive does not necessarily mean one *will* survive, however. The flip side of "Born in the U.S.A."—both literally and figuratively when the song peaked at #9 on the *Billboard* pop chart in January of 1985—is "Shut Out the Light," which was released as the B-side of the seven-inch vinyl single to "Born in the U.S.A." (It subsequently resurfaced on *Tracks* in 1998). "Shut Out the Light" is sung from the point of view of an exhausted vet for whom darkness invites horrifying flashbacks. Springsteen took the core of that song and incorporated it into "Born in the U.S.A." by having the narrator quietly say, "No, no, no" or "Oh my God, no" between the verses. Here, then, is one more countercurrent in the song, and powerful evidence that, for this man, the war is not, and will never be, over.

The music of "Born in the U.S.A." is also suggestively ambiguous. At the end of the song, Weinberg goes into an extended drum solo while the rest of the band seems to be straining simply to remain in the established chord progression. Eventually, it pulls together again—only to fade out. If there really is triumph here, it's only one part of our national story.

But triumph is mostly what was heard at the time. "Born in the U.S.A." has become a signature song for Springsteen, second only to "Born to Run" in establishing his fame. Though it was not the biggest hit from that album—"Dancing in the Dark" went to number two, blocked from the top spot by Prince's "When Doves Cry"—it has long been regarded as a kind of national anthem, particularly when augmented by the visual iconography of the time: a brawny Springsteen in a bandana wearing leather and denim (figure 4.1), as well as Annie Leibovitz's famous album cover showing Springsteen standing with his back to the camera in front of an American flag.

Springsteen did not regard the catchiness of the new tune as an unmixed blessing, however, and "Born in the U.S.A." proved to be something of a political football in the months that followed. As we've seen, President Reagan invoked the song at a 1984 reelection campaign rally in New Jersey, causing much outrage. Chrysler chairman Lee Iacocca offered Springsteen an estimated $12 million to use the song in an ad (he declined). Decades later, Springsteen was still ruminating ruefully about trick-or-treaters in red bandannas coming to his house and singing the song each Halloween. In later years he would perform much more spare and dark versions of the song, bringing its tragic dimensions into sharper focus.[4]

It's not exactly that Reagan and Iaccoca were wrong to hear what they did, however cynical they might have been: "Born in the U.S.A." really *is* about American resilience and pride. But that's not *all* it is. And by placing it in the context of its moment, one can see just how distinctive a statement it was and why it retains its cultural power. Amid forgetfulness and denial, Springsteen wove the experience of war back into the fabric of everyday American life—a recurring theme in his work ever since.

Generational Destruction

I know one of the worst effects of this whole thing is the way it's ravaged my own image of myself, taken my mind off higher things, restricted my ability to become involved with causes or people—I honestly feel so screwed up tight that I am incapable, I think, of giving myself, of really loving.
—Bill Clinton, writing to a friend about the draft, August 20, 1969

Don't fret too much over this Vietnam thing, Sam. You shouldn't feel bad about any of it. It had nothing to do with you.
—Irene Hughes, mother of Samantha Hughes, the protagonist of Bobbie Ann Mason's novel *In Country* (1985)

Even before Vietnam was a lost cause, it was an ambiguous one at best for millions of those who were chosen to fight it. Living in a post-draft era, it's hard for those born since it ended in 1973 to grasp how large a part the Selective Service played in shaping the lives of young men for twenty-five years following World War II, including its especially dramatic role during the Vietnam War. This was not simply because many young men did not wish to go to war, but also because that strong desire to evade or resist it was coupled with gnawing feelings that they really *should* go, whether as a matter of patriotism, equity, or solidarity with their peers. Through combinations of principle, luck, opportunism, and evasion, many men escaped the draft. But they could not escape being haunted by it, whether in terms of their subsequent career paths or by the knowledge that others were not so lucky.

Bruce Springsteen had no doubts about the Vietnam War or his participation in it: he was opposed to both. This was not a matter of careful consideration of the pros and cons, however. "There wasn't any kind of political consciousness down in Freehold in the late sixties," he explained later. "It was just a small town, and the war seemed very distant. I mean I was aware of it through some friends that went." One such friend was Bart Hanes, the drummer in Springsteen's first band. "'Well, I enlisted,'" Springsteen recalls Hanes telling him. "I remember he didn't even know where Vietnam *was*. And that was it. He left and he didn't come back. And the guys who did come back were not the same."[5]

Right around the time future president Bill Clinton was notified to appear at his local draft office (he maneuvered his way into a Rhodes Scholarship to Oxford), so was Bruce Springsteen (he had dropped out of Ocean County Community College, forfeiting any hope for deferment). Unlike Clinton, who wrung his hands and dragged his feet, Springsteen knew his course of action: "When I got on the bus to take my physical, I thought one thing: *I ain't goin.* I had tried to go to college, and I didn't really fit in. I went to a real narrow-minded school where people just gave me a lot of trouble and I was hounded off the campus—I just looked different and acted different, so I left school. And I remember bein' on that bus, me and a couple of guys in my band, and the rest of the bus was probably sixty, seventy percent black guys from Asbury Park. And I remember thinkin' like, 'What makes my life, or my friends' lives, more expendable than that of somebody who's goin' to school?' It just didn't seem right."[6]

However determined Springsteen may have been to resist the implacable force of the U.S. government, it was only one such force with which he had to contend. Another was family pressure—specifically that of his father, Douglas, a World War II veteran who, like many fathers of the era, bitterly resented the attitudes of the younger generation, which they considered self-absorbed and unpatriotic. Springsteen was not a hippie in the classic mold, but he did, however passively, oppose the war. And he exhibited the signal characteristic of the counterculture for men: long hair. The notion that hairstyle can make a powerful statement is not unfamiliar in the twenty-first century; many of us are aware, for example, of how fraught but potentially empowering it can be for African American women in particular. But we have forgotten what a pointed ideological statement it could make, or be perceived to make, in that period we think of as "the sixties."

Hair—the title of a hit musical in 1968—was also a source of considerable friction between Springsteen and his father that year, and it figures at the center of a monologue that would later be a staple of Springsteen's live shows. "When I was growing up, me and my dad used to go at it all the time over almost anything," he would begin. "I used to have really long hair, all the way down past my shoulders." For the elder Springsteen, long hair was symptomatic of his son's shortcomings, but there was nothing wrong with him that a tour of duty in a place like Vietnam couldn't fix. As Springsteen would go on to explain (this particular version comes from the live version of "The River" included on *Live 1975–85*):

> The first thing he would always ask me [when the younger Springsteen came home after the two had a fight] was what did I think I was doing with myself. And the worst part about it was that I could never explain it to him. I remember I got into a motorcycle accident once and I was laid up in bed, and he had a barber come in and cut my hair. And man, I could remember telling him that I hated him and that I would never, ever forget it. And he used to tell me, "Man, I can't wait till the army gets you. When the army gets you they're gonna make a

man outta you. They're gonna cut all that hair off of you and they're gonna make a man outta you."

According to the elder Springsteen, a man had short hair. And would stand up for a fight. This might not be masculinity in its entirety, but it was a start, one his son had not even made.

As it turned out, it was the cause of Springsteen's forced haircut—his motorcycle accident—that saved him from the draft, though for good measure he stayed up all night before the exam, claimed to be gay, and answered his questioners as erratically as he could. He was classified 4-F, effectively ending the possibility of his entering the army. By that point, of course, the Tet Offensive had demonstrated that the Viet Cong's will to fight was greater than the U.S. government had calculated. Realizing that public trust in him and the war effort had been permanently damaged, President Lyndon Johnson decided not to run for reelection. His successor, Richard Nixon, would soon be bogged down in his own Vietnam quagmire, and then a Watergate scandal, which further corroded the confidence the American people, young and old, had in their government.

And Douglas Springsteen? His son related what happened upon his return from his examination.

My dad said, "Where you been?"

I said, "I went to take my physical."

He said, "What happened?"

I said, "They didn't take me."

And he said, "That's good."

At this point, the crowd roars, as it did when Springsteen revealed earlier that he failed his physical ("Ain't nothing to applaud about," he tells them). The moral of the story is clear: Vietnam was a bad war, and in the end, even people like Douglas Springsteen could see that and allow the generation gap to close. The worst thing was that the son could never explain; the best was that he didn't have to. In a specific, limited, but important sense, this constitutes a happy ending.

And that may be fine as far as it goes. The crowd can even feel complacent that the villain of the piece is converted. But as Springsteen knew, it was not really the end of the story, and his subsequent career has become a sustained exploration of his recognition of the limits of his own vision as the boy on that bus.

A turning point came in 1981, when he read Ron Kovic's Vietnam memoir *Born on the Fourth of July,* which chronicled a naive young patriot's descent into Vietnam and his later opposition to the war as a matter of patriotism. With the memory of Bart Hanes in mind, Springsteen asked his manager Jon Landau to help him find a way to help Vietnam veterans. Landau, in turn, contacted Joe Klein, Woody Guthrie's biographer (and *Primary Colors* author), who put Springsteen in touch with Bob Muller, a former U.S. Marine Corps lieutenant who headed an organization called Vietnam Veterans of America. Springsteen went on to give a number of benefit performances for VVA that virtually single-handedly saved the organization from financial collapse. Muller himself went so far as to say that "without Bruce Springsteen, there would be no Vietnam veterans movement."[7]

This is surely an exaggeration, but it's fair to say that Springsteen was among the first to build bridges between veterans and rock-and-rollers—or, more pointedly, between those who served and those who didn't. In so doing, he made a powerful statement about the responsibility we have to those who acted in good faith on behalf of their government, even when others profoundly disagreed with its politics or believed it was wrong.

Other champions of veterans—like Ronald Reagan—would reject this approach by instead insisting on the winnability of the war and its moral legitimacy. "I think that what's happening now is that people want to forget," Springsteen said of this view around the time of Reagan's reelection. "There was Vietnam, there was Watergate, there was Iran [the Iranian hostage scandal of 1979–1981]: we were beaten, we were hustled, and then we were humiliated. And I think people got a need to feel good about the country again. But what's happening, I think, is that that need—which is a good thing—is gettin' manipulated and exploited."[8] For Springsteen, this meant glib flag-waving without consideration of the costs of the war, whether justified or not.

In any case, Springsteen's engagement with veterans had at least two other salutary consequences. The first is that it established a pattern he would later replicate in other kinds of philanthropic work. Throughout the *Born in the U.S.A.* tour, for example, he would devote one night's show to a particular charity—a food bank, for example— to which he would make a contribution and invite the audience to do so as well as part of a broader sense of republican citizenship. "I think people on their own can do a lot," he said. "I guess that's what I'm tryin' to figure out now: where do the aesthetic issues that you write about intersect with some sort of concrete action, some direct involvement, in the communities where your audiences come from?"[9] Such an approach suggested one answer.

The other consequence was in the artistic realm. Springsteen's VVA benefit took place at the end of his long tour to support *The River.* After the tour ended in 1981, he returned to New Jersey for his first sustained break from recording and performing in three years. One result of Springsteen's subsequent reflections—which included a period of depression reflected in the songs he wrote in these years[10]— was "Born in the U.S.A."

National Anthem

And always, they would ask you with an emotion whose intensity to shock you to please tell it, because they really did have the feeling that it wasn't all being told for them, that they were going through all of this and that somehow no one back in the world knew about it. They may have been a bunch of dumb, brutal, killer kids (a lot of correspondents privately felt that), but they were smart enough to know that much.

—Michael Herr, *Dispatches* (1977)

In the official ideology of the United States—in that mythic place where all people are equal before the law, where big dreams and hard work pay off, and where right makes might—there's relatively little room for defeat. Of course, we know that American history is not a string of effortless victories. The triumph of Yorktown was preceded by the bitter ordeal of Valley Forge; MacArthur had to lose the Philippines in order to take them back. And the Alamo is still remembered, albeit somewhat selectively, as a martyrs' grave rather than as a bunker for defenders of a land grab. Moreover, generations of grieving wives, sisters, and mothers know all too well the price of victory, a price that seldom leads to jubilation on the part of those who pay it. It's notable in this context that Springsteen chose to include on his 2007 album *Live in Dublin* the Irish folk song "Mrs. McGrath," which is rendered from the point of view of a woman emotionally crushed by a son's loss of both legs. "All foreign wars I do proclaim / Live only on blood and a mother's pain," she says.

To some extent, the lack of space for defeat in this country is historical: the United States, almost always the victor, has little lore of legends of invasions weathered, as in Mexico and Russia; millennial dynasties laid low, as in Egypt and China; or vanquished nationhood awaiting resurrection, as in Israel and Poland. To a great extent, our knowledge of what it means to lose a national struggle comes from the indigenous peoples we have defeated. That's something we have, or have allowed ourselves, a limited ability to understand, and something we've tried to grasp only fitfully, notably in a strain of the Western film tradition that includes *Cheyenne Autumn* (1964), *Little Big Man* (1970), and *Last of the Mohicans* (made a number of times, most memorably in 1992).

Prior to Vietnam, the most notable exception to this tradition of victory was the experience of the seceded Southern states in the Civil War. Here was a struggle that was an unambiguous failure, at least in military terms, but one that would capture the imagination of North and South for the next century as "the Lost Cause." The precise parameters of the term are rarely articulated; it's usually been a vague slogan that encompasses narrow interpretations of states' rights and a broad sense of the honor of fighting for family and home, but virtually never a confrontation with the institution of chattel slavery, which Confederate vice president Alexander Stephens (before the war, anyway) called the "cornerstone" of the Southern way of life. Though there have been some sober imaginative treatments in previous decades of the Southern white experience (notably Charles Frazier's 1997 novel *Cold Mountain*, which was made into a fine 2003 movie), only in the 2020s has there been a sustained attempt to literally dismantle this mythology as displayed in the plethora of Confederate monuments, most of which were erected in the period between the 1890s and 1920s, when the push for the Lost Cause was most energetically sustained.

"The Cause" was also promulgated in popular fiction, music, and eventually film, and some of the best-known works of American culture, notably *Birth of a Nation* (1915) and *Gone with the Wind* (1939), condensed and codified the mythology of a bucolic social order destroyed by hotheaded rebels or brutish Yankees. In any case, almost from the moment of Robert E. Lee's surrender, sober contemplation of Southern defeat shaded, almost imperceptibly, into defiant celebration that did little to examine the underlying causes of that defeat apart from the overwhelming numbers of the Northern forces. This impulse continued pretty much throughout the twentieth century. In rock music, for example, the Charlie Daniels Band told us that "The South's Gonna Do It Again" in his signature tune of the early 1970s, while in country music, Hank Williams, Jr., asserted that "If the South Would Have Won (Woulda Had It Made)" in the late 1980s. Just *what* the South's gonna do—or just *who* "we" are—is never explained. An explanation would undoubtedly have proven difficult, sticky, or repellent. Nevertheless, the Confederate flag remained a potent icon in college dorms, on pickup trucks, and in Southern state capitals into the twenty-first century.[11]

There has never been revelry surrounding the American memory of Vietnam, however. Whether those on the left who argue that we should never have gotten involved, or those on the right who argue that the left lost the war, all agree that our Vietnam experience was a nightmare best forgotten. It's an ironic consensus, and the ensuing mutual silence has permitted most Americans to ignore the literal devastation that blanketed Vietnam.

Comparisons with the collective memory of other wars makes the Vietnam case all the more striking. One gets a vivid sense of the basic national stance toward World War II, for instance, by looking to the culture of war movies during and after it: in the twenty-year period between *Casablanca* (1942) and *The Longest Day* (1962), the conflict is almost always portrayed as an essential—and triumphant—struggle of good over evil. Humphrey Bogart may be a little more reluctant than John Wayne, but there was never any doubt as to who the good guys and bad guys were. Wayne himself, with appearances in *The Fighting Seabees* (1944), *Sands of Iwo Jima* (1949), *In Harm's Way* (1965), and many other films, virtually defined the subgenre of heroic World War II movies.

While roughly 450 World War II movies were released during the war, only one Vietnam film came out during that conflict. This was *The Green Berets,* a 1968 release starring, of course, John Wayne. Made at the height of the war, it can be considered a kind of booster film of the type made during World War II. By the time of the Tet Offensive, however, doubts about the war made it difficult to sell an unalloyed celebration of the American effort—or, for that matter, anything at all about the war. For the next decade, Hollywood and pop culture generally avoided Vietnam altogether.

When the subject was taken up again in the late seventies, treatments of the war exhibited a pattern that would be common for over a decade: the depiction of Vietnam as a surreal, incomprehensible world in which all normal rules and expectations were ignored or inverted. This tendency was first manifest in writing on the war, notably journalist Michael Herr's *Dispatches* (1977), widely considered the finest reporting to come out of the conflict. It was not, however, reportage in the conventional sense of the word. Profane, iconoclastic, and avowedly subjective, Herr, a practitioner of the so-called New Journalism popularized by Tom Wolfe, went to great lengths to describe the war in perceptual terms at least as much as factual ones. So, for example, the Tet Offensive was "a huge collective nervous breakdown," conducted in a country that was "a dark room full of deadly objects."[12] The cinematic equivalent of such prose was director Francis Ford Coppola's epic *Apocalypse Now* (1979). Coppola and co-screenwriter John Milius made the film an Americanized version of Joseph Conrad's *Heart of Darkness,* with the search by Captain

Willard (Martin Sheen) for the ominously elusive Colonel Kurtz (Marlon Brando) as a parable of latent American savagery.

This approach to the Vietnam War, while compelling and incisive, was also somewhat problematic. First, however real such depictions might seem, they take American failure in the war—a failure that could plausibly be attributed to poor strategy, faulty intelligence, the hard-won resilience of the enemy, or moral weakness—and project it into the realm of the irrational, inscrutable, irredeemable. There's more than a little racism in this approach, too: the Vietnamese, instead of being portrayed as determined, tragic, and fallible people, tend to become an unknowable other—contemptible or terrifying, but rarely anything in between. In this line of thinking, we lost in Vietnam because we had to: the deck was stacked in a deadly game that we didn't have a clue how to play.

While a number of other movies would draw on a Coppola-esque sense of "The Horror" (notably Stanley Kubrick's 1987 *Full Metal Jacket*), a somewhat different, less ironic strategy was more common, especially among those movies that fall into the category of what communications scholar Pat Aufderheide has called the "noble-grunt film."[13] Its essence can be grasped in the most basic plot description of Michael Cimino's 1978 Best Picture winner *The Deer Hunter*: three basically decent guys from the heartland leave their mill town, experience The Horror, and return with wrecked lives. There's no mention of strategic objectives, national goals, or even brotherhood within any military unit, even when the three are imprisoned with other Americans. It's as if the only way to salvage the Vietnam movie as a credible form was to marginalize the big picture and project a small one.

This may be why so many movies about Vietnam—from *Coming Home* (1978) to *Born on the Fourth of July* (1989)—focus much of their action on the domestic scene, whether during the war or after it, and on the scars of the Vietnam vet and his loved ones. For the regular moviegoer in these years, a veteran who was not taciturn, self-pitying, and potentially violent seemed like an aberration. What makes these people sympathetic characters is not the cause that sent them overseas (they were lied to), or even the experience of combat (the enemy was invisible), but simply their returning home. Survival is heroism, and cynicism the final ideal. By the end of the decade, Aufderheide suggests, the noble-grunt movies may have helped Americans recover, "not for anything U.S. forces did in Vietnam, but simply for having felt so bad for so long."[14]

It was one thing to feel less bad; it was another to feel good. A number of American films in the 1980s attempted to portray military involvement in a more sympathetic light, only to reveal the limitations and contradictions involved in such an attempt. The most commercially successful version was *Top Gun* (1986), essentially a 110-minute recruiting commercial for the U.S. Navy. There's a hollowness at the core of the movie, though, because there's no real adversary. "If I can't shoot this sonofabitch, let's see if we can have some fun with him," says Tom Cruise's character, Pete Maverick, during an incident with a Soviet-made MiG fighter early in the film. By the time he finally gets his chance for some real action, a rescue mission on a disabled communications ship that "wandered" into foreign territory, one wonders if any of these characters—or any of the filmgoers who flocked to the movie in droves—had ever heard of the Gulf of Tonkin. (A similar vacancy characterizes the more emotionally resonant 2022 sequel, *Maverick*, where the mission at the center of the plot is again an unnamed enemy—perhaps an attempt to avoid angering the Chinese government, which has exerted increasing influence on the U.S. film industry.)[15]

Perhaps the pivotal figure in this quest for post-Vietnam heroism is a movie character who throughout the eighties was often cited as Bruce Springsteen's foil: Sylvester Stallone's John Rambo (figure 4.2). There are some important similarities between Springsteen's "Born in the U.S.A." persona and Stallone's alter ego. Both characters are emotionally scarred veterans. Both are prime specimens of masculinity. And both have a laconic vernacular style that seems to imply a repository of deep-seated moral certainty.

Actually, such qualities were hardly unique to Springsteen's and Stallone's characters; they represent sturdy American archetypes. From James Fenimore Cooper's Leatherstocking to the characters

FIGURE 4.2. Sylvester Stallone in *Rambo III* (1988). Rambo was often upheld as Springsteen's foil in the 1980s. But Rambo's sense of grievance contrasted with the sense of responsibility and empathy that characterized the soldiers and veterans in Springsteen's songs. (Source: Carolco Pictures)

played by John Wayne, such traits were considered emblematic of an ideal American male shaped by native soil. Indeed, Rambo himself has Indian blood, a symbolic explanation for his resilience and ingenuity, as well as his tragic view of life. A cursory look at the *Rambo* movies suggests, however, that his character is less a means for attaining mature masculine wisdom than for expressing macho resentment in the cowboy rhetoric of Ronald Reagan—himself often, and more plausibly, compared with Rambo than Springsteen.

The initial film in the series, *First Blood* (1982), introduces John Rambo. The plot unfolds with misunderstanding between the character and a local sheriff in Washington state that leads to car crashes, the arrival of the National Guard, and the incineration of much of a town before Rambo's superior officer, played by Richard Crenna, finally confronts him in an empty police station. "It's over, Johnny," Crenna advises, giving Stallone the chance to put his rage into words: "It wasn't my war. You asked me, I didn't ask you. And I did what I had to do to win. Then I come back to the world, and I see all those maggots at the airport protesting me, spitting, calling me baby killer and all kinds of crap. Who are they to protest me? Unless they've been me and been there?"

Rambo has a point, and it's one that no doubt represented the rage of many Vietnam veterans, as well as noncombatant war supporters at home. Yet his actions—and the depictions of those who oppose him—have something of a paranoid, even homicidal quality that competes with the viewer's sense of Rambo as a hapless victim. "They drew first blood" is his justification. These tendencies are even more pronounced in *Rambo: First Blood Part II* (1985), which implies that the U.S. government conspiratorially avoided retrieving its POWs and MIAs from Vietnam. *Rambo II* is one of a number of eighties movies (the 1984 film *Missing in Action* is another) that involve returning to Vietnam to set right some individual wrongs. When Crenna proposes an undercover mission to find American prisoners, Stallone asks, "Do we get to win this time?" Though a third Rambo film, *Rambo III*, set amid the Russian war in Afghanistan, was a box-office flop in 1998, there were further sequels in 2008 and 2019. The astonishing

persistence of this return-to-Vietnam trope is suggested in its perhaps unlikely reemergence in the 2020 Spike Lee film *Da 5 Bloods*, in
which a group of Black vets go back in country in search of a fallen
squad leader—and some buried treasure they left behind.

This brief, and necessarily simplistic, gloss of Vietnam in popular
culture overlooks important countercurrents. For example, Oliver
Stone's Vietnam movies include *Heaven & Earth* (1993), a notable
exploration of a female Vietnamese perspective. Brian De Palma's
Casualties of War (1989) depicts grunts who are not noble at all. Nor can
all the grief depicted in noble-grunt movies be reduced to by-products
of aggrievement. Robin Williams injects humor and humanity into
Barry Levinson's *Good Morning, Vietnam* (1987). Moreover, film was
not the only medium to engage with the topic in these years. Novelists like Bobbie Ann Mason and Tim O'Brien wrote nuanced works
that wrestled with Vietnam's ambiguous, ambivalent legacy to the
United States.

But the most immediate cultural backdrop for "Born in the U.S.A"
was not the intercultural dialogue across journalism, film, and fiction
media, but rather the intercultural dialogue in rock-and-roll music in
the years preceding Springsteen's song. In the sixties, of course, rock's
tendencies were overwhelmingly antiwar. Perhaps the defining song
of the Vietnam era was Country Joe and the Fish's "Feel-Like-I'm-
Fixin'-to-Die Rag." Released in 1967, it encapsulated the Summer of
Love: sarcastic, profane, and from San Francisco. Country Joe and
the Fish were on the roster at Woodstock two years later, and "Fixin'-
to-Die" was prominently featured in the 1970 film documenting the
event. There were a number of other important antiwar songs in the
era, among them Buffalo Springfield's "For What It's Worth" (1967)
and the Jefferson Airplane's "Volunteers" (1969). (A teenaged Springsteen himself made a foray into this territory in his unreleased 1967
song "All Man the Guns.")[16] But few were as memorable—or as
polarizing—as "Fixin'-to-Die."

Like Hollywood, the counterculture was relatively silent about
Vietnam in the later seventies. To some extent, this was surely a
matter of the war being viewed as a bad trip that most Americans

wanted to forget. But like Lyndon Johnson and Richard Nixon, rock and rollers suffered from a credibility gap. For musicians ignorant of and hostile toward the war experience, representing it may have seemed insuperably difficult or pointless.

There were a handful of performers who tried to explore military experience in the late seventies. Notably, however, such engagement was indirect. The Talking Heads song "Life during Wartime" (1979) depicts a protagonist involved in clandestine operations and stunned by how different it is from anything he has previously known ("This ain't no party, this ain't no disco"). In "Powderfinger," a song from his classic 1979 album *Rust Never Sleeps,* Neil Young posits an imaginary landscape in which an inarticulate young man instinctively responds to an invasion by grabbing a gun—and subsequently speaking from beyond the grave. Young sings the song with heartbreaking effect, and his backing band, Crazy Horse, provides a gnarled, dissonant backdrop. In its harrowing depiction of a life destroyed by a reflexive embrace of armed conflict, "Powderfinger" is one of the great antiwar songs in the history of popular music.

It was only in the early eighties, however, that Vietnam itself would be explicitly discussed in popular music. Billy Joel weighed in with "Goodnight Saigon" from *The Nylon Curtain* (1982), an album with thematic similarities to Springsteen's own *Nebraska.* "Goodnight Saigon" is a seven-minute epic, complete with the sound effects of crickets and helicopters—a kind of musical equivalent of *Apocalypse Now.* However, its incantation that "we would all go down together" suggests a fatalistic tone closer to the noble-grunt aesthetic of *The Deer Hunter* and subsequent Vietnam movies.

Somewhat simpler—and perhaps more affecting—is the Charlie Daniels Band's "Still in Saigon" (1982). Its dominant mood, however, is one of sheer confusion on the part of a veteran alienated from himself and others. "I can't tell no one I feel ashamed / Afraid someday I'll go insane," he muses. For this vet and others, Vietnam was less a foreign conflict than an inner civil war.

Considered against this backdrop, "Born in the U.S.A." is very much a product of its time. It does bear resemblance to the noble-grunt

Vietnam movies in that the perspective of its protagonist tends to be more local than global, tends to avoid ideology, and upholds resilience as the primary available virtue under the circumstances. But as indicated, his sense of grievance, while real, doesn't prevent him from accepting responsibility for his own mistakes, nor does he lose sight of victims—not all of whom were soldiers—other than himself. Which may just be a way of saying that "Born in the U.S.A." is a more nuanced work of art about Vietnam than the examples discussed above—perhaps one reason why it has survived while so many songs like it have receded into obscurity.

Another reason why the song is unusual in Springsteen's canon is that it represented a distinct departure from the preoccupations of civilian life that were—and to a great extent remained—at the center of his work. But war was still on his mind even as he returned to more parochial concerns in the 1990s. In his 1992 song "Souls of the Departed," from *Lucky Town*, an army officer in Basra, Iraq, is ordered to go through the clothes of dead soldiers during the Persian Gulf War of 1991. His haunted grief is compared with that of a mother in the virtual warzone in East Compton, where her seven-year-old boy is murdered by a gang. Here again, Springsteen links conflicts at home and abroad and contrasts the agony of these people with the complacent indifference of elites: "In the hills the self-made men just sighed and shook their heads." Little did he or anyone else know just how close to home a foreign war would come in a turbulent new century.

The Fight for Peace

I think one of the things that shocked people was the size of the sacrifice made on that day. There's nothing that I think could prepare people—I mean, whatever they're paying you to be a fireman or a policeman, they're not paying you for that. And that goes to some central point about how people experience their duty, their place in the world, their connection to the people alongside themselves and to complete strangers. If you look at the past twenty years, people might say, "Oh, that's disappeared from America." But if you look closely, it's there every day.

—Bruce Springsteen at Ground Zero, September 11, 2021

On the morning of September 11, 2001, Bruce Springsteen came down from his bedroom into his kitchen, where he was informed that a plane had flown into the World Trade Center. He watched the drama unfold on a television in his living room, transfixed and perplexed. That afternoon, he drove to a local bridge where it was possible to see the Twin Towers from the Jersey shore, and sat alone in his car watching the torrents of rising smoke. Upon leaving the parking lot, he encountered a passing motorist who rolled down his window. "Bruce, we need you!" he shouted from the moving vehicle, and disappeared without awaiting a reply.[17] The incident has since passed into that form of Springsteen lore known as a Bruce Story.

A lot of residents in northeastern New Jersey, the heart of Springsteen country, needed all the help they could get in those dark days. Commuters from that part of the state comprised the highest proportion of victims in the attacks in Manhattan, at the Pentagon, and in Pennsylvania. "The local communities were hit pretty hard," Springsteen told a reporter. "There were 150-plus casualties from Monmouth County alone. You would drive by the church every day and there was another funeral." In the days that followed, he was one of a number of celebrities who felt compelled to make gestures of solidarity. His responses included a live recording of himself singing "Thunder Road" to be played at a victim's funeral (he feared that actually attending would prove to be a media distraction), performing at a local theater with other musicians to raise a million dollars for the families of victims in Monmouth County, and premiering a new song, "My City of Ruins," for a fundraising telethon on September 21.The song, written about nearby Asbury Park, nevertheless seemed appropriate to the mood and conditions of New York City at the time.

As the motorist's unsolicited comment suggests, Springsteen's voice seemed especially welcome, even necessary, in the aftermath of September 11. A number of songs, particularly Irving Berlin's "God Bless

America," were widely embraced in the weeks and months that followed, and various performers, ranging from Bette Midler to Lee Greenwood, made commemorative appearances. There were benefit records and concerts, and a number of new songs, such as Paul McCartney's "Freedom" and Alan Jackson's "Where Were You (When the World Stopped Turning)?" were written in response to the tragedies. Yet more than any musician of his generation, Springsteen was widely seen as the foremost chronicler and poet of ordinary Americans, a man whose music spoke to—and for—the people. So his profile seemed especially prominent in those days; "My City of Ruins," for example, would be the lead track on the commemorative album *A Nation of Heroes*, which was released that fall.

In the months that followed, the attacks—which jarred a nation not used to experiencing devastation in the homeland, and which triggered two wars that would enmesh the United States for the next two decades—gradually became the centerpiece of Springsteen's artistic imagination. "When that guy yelled out, 'Bruce, we need you,' that was a tall order, but I knew what he meant," Springsteen remembered fifteen years later. "I needed something, someone, too. As I drove home that lonely day to find my wife, my children, my people and you [his fans] again, I turned to the only language I've ever known to fight off the night terrors, real and imagined, time and again. It was the only thing I could do."[18]

That said, "I didn't set out to write a 9/11 album," he explained. "I didn't want to write literally about what happened, but [about] the emotions in the air. In the purest sense, that's what a songwriter does." So it was that Springsteen wrote "Into the Fire," in which a bereaved narrator mourns a loved one who disappears into a burning building. That was followed by a thematically similar song, "You're Missing," and the pair proved to be what he calls "genesis" songs—songs that trigger a series of others. These pieces, combined with loose ends such as "Nothing Man," which Springsteen had been holding on to since 1994, became the core of a set of songs for a new album, *The Rising*, that he recorded in Atlanta with the help of a new producer, Brendan O'Brien, and released in the summer of 2002.

With the possible exception of *Tunnel of Love, The Rising* remains the most conceptually focused album Springsteen has ever made. But while the earlier album was centered on marriage, *The Rising* explores the many facets of grief in the new and unfamiliar world of wartime in the twenty-first century. As was his wont, Springsteen made no explicit references to 9/11 (though a couple of songs came close), instead allowing the songs to take on resonances that extend beyond that specific event. "Waitin' on a Sunny Day," a staple of Springsteen's recent tours, had also been written earlier, but aptly suggests the struggle to escape bereavement. So does the album's opening song, "Lonesome Day," whose bereaved narrator finds himself bewildered by loss and by a belated recognition of how little he really knew his loved one. ("It's all right, all right, all right," he sings, straining to console himself, in a song in which he pulls off an impressive falsetto.) The one unabashedly joyous song, "Mary's Place," was written to evoke the raucous spirit of his *The Wild, the Innocent & the E Street Shuffle* days, but in this context it takes on a charged air of catharsis.[19]

The most impressive tracks on *The Rising*, and the ones that really stitch it together, are those written in the wake of the attacks. "The Fuse" and "You're Missing" probe the experience of confronting emptiness ("Coffee cups on the counter, jackets on the chair / Papers on the doorstep, but you're not there," goes one pair of lines from the latter). "Paradise" contrasts visions of the afterlife between a Palestinian suicide bomber, a Navy wife mourning a husband killed at the Pentagon, and a third character swimming in a liminal space between life and death.[20] And "Empty Sky," with its percussive, suspended chords, cites the Plains of Jordan—site of the destroyed city of Sodom—while evoking both the longing of loss and a thirst for vengeance: "I want a kiss from your lips / I want an eye for an eye."

The Rising was Springsteen's first true E Street Band album since *Born in the U.S.A.* and was greeted as such with significant media attention. It instantly topped the *Billboard* album chart and remained there for three weeks (in the days before the iPod, released just months earlier, accelerated the transformation of music listening and sales into a digital realm). The *New York Times* film critic A. O. Scott reviewed the album for *Slate* in a piece headlined "The Poet Laureate of 9/11."[21] Indeed, it may well be that *The Rising* is the most significant work of popular culture to emerge from that event.

Springsteen was not done thinking about the impact of war in American life, however. In 2005 he made an additional commentary in one of the most dramatic songs in his canon: the title song of *Devils & Dust*. The album is largely a return to the terrain and themes of *The Ghost of Tom Joad*, rendered in an even grittier, even more squalid mode ("Reno," for example, is a graphic depiction of a session with a sex worker). But the setting of "Devils & Dust" is a wartime Iraq in the aftermath of the U.S. invasion in 2003. We meet our unnamed protagonist with his finger on the trigger of a rifle, assessing whether to fire (perhaps while observing an approaching vehicle, unsure whether its occupants are friend or foe). He addresses his remarks to a companion named "Bobbie"—the spelling suggests a female. "We've got God on our side," he asserts repeatedly, along with a haunting question: "What if what you do to survive kills the things you love?" It seems that he fears what will die inside him if he fires as much as he fears his actual death if he doesn't. The soldier knows what he believes—and yet faith may be insufficient. "Fear's a powerful thing," he notes twice, before it becomes "Fear's a dangerous thing" in the final verse. "It'll take your God-filled soul / Fill it with devils and dust." One is reminded of Mark Twain's famous line from "The Private History of a Campaign That Failed," about his two-week stint in the Confederate army at the outbreak of the Civil War: "All war must be just the killing of strangers against whom you feel no personal animosity; strangers whom, in other circumstances, you would help if you found them in trouble, and who would help you if you needed it."[22] If you succeed in killing a stranger, you kill a part of yourself. It may be a necessary price, but it's a costly one.

Bruce Springsteen has never witnessed war firsthand. Few of us have. One of our great privileges as Americans has been our relative insulation from great conflagrations abroad—even those in which the United States was implicated—protected as we are by hundreds of military bases of which most of us are blissfully unaware. This is partly why 9/11 was such a powerful event in American life, bringing the experience of war between nations home in a way that had not happened since Pearl Harbor in 1941, and before that the War of 1812.

But war is one of the most fundamental elements of human experience, and it powerfully shapes even those ignorant of its impact and legacy. So no attempt to render American life in its fullest dimensions can be complete without it. That's why Springsteen has gone there again and again.

MAX WEBER
OYANT
23/3/13

FIGURE 5.1. Pencil drawing of Max Weber, author of *The Protestant Ethic and the Spirit of Capitalism* (1905). Weber's book has been foundational in understanding what has come to be known as the Puritan work ethic. Springsteen's life and work reflect a countertradition that could plausibly be called a play ethic. (Source: Wikimedia Commons)

CHAPTER 5

The Good Life

Springsteen's Play Ethic

L IKE THE AMERICAN DREAM, the work ethic has long been a concept associated with national identity. In recent decades, however, it has become a source of unease. Celebrating Labor Day in 1971, for example, then-president Richard Nixon saluted "the dignity of work," but felt compelled to add, "Let us also recognize that the work ethic is undergoing some changes."[1] That Nixon regarded such changes as not for the better could be safely taken for granted. A half-century later, the conversation was less whether the work ethic was in decline than whether it was a worthy goal in the first place. There was much talk of "quiet quitting" on the part of among Generation Z (those born between 1997 and 2012), who saw little point in subsuming their identities in their work.[2] But such resistance was not a new development. "God sent you unto this world as unto a Workhouse, not a Playhouse," read one Puritan maxim.[3] Even in the era most observers consider the heyday of the work ethic, the very necessity for such an admonition suggests that countertendencies abounded. And yet it remains the case that Americans work more hours, and get—as well as take—less vacation time than their international peers.[4]

The American Dream has always been an elastic term whose definition has not been fixed. The definition of the work ethic, by contrast, has. It received its best-known elaboration in sociologist Max Weber's classic book *The Protestant Ethic and the Spirit of Capitalism,* first published in a German scholarly journal in 1904–1905 and translated into an English edition in 1930. Rooted in the ascetic Protestantism of the Reformation, Weber (figure 5.1) described the emergence of a conception of work not as a brutal necessity but rather as a calling.[5] Far more than most academic theories, Weber's work has proven durable not only in the academy—where, naturally, it has been under steady assault without ever fully losing its explanatory power—but also in the popular discourse of journalists, businessmen, and even ordinary working people. In the second half of the twentieth century, the common lament was that the old focus on work had degenerated into an obsession with leisure; a society once focused on making things now seemed hell-bent on consuming them—and borrowing money to do so. Such complaints took on particular intensity as the United States' economic preeminence in the world gradually diminished.

Yet even when it was at its height, the work ethic was never the only model for thought and behavior in the United States for a number of reasons. First, a large segment of the population was not Protestant, and while it would be fair to suggest that the work ethic affected ethnic Catholics or Jews in the nineteenth and twentieth centuries, and the so-called "Nones" in the twenty-first, these groups never shed their cultural identities altogether, even when their behavior corresponded to white, Anglo-Saxon, Protestant norms. Second, a large segment that *was* largely Protestant—that is, African Americans—was largely enslaved for 250 years and could not share the hope for upward mobility that lies at the core of the work ethic. Nor, for that matter, could many white Protestants, who for any number of reasons—fractured family life, a lack of will or talent, repeated failure in the marketplace—found the work ethic an impractical strategy for making their way in the world.

For these and other people, an alternative model was available, one which could be called a *play* ethic. The play ethic is not a simple negation of the work ethic that celebrates idleness. Nor is it a more philosophical sensibility that prizes sedentary contemplation. Rather, it involves a focused, energetic commitment to play not for a livelihood, personal advancement, or social obligation, but as an end in itself.

Having said that, there's a paradox at the heart of the play ethic. Just as the worldly work ethic had otherworldly implications (since it could provide clues as to whether one would be among the saved), so, too, the play ethic connotes much more than mere play. It's not so much an escape from everyday life as a means to enrich, even redeem, it, and in the process become part of a broader community. It is in this way that one can really speak of a play *ethic*.

It's not always easy to take play seriously. Nowhere is this more true than in popular music. "It's only rock & roll," the Rolling Stones told their listeners in their song and album of 1974. Most rock and rollers before and since, from garage-band guitarists to superstar vocalists, define what they do *in opposition to* the workaday world.

Bruce Springsteen does not. The great irony of his career is that a man who makes a living through play plies his trade with exhausting intensity. In a way, that makes sense; anyone who gets paid as handsomely to do what he wants can be expected to put in long hours. But perhaps the most revealing aspect of Springsteen's vocation—a word that points to the almost religious way in which he practices his profession—is not what it reveals about him. Rather, it's the possibilities of both work and play for the rest of us in a country where the value of both has long been challenged.

Working Solutions

I think that all the great records and great songs say, "Hey, take this and find your place in the world. Do something with it, do anything with it. Find some place to make your stand, no matter how big or small it is." That's a pretty wonderful thing for a record to do.

—Bruce Springsteen, 1981

If some people have been lamenting the decline of the work ethic from almost the moment of its inception, others have experienced the decline of work itself for about as long. Whatever the real defects of Puritan society, it was possible there to believe that the work one did could be personal, communal, and sacred all at the same time. While the fruits of one's labors were often siphoned off to a landlord, even an African American in colonial New England could reasonably hope to be a landlord oneself (or, at any rate, to own property) one day.[6] And *all* work was seen as part of a vast project to build a city on a hill.

In fact, a number of observers have noted the extraordinary social fluidity, not just in New England but throughout early Anglo-American society, fluidity that scared some but was positively liberating to others. A mix of pilgrims, entrepreneurs, journeymen, and indentured servants jostled in colonial society, the lines between them often blurred. Even the great evil of slavery was less rigid than it became in the late eighteenth and early nineteenth centuries; major urban slave revolts in New York City in 1741 and Richmond in 1800—the mere fact of which indicated at least some resistance to labor subordination—included white participants.[7]

The advent of industrialization in the nineteenth century decisively reorganized American life in a number of ways. First, workers themselves were separated from each other as work was increasingly split into smaller, more repetitive, and less satisfying tasks characteristic of the assembly line. Second, American families became increasingly segmented; the origins of the perception of the stay-at-home mother and off-site laboring father as the dominant social model had its roots in industrial capitalism, although generally only well-to-do mothers could actually afford to stay at home, and even many of those performed paid labor. Finally, work itself was increasingly segregated from the rest of the workers' lives, less a calling than a matter of brute survival.

In the twentieth century, there was a widespread sense that work had become less oppressive. In part, this is because the advent of the labor movement gave some workers a measure of leverage over their bosses, though that ebbed with the decline of unions in the second half of the century. In part, too, governments sometimes arrested the worst abuses of private power—from child labor to cartels—that have typified unchecked corporate growth. Another reason, and one that should not be underestimated, is the obvious benefit that industrial capitalism has conferred in providing safety, convenience, and pleasure to those able to afford them. From air-conditioning to smart-phones, the fruits of mass labor, and the morphing of industrial capitalism into consumer capitalism, have made even the most difficult lives more comfortable. (The latest iteration of capitalism, financial capitalism, seems more precarious and problematic.)

But perhaps the most valuable coin in the realm of modern work—to many, its sole justification—is leisure. Leisure is a somewhat different thing than play. Its connotations are not so much the kind of emotional and physical engagement required of play, but freedom from any kind of engagement at all. For the most thoroughly drained workers, the freedom to do nothing is especially prized. For more privileged workers, leisure represents the opposite of production: consumption.

Indeed, consumption—buying things or experiences—is the favored form of leisure in contemporary American society and one that helps sustain the economy as a whole. Obviously, a good deal of consumption in daily life, such as of food, clothing, and shelter, is essential and is done by everyone. And some can literally or figuratively be seen as an investment in the building of something better. But much of it is conducted solely as a form of leisure. Shopping (or, more specifically, spending) has become *the* national pastime. There's nothing inherently wrong with that. For some, shopping—including bargain-hunting, buying and selling via internet commerce, and the like—is, in fact, a form of play.

But long after such practices became widespread, older traditions of play continued to offer relief from new forms of work. The principal repository of these traditions is popular culture. Like preindustrial folk culture—which continues to exist to this day in the rich traditions of handicrafts and communal rituals that range from ethnic cuisines to parades—much popular culture relies, like performing music or writing a book, on readily available materials and common techniques. The difference is that popular culture is refracted (and magnified) through the prism of mass production. One historian has elegantly defined popular culture as "the folklore of industrial society."[8]

Popular culture, of course, has itself become a highly elaborate form of consumption in its own right. In the narrowest sense, paperback

novels, vinyl records, and other cultural documents are savored precisely because they're perfectly useless things. In some cases, they've
completed the process of melting into air[9] and taken virtual form, as
in digitized movies, music, television shows, and e-books, untethered
from their original contexts.

Whatever forms such culture takes, it's no accident that many of
the most cherished forms of earlier pop culture were produced by
people of modest backgrounds and few illusions about the laboring
life—women novelists (from Fanny Fern to Willa Cather), Black
musicians (from Bessie Smith to Louis Armstrong), ethnic stage and
screen actors (from Sophie Tucker to Abbott and Costello). Though
such figures had distinguished and often satisfying *careers,* most of
their audiences simply had *jobs,* which had important implications for
the tenor of the art produced by these luminaries. While the popular
culture they and others produced was a part of the world of consumption, it offered critiques of work and leisure from within.

Bruce Springsteen is very much an artist in this tradition. For all the
commentary on Springsteen's earnestness, his wholesomeness, and
his embodiment of durable American values, it's striking to realize
how infrequently his characters celebrate the dignity of work, declaim
it as a source of strength or self-worth, or prescribe it as a cure for personal or social ills. Their real interests lie elsewhere.

No one really works on Springsteen's early records. The only song
that even hints at wage-earning is "Does This Bus Stop at 82nd Street?"
in which an insouciant narrator wanders an urban landscape "where
dockworker's dreams mix with panther's schemes to someday own
the rodeo." Even here, the clear implication is that work, like the radical politics of Black nationalism, is something of a game.

Beginning with *Born to Run,* however, Springsteen characters
increasingly become aware of the way in which working-class adult
life is tethered to labor. Without exception, they speak about it in negative terms. So, for example, the passionate motorcyclist of "Night"
begins by saying, "You get up every morning at the sound of the bell /
You get to work late and the boss man's giving you hell." Even in songs
where work isn't discussed directly, like "Born to Run," one neverthe-

less senses its oppressive reach as the very thing that "rips the bones from your back"—*the* reason why the narrator and his partner "gotta get out while we're young."

This stance toward alienated labor intensifies on subsequent albums, as even the briefest survey suggests. "Daddy worked his whole life for nothing but the pain," observes the narrator of "Adam Raised a Cain," seeking to escape a similar fate. The son of "Independence Day" declares his freedom from a similarly alienated father by asserting, "They ain't gonna do to me what I watched them do to you." On *Born in the U.S.A.*, the protagonists of two successive songs, "Working on the Highway" and "Downbound Train," work on chain gangs, their bondage literal as well as figurative. Work is only one part of the lives depicted on these records, and there is some real happiness. But it doesn't come from a job.

This is not to say that these people don't recognize the necessity for work, or acknowledge its stabilizing role in their lives. Unemployment figuratively destroys characters in songs like "The River" and literally does so in the case of "Johnny 99." Occasionally, some joy can even be wrested out of work, as when the driver of "Open All Night" savors fried chicken from Bob's Big Boy with his favorite waitress while out on the road (of course he's taking a break when he does so). But work is never an end in itself.

Nor is consumption much in the way of compensation. Springsteen is not a doctrinaire critic of consumerism—"People never sold out by buying something," he has said—but he has an acute eye for its sheer ruthlessness.[10] In "You Can Look (But You Better Not Touch)," we hear about a television advertisement where a woman entices a viewer to conflate sexual and consumer transactions: "I watched as she wiggled back and forth across the screen / She didn't get me excited, she just made me feel mean." Part of the insidious quality of capitalism is the way in which it objectifies everything in sight—notably, in the case of social media, consumers themselves—into commodities that can be bought and sold. In this regard, the word "mean," which suggests not only frustration but parsimony, even impoverishment, is especially appropriate.

Play is a very different matter. To a striking degree, it is a source of epiphany. Nightclubs, boardwalks, even fishing expeditions—these are sites where Springsteen's characters find true romance, demonstrate heroism, come to understand themselves. Sometimes simply not working turns out to be an end in itself, so valuable that characters declaim such freedom as a source of strength and self-worth: "When I'm out in the street, I walk the way I wanna walk," says the dockworker of "Out in the Street." And people find—as well as make—beauty from the flotsam of consumer culture: Roy Orbison records ("Thunder Road"), photographs on walls ("Candy's Room"), even gas-station signs ("Jungleland").

This depiction of play as a source of insight is especially apparent in one of Springsteen's favorite settings, amusement parks. One good example is "4th of July, Asbury Park (Sandy)." Like many of his early songs, this one is a love song about two boardwalk drifters, and characterized by affectionate descriptions of beach bums. But there's a sense of irony directed at "the boys from the casino who dance with their shirts open like Latin lovers on the shore," one that suggests a new level of sophistication about the world beyond the boardwalk. Then the singer turns that irony on himself: "I just got tired of... banging those pleasure machines," he says, making a double entendre of playing pinball. Later in that verse, he uses an amusement-park ride to capture his dilemma: "And you know that Tilt-a-Whirl down on the South Beach drag?" he asks. "I got on it last night and my shirt got caught / And they kept me spinning, babe, / Didn't think I'd ever get off." Being trapped on an amusement-park ride—on the "drag," no less—becomes a symbol for mechanical forms of leisure and a yearning for more satisfying forms of play. He confesses that his affair with a waitress is now over, and he asks his Sandy to be his companion in a quest for something better: "For me this boardwalk life's through, babe, / You oughta quit this scene, too."

Amusement parks are only one example of the prominent role of play in Springsteen's art; there are, of course, a number of others. One of the most important, not surprisingly, is playing music. "We learned more from a three-minute record, baby, / Than we ever learned in school," asserts the singer of "No Surrender," who later speculates to a friend that "maybe we could cut someplace of our own / With these drums and these guitars." In the autobiographically based "Rosalita (Come Out Tonight)," this aspiration becomes a reality, as the protagonist joyfully reveals to Rosie that he has received a record contract and should now be able to gain her parents' blessing. Songs such as these suggest the centrality of play in these peoples' lives, and the intensity of their hope that it can furnish the basis of material blessings as well as psychological ones.

Only Rock & Roll

When Bruce Springsteen sings on his new album, that's not about "fun." That's fucking triumph, man.

—Pete Townshend of the Who on *Born to Run*, 1975

Charles Cross attended his first Bruce Springsteen concert in the summer of 1974, when he was sixteen, using fake identification to gain admittance to New York's fabled Bottom Line nightclub. Cross was unfamiliar with the emerging artist's work. But as Springsteen played a guitar solo on a tabletop, his sweat dripping on Cross, the future founder of a Springsteen fan magazine imagined that he had been "baptized in some alien way." Over the next four years Cross would roam venues from coast to coast to catch Springsteen shows.

Cross's true conversion experience, however, took place on December 20, 1978, when he saw a Springsteen show at the 5,000-seat Seattle Center Arena. When it was over, he felt exhilarating exhaustion. "I'd been on twenty-mile runs that had left me with more energy," he recalled. "My knuckles were bleeding, my ears were ringing like an errant auto alarm, and I was so hoarse from shouting that I sounded like Sally Kellerman [a famous actress of the time] with a head cold." Wandering up to the stage, he saw the set list Springsteen had used to plan the concert and realized that he had run through it hours before, making much of the show wholly uncharted. Dazed, he watched roadies dismantle the sound system.

Suddenly, Springsteen ran on stage with a towel around his neck, stood in front of a band member's microphone with an unamplified guitar, and launched into a version of Buddy Holly's "Rave On." The crew managed to get the sound system working in the middle of this, his fourth encore, and fans began streaming back into the hall. When Springsteen left the stage again, security guards tried to move the crowd out of the building, but fans resisted leaving until the lights went out, leaving them to find their way in the dark. Cross finally returned home in the snow sometime after four a.m. "It had never felt more like Christmas," he wrote.[11]

There have been many live performers in the rock era who attracted passionate followings comparable to that of Bruce Springsteen. The Grateful Dead sold relatively few records over the course of its thirty-year career, but the band's concerts were always a cause for celebration. A Rolling Stones tour was usually an international media event. And James Brown was known to generations of concertgoers as "the hardest-working man in show business."

But Springsteen may well be unique in the degree to which he has sought to make playing—in the general and specifically musical sense of the term—a form of joyful work. This intensity is obvious during his shows, but it's discernible offstage, too. "At every date he goes out and sits in every section of the hall to listen to the sound," technician Bruce Jackson observed in 1978. "And if it isn't right, even in the last row, I hear about it and we make changes. I mean every date, too."[12] The photograph accompanying Springsteen's liner notes to *Live 1975–85* shows him with a guitar roaming the aisles of an arena as part of a sound check, suggesting diligent attention to detail sustaining his apparent spontaneity on stage.

Indeed, for Springsteen at least, a concert seems to have less in common with a frat party than a barn raising; while there's an undeniable sense of pleasure in the proceedings, one senses a desire for exertion as well. "An evening with Springsteen—an evening tends to wash over into the a.m., the concerts lasting four hours—is vivid proof that the work ethic is alive and well," wrote conservative columnist George Will in his notorious Springsteen profile of 1984.[13]

Yet as satisfying as Springsteen's concerts may be for him and his fans, a pressing question remains: What utility or relevance does this play-as-work ethic have for those of us who are not well-paid rock stars (or newspaper columnists)? What are *we* supposed to do? Is there any way we can recapture the spiritual sustenance and vitality that the work ethic at its best may confer? Springsteen provided an answer to this question by way of the most celebrated consumer product of all: the automobile.

Vehicles of Meaning

I think that cars today are almost the exact equivalent of the great Gothic cathedrals. I mean the supreme creation of an era, conceived with passion by unknown artists, and consumed in image if not in usage by a whole population which appropriates them as a purely magical object.

—Roland Barthes, *Mythologies* (1957)

Play, we began by saying, lies outside morals. In itself it is neither good nor bad. But if we have to decide whether an action to which our will impels us is a serious duty or is licit as play, our moral conscience will at once provide the touchstone. As soon as truth and justice, compassion and forgiveness have part in our resolve to act, our anxious question loses all meaning. One drop of pity is enough to lift our doing beyond intellectual distinctions.

—Johan Huizinga, *Homo Ludens* [Man the Player] (1938)

I love those Beach Boy songs. I love "Don't Worry Baby." If I hear that thing in the right mood, forget it. I go over the edge, you know? . . . So I write "Racing in the Street" and that felt good.

—Bruce Springsteen, 1985

For the last century, the most important means used for Americans to go to work—or to go play, or to go do just about anything else—has been the automobile. The story of the development and proliferation of cars is one that intersects with many others: the evolution of technology, the advent of mass production, the growth of organized labor, the acceleration of consumerism, etc. And surrounding these broad, impersonal processes, a number of myths and symbols (cars = freedom) have developed, which have been woven into the fabric of everyday life. Not surprisingly in an age of skepticism of received wisdom, cars have also been suspiciously regarded as the root of any number of social ills, among them inequality and environmental despoliation, amid recent hopes that electric cars will mitigate the worst effects of car culture.

For better or worse, cars became emblems of modernity when they emerged a century ago—supplanting railroads, the emblem of modernity in the nineteenth century—because they resonated with longstanding American obsessions. Neither cars nor railroads (nor movies, another symbol of modernity) can be said to have been *invented* in the United States, as they have important European antecedents or origins. But they have been uniquely embraced by, and identified with, this country because of specific historical conditions that made them flourish here: the nation's huge size, its infatuation with technological innovation, and the relative affluence of its middle class, among other factors. These conditions crystallized most clearly in Henry Ford's assembly-line production of the Model T, a car he unveiled with great success in 1907, in part because he paid his workers enough money so that they could think about buying one themselves.

Ever since the advent of the Model T, cars have been a kind of fulcrum between work and play. Usually paid for with wages, they have been both a means and an end of labor. No one, however, has ever written a great book or made a great movie about driving to work. For most Americans, the *real* value in owning a car is what you can do with it when you're *not* working.

The car has a venerable history in all the popular arts, but its appeal has nowhere been greater than in rock-and-roll music. Perhaps this is because both cars and rock and roll were emblems of U.S. economic and cultural supremacy in the mid-twentieth century, when unprecedented levels of disposable income fueled their growth. It is surely more

DRIVING AMBITIONS

FIGURE 5.2. Chuck Berry's Cadillac on display at the National Museum of African American History. Berry, a gifted guitarist and songwriter, was a major influence on Bruce Springsteen, and both men had a penchant for writing about cars as fact and metaphor. (Source: Wikimedia Commons)

than coincidental that a song many popular-music historians consider the first rock-and-roll record, Jackie Brenston's 1951 hit "Rocket 88," is about a car. Elvis Presley ratified his transformation from poor white trash to *nouveau riche* white trash by purchasing cars compulsively, and the model he sang about most often and most lustily (in, for example, "Baby, Let's Play House") is a pink Cadillac—a car largely inappropriate for anything *but* play in socially unsanctioned ways.

The consummate rock poet of the automobile, however, was Chuck Berry (figure 5.2). Long underrecognized as one of the greatest American popular songwriters of the twentieth century, Berry wrote a series of deceptively complex songs with automotive themes throughout his career. The most famous was his 1955 hit "Maybelline," in which the narrator, driving a plebeian Ford, tries to overtake the Cadillac that carries his girlfriend away. (For Berry, play, no less than work, is a site of class struggle. His song "No Money Down," a loving

FUN FUN FUN

FIGURE 5.3. The Beach Boys performing at the Hollywood Bowl, November 1, 1963. The band offered a shimmering version of play that captivated the Baby Boom generation. Springsteen absorbed—and reconfigured—that tradition in his body of work. (Source: Photofest)

description of a new car, is haunted by the specter of the finance company that will take it away.) Deploying a guitar sound that evoked a running engine—Berry did win lasting renown as a guitarist, perhaps because of his flamboyant performance style—"Maybelline" is one of the canonical works of early rock and roll.[14] Berry went to jail in 1962 on a trumped-up charge of transporting a Mexican prostitute across state lines, suggesting the potency of race, sex, rock, and cars for those who sought to police behavior.

In the early sixties, the preeminent poets of the automobile were the Beach Boys (figure 5.3), who in songs like "Little Deuce Coupe," "Fun Fun Fun" (both 1963), and "I Get Around" (1964), offered an even more shimmering vision of automotive play than Presley had. The power of Beach Boys music lay less in their lyrics or public image than in the soaring beauty of their harmonies, which evoke the happiest moments of the American Century. Their voices conjured up a world that was largely a fantasy, though even its sternest critics would concede its charm.

Given their centrality in American life in these years, it's not surprising that cars would be included as part of the indictment against "the system" made by the radicals of the late sixties. As the civil rights movement crested and protest over the Vietnam War rose, cars were regarded by the counterculture as just another symbol of a corrupt technocratic order that was materialistic, wasteful, and bad for the environment. Rather than lovingly describing a car the way Berry did, the hippies of the late sixties preferred Volkswagen Beetles (a pointedly foreign car) or beat-up vans as the automotive statement of choice.[15] Psychedelic indulgence, not loving craftsmanship, was celebrated in The Who's "Magic Bus" (1967). For Carole King the road became the basis of a lament in "So Far Away" (1971).[16]

Meanwhile, American mastery of the automotive market, itself an index of American mastery of the global economy, was slipping. The energy crisis of the seventies revealed the degree to which the freedom that a car supposedly offered was now dependent on Arab oil. Functional, inexpensive Japanese cars began beating the heirs of Henry Ford at their own game. The so-called "malaise" of American society in the era could be seen on any parking lot or in any gas station.

It was within this context of skepticism and even decline that, automotively speaking, Bruce Springsteen came of age. But as anyone with even a passing familiarity with his music knows, cars are absolutely central to Springsteen's music in a Presley/Berry kind of way—his favored subject, setting, and symbol. "Everybody is saying that cars and girls are all I sing about!" he observed in 1987. "Then I realized, 'Hey! That's what Chuck Berry wrote about!' So it wasn't my idea. It was a genre thing, like detective movies."[17]

Springsteen has used cars in all kinds of ways. Sometimes, they are the explicit subjects of celebration. "Well, there she sits, buddy, just gleaming in the sun / There to greet the working man when his day is done," says the singer of "Cadillac Ranch," in which cars connote the opposite of work. Yet even such seemingly straightforward songs can have ambiguous overtones. Springsteen has called "Ramrod," another paean to cars and girls from *The River*, "one of the saddest songs I've ever written."[18] This is not only because of the powerful sense of anachronism that characterizes it ("Hey, little dolly with the blue jeans on," goes the opening line), but also because of the grim realities that are always a backdrop for fun ("I've been working all week, I'm up to my neck in hock / Come Saturday night I let my ramrod rock").

Springsteen also uses cars to chart psychological stress, and even collapse. One of the most poignant examples is "Used Cars," one of a number of songs from *Nebraska* where automobiles and driving play pivotal roles. The novel concept here is that of a *used* car, with its implications of limited means and shopworn aspirations. "Now, mister, the day the lottery I win / I ain't never gonna ride no used car again," its boy protagonist declares, his very determination a form of pathos.

On no album, however, are automobiles more important than *Darkness on the Edge of Town*. With one (significant) exception, every song at least mentions cars and/or driving. And more than on any other album, cars are intimately bound up in questions of work and play.

Tellingly, those who have given up—the men of "Factory"—walk. Sung from the point of view of a son sadly observing his father, "Factory" describes men who have lost the will to make a break: "End of the day, factory whistle cries / Men walk through these gates with death in their eyes." And, he notes, the specter of violence looms: "You just better believe, boy, somebody's gonna get hurt tonight." Lacking anywhere to go after work, these men project their aggressions onto themselves and others. In the words of another son, that of "Adam Raised a Cain," "Daddy worked his whole life for nothing but the pain / Now he walks these empty rooms looking for someone to blame." A lack of play is not simply unfortunate, but dangerous.

"Racing in the Street," by contrast, is essentially Springsteen's manifesto on the value of play. The song is also a commentary on rock history, making subtle connections to—and subtle departures from—his rock-and-roll forebears and their visions of play.

One can begin seeing what Springsteen is up to in "Racing in the Street" by looking at the first verse of the song. "I got a '69 Chevy with a 396 / Fuelie heads and a Hurst on the floor," the narrator begins, lovingly describing a vehicle that he and his partner Sonny built from scratch. "We only run for the money, got no strings attached," he says of his racing habit. If one had never actually heard the music, one might imagine it having a raucous, playful beat. The lyrics seem like something the Beach Boys or a like-minded inheritor such as Van Halen might perform: a chronicle of cars, young women, and good times rooted in a working-class life of auto parts, a girl waiting at 7-Eleven, and adolescent braggadocio.

But "Racing in the Street" lacks any such buoyancy. In fact, the song is a ballad. It begins with an almost dirgelike piano, and Springsteen sings the lines slowly, even reverently, with no further accompaniment. Insofar as a specific time is evoked (sometime after 1969), it is the turbulent Vietnam era.

This becomes clear in the next verse, which suggests an acute consciousness of popular-musical history: "Summer's here and the time is right / For racing in the streets." Here Springsteen is making an important allusion in the rock canon. In the summer of 1964, Martha and the Vandellas had a huge smash for Motown Records with "Dancing in the Street." The song, while not overtly political, nevertheless became a Black anthem during the urban riots of the sixties. Four years later, wryly inverting any innocuous overtones in "Dancing in the Street," the Rolling Stones released "Street Fightin' Man," a song in which summer provided the perfect opportunity for *fighting* in the streets. Best known for its famous rhetorical question about what can a poor boy do but play in a rock-and-roll band, the song was a fixture of Springsteen set lists in his live shows for many years.

Again, however, the important issue here is mood. Whether in joy or anger, both "Dancing in the Street" and "Street Fightin' Man" are marked by an ebullience notably absent in "Racing in the Street." But if Springsteen's song lacks the spontaneity of the others, one does sense the quiet confidence that competence brings: "We take all the action we can meet," he says. There's a perceptible quickening of the song's pace by this point, attributable in large part to drummer Max Weinberg's measured rim taps and subtle use of the hi-hat. It's as if the narrator of the song is warming up, like one of his engines.

The entry of Danny Federici's organ at the end of the first verse signals the arrival of the song's key assertion: "Some guys they just give up on living / And start dying little by little, piece by piece." But then, he notes, there are others like himself, who "come home and wash up / And go racing in the street." These lines encapsulate Springsteen's vision of work and play. In one sense, it's a fairly straightforward matter: work destroys, play preserves; work pollutes, play purifies. But in this description, grace is not simply conferred to all. Rather, the elect are those who have the strength to play. As in the case of Puritan religion, however, there's no straightforward equation as to who is saved and who is not; we're not told *which* guys start dying, or *why* some come home and wash up, only that some do. For those who do, such salvation, however fleeting or even misleading, is a palpable experience. Springsteen sings the chorus more expressively (his *"Tonight,* tonight the strip's just right" has bite), and the entrance of the whole-band arrangement suggests that the song has opened up full-throttle. In this sense, the serene musical bridge that follows is figurative as well as literal: we're hearing the sound of a man who has made it to the other side.

And then something surprising happens. As the bridge comes to a close, the music tapers off, leaving just a piano and a singer again. It's as if he's crossed back into darkness. But he has a reason: a woman. He met her when she was with a Camaro owner from Los Angeles. "I blew that Camaro off my back / And drove that little girl away," he reports. Here we seem to be back in the realm of the Beach Boys, though again the tone is somber. Perhaps a better analogy would be with Berry's "Maybelline," in its sense of class conflict and a struggle for the heart of a woman. Unlike Berry's protagonist, however, this one is a winner. But the woman in question is not: "There's wrinkles around my baby's eyes / And she cries herself to sleep at night."

For Berry, the Beach Boys, and in the songs of countless other rock artists, women are trophies won and lost in contests, and "Racing in the Street" would appear to be no exception. What's different here, though, is an unusual sense of compassion and clarity of description. Moreover, Berry's Maybelline, however compelling she may be, is mute. This woman is not: she speaks listlessly, but clearly, in body language as well as speech: "she sighs, 'Baby did you make it all right?,'" he notes, a woman whose "dreams are torn" and with "the eyes of one who hates for just being born." Never mind the guys—*she's* "dying little by little, piece by piece." The protagonist notices this, and responds: "Tonight my baby and me, we're gonna ride to the sea / And wash these sins off our hands."

In earlier versions of the chorus, Springsteen uses a singular pronoun: "*I* wanna blow 'em off in my first heat"; "*I* wanna blow 'em all out of their seats." In the final chorus, the pronoun becomes plural: "Out of *our* way." Play becomes communitarian, something one does not only to save oneself, but also something one does for (as well as in honor of) others—which includes the "shut down strangers and hot rod angels" this racer has vanquished. One could argue that this woman is only coming along for the ride, but previous evidence (that Camaro) suggests that the road has some romance for her, too, even if this isn't a perfect vision of gender equality. Far from mindless amusement, this is deeply engaged play that takes on a moral dimension.

Good Work

We refer to the exceptionally talented artist as gifted, conceive her work as a gift to the world, and focus on the spontaneous self-forgetfulness that is often said to characterize play and the creative process. Only our reduction of work to labor has led us to stigmatize play as frivolous.
—Jackson Lears, *Fables of Abundance* (1994)

Hannah Arendt was perplexed. The noted philosopher and critic of fascism (she had come to the United States as a refugee from Hitler's Germany) had been deeply impressed by the launching of the Soviet *Sputnik* satellite in 1957, which she considered the most momentous development in human history, greater even than nuclear fission. Like splitting the atom, however, human mastery of the heavens was not to be celebrated as an occasion of joy, but rather of mounting anxiety. A space race—one more front in a tense Cold War—was underway, fueling a current of unease in the most prosperous society the world had ever known. Insofar as there was any shared feeling of optimism, Arendt noted, it took the form of hope that it was now finally possible to escape the earth.

In her 1958 book *The Human Condition*, Arendt tried to understand how the world had reached this state of affairs. She believed a good deal of the problem derived from modern conceptions of work and leisure. To explore the matter, she defined three key terms: "labor," that which is done to maintain everyday life; "work," which involves making durable things; and "action," or memorable behavior in the public sphere. In ancient society, action was considered the greatest activity, usually performed in the realm of politics. In Periclean Greece, action was predicated on freedom from labor, and in some sense, then, was dependent on having others—wives and/or slaves—to do an actor's labor for him.[19]

The advent of industrialization gave labor new importance in capitalist societies, Arendt noted. Ironically, however, the growing wealth and leisure of such societies had not resulted in a diminution of labor, but instead its near overthrow of work and action, as "making a living" had become our paramount preoccupation. As Arendt explained, leisure was "never spent in anything but consumption, and the more time left to [a laborer], the greedier and more craving his appetites."[20] In such an environment, work was increasingly a matter of producing disposable commodities, and action (which, in an age of labor-saving devices, no longer depended on slavery) was viewed as an irrelevant or unnecessary distraction. The essential symbol of modern life, then, had become an ever more elaborate treadmill.

Arendt saw alternatives to this set of arrangements, alternatives that could mean the difference between life and death (spiritual and literal, individual and collective). At the core of those alternatives is a sense of play, a willingness to think and act independently of the vicissitudes of labor. In such an enterprise, Bruce Springsteen provides a worthy example. It may seem ridiculous to consider him a latter-day Pericles—or, for that matter, a Hannah Arendt. But if we are willing to suspend our disbelief, it becomes possible to see his music as work and his concerts as action. All it takes is a willingness to play along.

The Devil's Play

Now I see that two of the best days of my life were the day I picked up the guitar and the day that I learned how to put it down. Somebody said, "Man, how did you play for so long?" I said: "That's the easy part. It's stopping that's hard."

—Bruce Springsteen, 1992

One of the realities of both work and play is growing sense of awareness, even dread, that one won't be doing either forever. Bodies age; opportunities wither; energy ebbs. Play, whose joy inheres in a lack of productive purpose, can also lead to a sense of pointlessness. But the alternative doesn't always seem much better. Sometimes you keep working or playing because you're afraid of what will happen if you stop.

Springsteen has acknowledged that fear. "I had locked into what was pretty much a hectic obsession, which gave me enormous focus and energy and fire to burn, because it was coming out of pure fear and self-loathing and self-hatred," he explained. "I'd get onstage and it was hard for me to stop. That's why my shows were so long. They weren't long because I had an idea or a plan that they should be that long. I couldn't stop until I felt burnt."[21]

One of the more striking aspects of Bruce Springsteen's life is the way this highly talented and richly rewarded man has struggled with depression, something he chronicles throughout his 2016 memoir *Born to Run*. He grew up in the shadow of his late father's mental illness (in 2021, he described him as having suffered from schizophrenia),[22] and has been on antidepressants at different points in his life. It was nevertheless surprising—and, given all he has done and the honors he has received, sobering—to learn that as recently as 2014, on the eve of his sixty-fifth birthday, he found himself in a six-week stretch during which he could barely get out of bed, "an empty husk" who for the first time "felt I understood what drives people toward the abyss."[23] Such a disclosure was, in an important sense, a gift—a reminder of his humanity and fallibility that keeps alive the possibility that even those whose lives are remote from our own may still be collectively engaged in the shared, hard, good work of growing old.

For Springsteen, that has been a matter not only of confronting bodily mortality, but also waning influence in a national culture in which he once occupied a central place. The first intimations of this came in the early nineties, when he broke up the E Street Band and produced two indifferently received albums in *Human Touch* and *Lucky Town*. He spent much of the next decade focused on the work of being a husband and father to his three children—playing of a different, more literal kind—and putting down that guitar. He made a return to the spotlight with the release of *The Rising*, which followed a hiatus of seven years between 1995 and 2002 when he had not released a studio album, the longest such stretch of his career.

After that, though, Springsteen embarked on a stretch of steady professional activity in which he released ten albums in the next twenty years. He also toured extensively, gave 236 performances of his one-man Broadway show over 471 days, and wrote a 500-page memoir.[24] Though much of this work went unnoticed except by his most devoted fans, it represents a stretch of productivity that would tax an artist half his age.

He wasn't really doing it for the money. For one thing, he had made more than enough of that. Certainly, some of these enterprises were more profitable than others, but Springsteen's career as a pop hitmaker was over. His albums of the twenty-first century routinely hit number one, though that metric had ceased to mean much in an age of streaming. Springsteen himself was disappointed in what he hoped would mark a comeback with *Wrecking Ball*. Though President Obama used the leadoff track, the anthemic "We Take Care of Our Own," as a campaign song in his 2012 reelection campaign, the album cooled quickly. "I thought this was one of my most powerful records and I went out looking for it all," he mused in his memoir.[25] None of the albums that followed had even that high a profile. Moreover, *High*

Hopes (2014) and *Letter to You* (2020) were marked by what could be termed filler: cover tunes and re-recordings of songs that were already part of his catalog. An increasingly retrospective air has characterized his work.

The question for Springsteen—the question for all of us—is what to do when our horizons narrow. His answer: keep playing. Perhaps ironically, he does it now in a purer sense, with little expectation of reward from anything beyond the activity itself. This context is important to consider in light of *Only the Strong Survive* (2022), the first of what he has indicated will be a string of cover albums.[26] The hitmaking veteran recording an album of standards has a long and venerable tradition in pop music. But such records also usually speak to an implicit ebbing of creativity. Springsteen has been paying homage to his predecessors for over half a century, and a playful willingness to perform songs by younger peers has been a staple of his recent live shows. (He gave a rousing, acoustic-guitar-whacking solo rendition of 17-year-old Lorde's "Royals" in Auckland in 2014.)[27] Such performances have always been in active dialogue with his own mountainous body of work. Such creative friction is what quietly drives *Western Stars* (2019), an album of original songs that's probably Springsteen's best work of the last decade. But that dialogic dynamic is not as strong on *Only the Strong Survive*, a collection of mostly Motown and soul classics. Perhaps he believes, not implausibly, that at this point in his life the effort is more important than the outcome.

In an important sense, however, Springsteen is ending his career back where he began it: on stage—and on top. His tours remain international events, notably the one he undertook in 2023–24 at the tender young age of seventy-three. His life on the concert circuit has been the one constant of his career. And long after he has left it, that stage—where he has enacted a life of play—will be his legacy.[28]

FIGURE 6.1. Still of Bruce Springsteen dancing with Courtney Cox in Brian De Palma's 1984 video for "Dancing in the Dark." Springsteen's life as a man has included a long stretch as a sex symbol. "What do I like about him? He's a fox!" explained one fifteen-year-old when queried about Springsteen's appeal in 1985. (Source: Columbia Records)

CHAPTER 6

Man's Job

Springsteen's Masculinity

O N JUNE 29, 1984, during the opening night of the *Born in the U.S.A.* tour in St. Paul, Minnesota, Bruce Springsteen made his first Music Television Video, "Dancing in the Dark."[1] Technically, this was actually the second Springsteen video; "Atlantic City,"' released in late 1982, was composed of spare black-and-white footage of that city shot from a car. But "Dancing in the Dark"—the single had been released a month earlier and was moving up the pop charts—was the first in which Springsteen decided he would actually appear, and as such it marked his debut in the MTV era.

The video (figure 6.1) was directed by Brian De Palma, an accomplished Hollywood director best known then for his hit films *Carrie* (1976), *Dressed to Kill* (1980), and *Scarface* (1983). Originally, "Dancing in the Dark" was to have a storyline, but Springsteen and De Palma decided to make it a simple performance video that reenacted a common scene at Springsteen concerts: his extending a hand to a woman in the audience to come on stage and dance with him. For this role, De Palma cast Courtney Cox (future star of the hit television series *Friends*).

The Bruce Springsteen who appears in "Dancing in the Dark"— the camera begins at his feet and moves upward, pausing with a tight shot of his crotch—is noticeably different from the blurred, but unmistakably slight, figure pictured on the album sleeve of *Nebraska* less than two years before. Springsteen has always been an attractive person, but prior to the release of *Born in the U.S.A.* he was not a beef-cake specimen of masculinity. He was never a big man (Clarence Clemons played that part), and his early-seventies image was that of a Beat poet: skinny, bearded, unkempt. He changed his look slightly in the late seventies by shaving his beard and donning an occasional sports jacket, though his scruffiness never entirely disappeared.

The Springsteen of "Dancing in the Dark," by contrast, sports per-ceptibly larger biceps and a much broader chest. The man who refused to have his picture retouched for album covers was now a plausible subject of teen fantasy. "His jeans were as tight as rubber gloves, and he danced like a revved-up sports car about to take off," thinks Sam Hughes, the adolescent female protagonist of Bobbie Ann Mason's 1985 novel *In Country,* as she watches the video in her Kentucky home. Later, Sam daydreams about hitting the road and finding a Springs-teen concert. "And he would pull her out of the front row and dance with her in the dark," she imagines.[2]

In the months that followed, the handsome, youthfully thirty-something Springsteen came to represent a vibrant, working-class, white male heterosexuality in pop music. At a time when Michael Jackson's sexual identity was unclear, Prince's eroticism boldly crossed gender boundaries, and Madonna turned femininity into a series of disposable images, Springsteen represented the vital center: short hair, blue jeans, work shirt, and an occasional bandanna or baseball cap to absorb the sweat of his brow. "What do I like about him? He's a fox!" explained one fifteen-year-old when queried about Springs-teen's appeal in 1985. "He's down to earth. He's so cool, he's not like any other rock star. He acts normal."[3] Springsteen may have been down-to-earth, but his appearance in the *Born in the U.S.A.* era was not exactly unselfconscious. As British sociologist Simon Frith wrote at the time, Springsteen was dressed up as a worker even when he wasn't working; "He's never even seen flashily attired for a night out, the way a real working-class person would be." (Undoubtedly recogniz-ing the contradictions involved in his life, Springsteen began don-ning more formal garb in the late eighties and nineties, though to this day he still seems most comfortable in casual clothes.) No less than his contemporary Boy George of Culture Club, Springsteen's gender presentation was socially constructed from a gallery of historically determined choices.

Figures from Boy George to Lil Nas X have long attracted attention among such scholars because their extravagant, iconoclastic personae serve as an inverted mirror to society at large; by adopting an "abnormal" appearance, they help clarify—and challenge—just what we consider "normal" to be. Because conventionality can be boring or even oppressive, those who reject it are often discussed in a positive, even celebratory fashion.

Less, it seems, has been said about what healthy masculinity looks or sounds like in contemporary American life. That was true in the early 1980s, and it remains even more true in the 2020s, when the terms "toxic" and "masculinity" can seem figuratively joined at the hip. The effort to define healthy masculinity has taken on even more complexity in a time when sex and gender—two distinct, though overlapping, terms—have been more separated than ever before in elite discourse. (I'm using the term "masculinity" here to describe people whose male sexual and gender identities are in alignment.) In such a context, Springsteen offers observers an unusually vivid picture of what might be termed majoritarian manhood. He's a useful case study in the sense that he has grown up in public; since the release of his first album in 1973, he has revealed himself as, successively, a carefree youth, an angry young man, a troubled husband, a mature father, and a senior citizen.

Moreover, there's a very self-conscious, even autobiographical, dimension to Springsteen's gender presentation, one that makes this chapter somewhat different from those preceding it. Springsteen may be a sometimes unwitting commentator on republicanism or the work ethic, but his stances on such subjects are not necessarily central to what he thinks his work is about. The same cannot be said of this topic. "A lot of [my] music is focused around what defines my manhood to me, what are my commitments—how to try to stick by them as best as possible," he said in 1992.[4] Far more than elsewhere, then, tracking Springsteen's own personal development through a series of male roles he has played is crucial to understanding that music. Such an effort, in turn, is a part of an older, much larger, ongoing national drama about manhood in America.

Brotherhood

The one I love lay sleeping by me under the same cover in the
    cool night,
In the stillness in the autumn moonbeams his face was inclined
    toward me,
And his arm lay lightly around my breast—and that night I was happy.
           —Walt Whitman, "When I Heard at the Close of Day"

The boys of Clary's gang had heard that Abe Lincoln was not a bad fellow. Bill Clary, who ran a saloon in the growing frontier settlement of New Salem, had heard the nineteen-year-old newcomer described at length by his friend Denton Offutt, who had teamed up with Lincoln in 1831 and started a general store. There were stories about Lincoln's honesty, like the one in which he had walked six miles to pay back a woman a few cents he had accidentally overcharged her. But what really interested Clary was Offutt's claim that Lincoln was an excellent wrestler. He bet Offutt the princely sum of ten dollars that Lincoln could not defeat Jack Armstrong, the reigning Clary's Grove champion. At Offutt's urging, Lincoln reluctantly accepted the challenge.

Spectators came from miles around to witness the event, wagering knives, trinkets, drinks, and cash. Armstrong, short and powerful, sought to close in on Lincoln and exploit his own superior strength. The gangly Lincoln literally sought to keep Armstrong at arm's length and wear him down (figure 6.2). There are conflicting accounts of what happened next; a number of historians think Lincoln may have beaten Armstrong, only to be threatened en masse by the gang. In any case, all accounts agree that Armstrong stepped forward and offered Lincoln his hand. From then on, the new arrival had the permanent respect and affection of the boys of Clary's Grove.[5]

BLOOD BROTHERS

FIGURE 6.2. Illustration of Abraham Lincoln taking on the Clary's Grove Boys as a young man in New Salem, Illinois, from the 1904 book *Statesmen*. Lincoln has long been upheld as an embodiment of male virtue in his ability to hold his own with his adversaries—and, as was the case here, to befriend them. (Source: Wikimedia Commons)

This is an old, perhaps apocryphal story, from a world very different than ours. And yet the fundamental dynamics of the situation are very familiar. In fact, they elucidate the values of what historian E. Anthony Rotundo describes as the "boy culture" of the nineteenth century, values that remain a part of the boy culture of our time: courage (in this case, a physical challenge and a willingness to take on all comers); loyalty (for Lincoln, in honoring Offutt's commitment; for the Clary's Grove boys, in defending Armstrong—and befriending Lincoln); mastery (wrestling talent on Armstrong's part, and probably Lincoln's as well); and, above all, independence (Lincoln's willingness to enter an unfamiliar social milieu). Certainly, these are not values limited to boys, who in this story were probably what we would call adolescents or even young adults, nor are they without appeal to women. But it is also clear that boy-culture values have distinctive accents, such as an emphasis on physical prowess and a tendency to resist adult authority.[6]

Contemporary popular culture is a vast repository for depictions of boy culture. Hollywood is a particular storehouse; *Diner, Glory,* and *Dead Poets Society,* to cite three very different movies from the 1980s, all depict groups of young males trying to maintain a code of boy-culture values even as they navigate the shoals of the larger society. But perhaps the preeminent home for boy culture is popular music, which, from the relative innocuousness of the Beatles to the deadly stakes of Tupac Shakur, has been an often obsessive focus in art and life.

Few artists have premised their careers on male bonding to the extent Bruce Springsteen has. More important, however, is the high degree of self-consciousness that has accompanied Springsteen's depiction of same-sex friendship, and his evolution over time. While for most men such relationships tend to be outgrown, for him they have been a matter of lifelong exploration.

Springsteen's early albums depict an adolescent milieu of street brawling, car racing, and constant partying, one usually dominated by boys. With a cast of characters with names like Hazy Davy, Wild Billy, and Killer Joe, "Spirit in the Night" typifies this world. "Now the night was bright and the stars threw light," he notes of the vividly animated setting for their antics. Springsteen elsewhere describes these characters as built like light, and their dance reflects a kind of boundless energy. Such images are common on Springsteen's first two albums. "The kids down there are either dancin' or hooked up in a scuffle," observes the narrator of "The E Street Shuffle" of a typical street scene of stylized mayhem.

The narrators of these songs note such activities with amusement, but they're never wholly detached from this adolescent world, even when they've presumably outgrown it. "Well, my feet finally took root in the earth," says the narrator of "Growin' Up," in one of the rare uses of the past tense on either *Greetings from Asbury Park* or *The Wild, the*

Innocent, and the E Street Shuffle. "But I got me a nice little place in the stars." And with that he's off again, resuming a catalog of further adventures with a zeal that seems very much present-tense.

Women (or, perhaps more accurately, girls) are present on these albums, not only as the romantic interests that have been part of Springsteen's music from the very beginning but also in his accounts of boyish adventure. They really are allowed in the clubhouse—Crazy Janey of "Spirit in the Night," who joins Hazy Davy and company at Greasy Lake, is essentially one of the guys. More often, however, young women are the "little pretties" of "Tenth Avenue Freeze-Out," who are appreciated but viewed largely from a distance. Springsteen's sexism at this phase of his life, typical of the time, led the New York chapter of the National Organization of Women to initiate a 1981 letter and phone-call campaign to demand that his songs stop referring to women as "little girls" (as in "I Wanna Marry You," from *The River*).[7]

Perhaps the most striking characteristic of Springsteen's first three albums is the intensely social quality of his settings: his characters are almost always in groups, reflecting a kind of pack mentality characteristic of young males. "The midnight gang's assembled, and picked a rendezvous for the night," explains the narrator of "Jungleland." Later, he notes, there will be an "opera" on the turnpike and a "ballet" in the alley, metaphors for street fights that emphasize their collective—and romantic—qualities in a song that sounds like a 1970s version of *West Side Story*.

There's an almost erotic subtext animating many of these encounters. Here again, there is little that is new. When Abraham Lincoln left New Salem for the growing city of Springfield in 1837, he kept his lodging costs low by sharing a bed with his friend Joshua Speed.[8] It's questionable whether they ever did more than that. Ironically, the fact that same-sex relations were widely considered so thoroughly beyond the pale legitimated a much wider range of contact than was common later. As Rotundo explains, "a man who kissed or embraced an intimate male friend in bed did not worry about homosexual impulses because he did not assume he had them." Only after anxieties about gender began intensifying at the turn of the century—typified by Theodore Roosevelt's insistence on "the strenuous life"—did the line between queer and straight sharpen.[9]

Yet even in a century with pronounced sexual anxiety over homosexuality, "boy culture" has always allowed a measure of what Walt Whitman called "adhesiveness" between men. Nowhere has this continuity with older forms of male bonding been more obvious than in the archetypal rock-and-roll band. The reasons are obvious enough: for much of its history, rock and roll has been a largely male enclave. It has celebrated the rootlessness and antiauthoritarianism characteristic of boy culture, and it has made male bonding a virtual fetish, from the coy dancing inmates of "Jailhouse Rock" (1957) to Thin Lizzy's "The Boys Are Back in Town" (1976). Indeed, rock has allowed presumably heterosexual men so much homoerotic license—consider all that makeup Mick Jagger wore in the sixties and seventies—that it provided more than adequate cover for closeted gay men, like Elton John and Freddie Mercury of Queen, to do likewise without the fear of reprisals from rock fans whose hatred of disco in the seventies was partly rooted in homophobia.

Like other classic rock groups, Bruce Springsteen's E Street Band was celebrated as a male fraternity by members and fans alike (at least until the mid-eighties, when Patti Scialfa joined it). Springsteen has never exhibited the sexual flamboyance of the Rolling Stones or David Bowie—his work lacks their subtext of decadence, though Bowie, as usual ahead of the curve, did record a stylized cover of "It's Hard to Be a Saint in the City" in 1974—but his performances are marked by a surprising amount of sexual subversion. It's most apparent in the case of his relationship with Clarence Clemons, with whom his contact ranged from their affectionate pose on the cover of *Born to Run* to the exuberant kisses they routinely exchanged during live shows. Springsteen showed similar intimacy with guitarist Steve Van Zandt in the way they gazed into each other's eyes while sharing a microphone throughout any given evening.[10]

Such intimacy, sexual or otherwise, diminishes markedly with the release of *Darkness on the Edge of Town* in 1978. It's not altogether clear why. Perhaps Springsteen's legal problems with manager Mike Appel, problems that put his career on hiatus for months (and delayed his next album for years), played a role in distancing him from a carefree boy culture still very much evident on *Born to Run*. More generally, simple aging may have played a role. In any case, the men of *Darkness* are largely isolated. Although many of these songs do feature men in groups, a feeling of solidarity is largely missing, unless it is that of a passively shared oppression. In a sense, *Darkness* is an album about the transition to adulthood—"Mister, I ain't a boy, no, I'm a man," declares the protagonist of "The Promised Land"—and the end of the often nurturing relationships of adolescence. To become a man, apparently, means going off on one's own. So, for example, the narrator of "Darkness on the Edge of Town" stands alone on a hill, cut off not only from his wife but also from the strip racing that used to be a big part of his life. Never again would Springsteen *write* about brotherhood with quite the same insouciance of his early career, even if he continued to *perform* rituals of brotherhood on stage.

This is not to say that Springsteen lost sincere feelings of fraternity with his fellow men. Quite the contrary. But his records of the eighties and nineties were marked by a more bittersweet quality, a consciousness of loss that always seems at least implicit and is sometimes a good deal more than that.

This sense of love and loss is especially powerful in one of Springsteen's few songs that explicitly deals with brotherhood in a literal sense: "Highway Patrolman," from *Nebraska*. "Highway Patrolman" tells the story of Joe Roberts and his wayward sibling Franky. The two men are bound by a lifetime of shared experiences, which extends to both of them dancing with Joe's wife, Maria. From such past pleasures a bond has formed. This sense of loyalty has a dark side—Joe is, after all, abetting the escape of a likely felon—but as he explains, "when it's your brother sometimes you look the other way." The brother here is literal, of course, but the implications are broader. (Johnny Cash—a paradigmatic figure of masculinity for decades in the second half of the twentieth century—recorded an affecting cover of "Highway Patrolman" as the lead track on his 1983 album *Johnny 99*, which also includes a cover of that song. "Highway Patrolman" was the inspiration for Sean Penn's 1991 directorial debut *The Indian Runner*, clips of which were later made into a video for the song.)[11]

By the time of *Born in the U.S.A.*, the valedictory strain in Springsteen's vision of brotherhood had become the central theme of a number of tracks, notably "Bobby Jean." A song of farewell to a cherished friend (based on Steve Van Zandt, who left the E Street Band in 1984),[12] "Bobby Jean" describes two sixteen-year-olds who were inseparable companions. "There ain't nobody, nowhere, nohow / gonna ever understand me the way you did," explains the singer. The language here might be that used by a lover; indeed, the name Bobby Jean is ambiguous enough to refer to a female as well as a male. Only the typically male wanderlust and rock-band solidarity the song describes lead one to conclude that it is an ode to friendship rather than romance. But in contrast to "Growin' Up," the pastness of these experiences is emphatic, so much so that, for characters like the aging baseball player of "Glory Days," the memories become oppressive, almost pathetic.

At their best, however, memories of a shared past are not a burden but a valuable resource that enriches the present. "No Surrender," which precedes "Bobby Jean" on the second side of *Born in the U.S.A.*, includes accounts of happy childhood memories—cutting classes, listening to music, and swearing blood oaths. But harsh realities also intrude: "Well, now young faces grow sad and old / And hearts of fire grow cold." Still, there's a determination to move forward together: "Maybe we could cut some place of our own / With these drums and these guitars." As with "Bobby Jean," it's easy to see an autobiographical subtext here, for Springsteen did indeed "cut some place of [his] own." But what does it mean to grow young again? Springsteen offers his answer in the final verse: "I want to sleep beneath peaceful skies in my lover's bed / With a wide-open country in my eyes and these romantic dreams in my head." What seems to happen is that a boy's aspirations for male friendship get transferred to another person (usually a woman) with whom such possibilities may yet be realized. In other words, this character grows up—but doesn't give up. There is loss in this development, but hope too, and this version of the song, buoyed by its garage-rock arrangement, is more hopeful than elegiac.

In the decade following *Born in the U.S.A.*, however, Springsteen showed distinctly less interest in male friendship. *Tunnel of Love, Human Touch,* and *Lucky Town* all focus on other aspects of masculinity. When Springsteen included "No Surrender" on *Live 1975–85,* he chose a slow, acoustic version that underlined the song's elegiac elements. In these years, marriage and children were his primary interest.

The release of *Greatest Hits* in 1995 spurred Springsteen to make, in the words of Walt Whitman's title to the epilogue of *Leaves of Grass,* "a backward glance o'er travel'd roads." In the case of male relationships, the primary evidence for this reassessment is two previously unreleased songs included at the end of the album, "Blood Brothers" and "This Hard Land." "The world come charging up the hill / and we were women and men," begins the narrator of the former, neatly encapsulating many of the elements of boy culture discussed here. Yet it's the burdens of adulthood that dominate the song, from the mundane struggles of everyday life to the memories of those who have "fallen in their tracks." Unlike the singer of "No Surrender," the key issue for this man is not to grow young again, but rather to find a way to age gracefully. "I'll keep movin' through the dark with you in my heart," he concludes, offering a vision of dignified adulthood that rejects stasis even as it honors the past.

Somewhat more romantic in outlook is "This Hard Land," which dates back to 1982. A song about frustrated dreams, "This Hard Land" does not really focus on brotherhood until its conclusion, but does so there in an unusually vivid way. "Meet me tonight at Liberty Hall," the narrator tells his buddy Frank, perhaps referring to a Houston concert venue Springsteen played in the seventies. "Just one kiss from you, my brother, and we'll ride until we fall." He conjures up a vision of sleeping in fields and by rivers, even as he seems to understand it's a hope that's more fond than realistic: "Well, if you can't make it / Stay hard, stay hungry / Stay alive, if you can / And meet me in a dream of this hard land." But even unrealized dreams seem to strengthen, rather than weaken, those that embrace them. To Springsteen, it would seem that this combination of memory and hope, expressed in a boyish idiom, forms the essence of brotherhood.

If this was the end of the story, one might conclude that Springsteen had a positive—but limited—view of the role men play in each other's lives. Essentially, his work tells a tale of bonds formed in childhood that get lost in adulthood but that cast a rosy afterglow. In Springsteen's records of the seventies and eighties, there's little sense of men having *ongoing* relationships as adults. In the nineties, however, a richer picture of brotherhood comes into view.

The most notable example of this development is "Streets of Philadelphia," which moves brotherhood into new realms—not simply that of a bond of blood, sex, or friendship, but love in its most physical and metaphysical dimensions. Like "Highway Patrolman," "Streets of Philadelphia" is, on the surface at least, about loss: a dying man addresses his companion. Their connection is all the more important because his isolation is so great; as he explains to his partner, "Ain't no angel gonna greet me / It's just you and I, my friend."

There are many dimensions to this song, but one of the most important is largely implicit: that these are two people deeply involved with each other, in a relationship that has little to do with childish antics or otherwise pressing rituals of domesticity. Indeed, their very unselfconsciousness is indicative of Springsteen's maturity; only a grown man comfortable with himself could sing these words—not simply as an act of sympathetic imagination, but as a matter of earned wisdom. (We'll return to the spiritual dimensions of "Streets of Philadelphia" in the next chapter.)

This broadening and deepening of brotherhood is reinforced throughout *The Ghost of Tom Joad*. "Sinaloa Cowboys," a starker version of "Highway Patrolman," also deals with two siblings on the edge of the law. This time, however, both (Mexican) brothers are on the wrong side of it. Even before they entered the drug trade, their father had warned them that El Norte would extract a price from them, and indeed one of them is killed (blood brothers indeed). And while their tie will sustain the surviving brother—during the burial he extracts the ten thousand dollars they had hidden in the ground—it will cast an undying shadow of sorrow.

Ultimately, however, *Tom Joad*'s importance as a statement about brotherhood has less to do with a particular story or lyrics than about the way the album as a whole invites us to think of brotherhood as extending beyond the realm of immediate family or friends. The uncle of the narrator in "Straight Time" urges his nephew to resume a life of crime by saying "Charlie, remember who your friends are"—a statement which, however misguided, suggests that some ties are more important than blood. In a more positive vein, the resolution of the racial conflict at the heart of "Galveston Bay" (also to be discussed in the next chapter) makes an argument for all men—even enemies— as brothers. Here is the ultimate definition of brotherhood: love that transcends boundaries.

Husbandry

hus•ban•dry (noun) 1: the care of a household 2: the control or judi-cious use of resources: CONSERVATION
                                        —*Webster's Seventh New Collegiate Dictionary* (1965)

Bruce Springsteen emerged as a songwriter in the 1970s at a crucial juncture in the history of love and marriage, when the women's move-ment was actively questioning—and altering—the social rules gov-erning relations between partners. There is little indication, either in his public statements or in his songs, that he took any formal interest in the movement. Nonetheless, in tracing the trajectory of his music in the half-century since he began making records, one can discern a clear pattern of accommodation to the social changes wrought by feminism and other movements involving gender without an ener-vating compromise of his male sexual identity.

Like many boys who grew up where and when he did, Springsteen was no paragon of gender enlightenment. His childhood years of the 1950s are widely considered a time of traditional gender roles, the age of *Father Knows Best,* when men labored in the workforce, women stayed at home to raise children, and sexual inequality was a fact of life. While this perception is something of a distortion—Springsteen's mother, Adele, like many working-class women of the time, continued to work for wages and wielded power in ways that escape conventional calculation—its accuracy was greater in the early postwar era than it was before or after the Cold War.

There is little indication that Springsteen ever aspired to be a traditional family man. But even as a self-styled rebel against the deadening conventions of working-class life, he absorbed traditional ideas about women and sex. In many of his most famous songs—including "Thunder Road," "Born to Run," and "Racing in the Street"—it is the man who unambiguously (and uncritically) occupies the driver's seat.

There is, however, another side to this story: a strain of egalitarianism, one that corresponds to other forms of egalitarianism in Springsteen's work, that has been apparent from the very beginning. At a 1972 performance of "Growin' Up" at Max's Kansas City, Springsteen described it as a song about becoming a man—adding that "it could be a song about becoming a woman, too." Around this time he also performed a heavy-metal reading of Carole King's "Will You Still Love Me Tomorrow," suggesting his capacity to think beyond typical categories of gender.[13]

When Springsteen moved away from writing songs in group settings into those of intimacy in his early work, women came into their own more decisively. There is no finer example of this egalitarianism than "For You," from *Greetings*. Though an insouciant song with prolix lyrics of the kind so characteristic of Springsteen's early compositions, it is more focused than most of them, and, despite its breezy tone, more serious. Its narrator addresses a woman who has apparently attempted suicide. But he refuses to let her mental illness excuse her behavior, and for all his obvious affection, he's mad at her. Ensuing verses describe a relationship between outsiders, outsiders who have generally interacted as equals but who have periodically exchanged the upper hand: "Remember how I kept you waiting when it was my turn to be the God?" It's not clear why this woman is in such trouble, but the sheer energy of the song makes it hard not to believe the kids are all right. In any case, "For You" showcases a recurrent Springsteen vision of love as partnership.

"4th of July, Asbury Park (Sandy)" also illuminates Springsteen's vision of romance as egalitarian partnership. Like many of his early songs, "Sandy" is characterized by the usual affectionate descriptions of boy culture, but now there's an air of irony directed at the adolescent narcissism of "the boys from the casino who dance with their shirts half open." His relationship with a waitress, marked by a similar vanity, is now over ("she won't set herself on fire for me anymore"), and he asks Sandy to be his companion on a quest for something more meaningful: "For me this boardwalk life's through, babe / You oughta quit this scene too." Here again, friend becomes lover while remaining equal.

Such an approach to romance has its risks. "Backstreets," from *Born to Run*, shows what happens when the foundations of an egalitarian relationship are shattered. "One soft infested summer me and Terry became friends," this narrator begins (note Terry's androgynous name, and the description of their relationship as a friendship). They're romantic rebels who dance in the dark, huddle together in cars, and roam the backstreets of the title until Terry leaves him for another man. Terry ultimately returns, but this cannot erase the narrator's bitterness in realizing that "after all this time we're just like the rest" in the ordinariness, even tawdriness, of their shared romantic myth. Maybe this man, who sings these lines in agony, is being a little histrionic here, perhaps even vindictive. He's less mature, still invested in fantasies that the protagonist of the later "Sandy," for example, has begun to question. As a character in a story, however, he's quite compelling, and it's clear that in this moment of disillusionment what he mourns is not simply one person's unfaithfulness but the loss of a sense of shared hope between equals.

The women of Springsteen's best songs are also girls who want to have fun, gaining rights of uncensored expression generally denied women in pop music until the 1980s. "Fire," the song he wrote for Elvis Presley but which became a top-ten hit for the Pointer Sisters in 1978 (it is included on *Live 1975–85*), is about the joy of sex. The narrator of "Open All Night," from *Nebraska,* describes his paramour Wanda taking so much pleasure from eating fried chicken that it takes on tactile overtones: "On the front seat, she's sitting on my lap / We're wiping our fingers on a Texaco road map."

At the same time, neither sex in particular nor any man in general can always be an adequate source of satisfaction. As queer scholar Martha Nell Smith notes in her insightful essay on sexuality in Springsteen's music, in "Candy's Room" there is "no man," not even the one who loves her, "who can keep Candy safe."[14] This is a point Springsteen would go on to make repeatedly, as in *The River*'s "Point Blank," whose female character waits not on Romeos but on welfare checks; in *Nebraska*'s "Used Cars," in which a mother nervously fingers her wedding band while her husband unsuccessfully negotiates with a car salesman; and in *Tunnel of Love*'s "Spare Parts," in which a mother discards her hope of romance in order to become a more focused and effective parent.

What's really striking about Springsteen's vision of women, though, is the way neither sexual aggression nor economic independence need compromise a femininity valued by many men and women alike. He affirms this non-universal—though nevertheless widely shared and compelling—vision in his decision to perform and record the Tom Waits song "Jersey Girl," which closes *Live 1975-85*. In the song, a man's efforts on his lover's behalf are rooted in a deep understanding of her (ongoing) struggles as a worker and a mother, as well as her desire to express herself through heterosexual romance. "I see you on the street and you look so tired," he says, noting her dead-end job—and his intention to give her some relief. "Go in the bathroom and put your makeup on," he tells her. "We're gonna take that little brat of yours and drop her off at your mom's."

This sense of empathy also animates Springsteen's more traditionally male stances. By the 1980s, even his odes to lust implicitly acknowledge other perspectives. "Darlington County" is sung from the point of view of a guy trying to pick up women, but his charm stems from his sense of irony, even absurdity: "Our pa's each own one of the World Trade Centers / For a kiss and a smile I'll give mine all to you." The narrator of "Dancing in the Dark" makes a macho declaration that "This gun's for hire," but does so acknowledging his personal frustrations (the very title of the song is a metaphor for making the most of a life constrained by limitations).

Even "I'm on Fire," arguably Springsteen's most sexually aggressive song, is marked by such countercurrents. "Hey little girl is your daddy home? / Did he go and leave you all alone?" this man begins, the understated, even smoldering mood of the synthesizers and snare drum greatly contributing to the power of the song. The narrator's characterization of his rival is plain: he's inadequate—and absent. But then he makes a stark confession: "Sometimes it's like someone took a knife, baby, edgy and dull / And cut a six-inch valley in the middle of my skull." Far from playing hard to get—"only you can cool my desire"—he's conveying need with unfeigned intensity.

The complexities of "I'm on Fire" to some degree reflect Springsteen's own personal development and evolving preoccupations. By the time he was writing this material, he was well into his thirties, a time when a man is often making, or consolidating, lifetime commitments. "Everyone seems to hunger for THAT relationship and you never seem happy without it. I think you do tend to think about that particular thing around thirty," he said in 1981, when he was thirty-one and still years away from marriage himself but apparently considering it. "But even up until then, when I was writing all the earlier songs, 'Born to Run' and stuff, they just never seemed right without the girl. It was just part of whatever that person was doing. It wasn't gonna be any good without her."[15]

Still, however important love is to the men who populate the Springsteen albums from *Greetings* to *Born in the U.S.A.*, it's always to some degree secondary. To invoke Springsteen's formulation, "Born to Run" wouldn't quite sound right without the girl, but the girl somehow wasn't the core issue. How a man might *sustain* a relationship; whether a life *centered* on romantic partnership might be worth pursuing; what it actually *means* to be a man: these are questions that went largely unexplored from the early seventies through the mid-eighties.

Then, during his tour to support *Born in the U.S.A.*, Springsteen met the actress/model Julianne Phillips, whom he would marry in

1985. This seemed like a typical move in an age of postfeminist celebrity, when marriages of rock stars and model-actresses were common. In the mid-eighties, Billy Joel and Christie Brinkley, Motley Crüe drummer Tommy Lee and Heather Locklear, and Whitesnake vocalist David Coverdale and Tawny Kitaen were all celebrated as two-career couples who also happened to be sex symbols—though sex symbols whose beauty and flaunted sexuality nevertheless embodied very conventional notions of manhood and womanhood. (All of these marriages, perhaps not coincidentally, ended in divorce.)

But while Springsteen shared space in *People* with all these figures, it became clear relatively quickly that for him marriage was much more than a good public-relations move. Upon completing his tour, he established a new life rooted in heterosexual domesticity, and with the release of *Tunnel of Love* in 1987, he inaugurated a new phase in his life and work. Unlike any record he had made before, *Tunnel of Love* was a virtual concept album about love and marriage, with romance as the explicit theme of every song. While this is not especially surprising, the degree of complexity and turbulence that marked the record far exceeded the intensity in the recordings of any of his newly wedded counterparts, including the often reflective Billy Joel.[16]

But *Tunnel of Love* is more than a document of Springsteen's marital difficulties. It also charts the difficulties for men and women grappling with changing expectations at the end of the twentieth century, as women increasingly took on roles that had once been the sole province of men, and men were expected to show a new awareness of, and willingness to adjust to, the wishes of women. Springsteen's strategy in navigating these currents has involved retaining traditionally gendered words and concepts but endowing them with a broader, more flexible meaning.

Take, for example, toughness, a longstanding masculine ideal. "Well it's Saturday night / You're all dressed up in blue," begins "Tougher than the Rest," which Springsteen drawls to a slow, chugging rhythm. (It's worth noting that the girl wears blue, stereotypically a "boy" color, and that the video for the song features gay couples fleetingly interspersed with straight ones.)[17] But what exactly does toughness mean? Physical strength? A hard-boiled style? This character elaborates an answer in the final verse: "If you're rough and ready for love / I'm tougher than the rest." For all his laconic, competitive assertions, it's clear that for this man, toughness means a willingness to work at romance and to endure its disappointments. By this standard, women have to be tough as well.

Although never invoked so directly, toughness is upheld as a necessary quality throughout *Tunnel of Love*, because even the most successful relationships, far from offering refuge or release, are depicted as often dogged struggles. If amusement-park rides in "Sandy" were an *unwanted* diversion from the real world, and those of "Jersey Girl" a *welcome* diversion from the real world, the roller coaster of "Tunnel of Love" is inextricably *part of* the real world, where hopes and fears surrounding romance are as present as anywhere else. Nevertheless, while love may be a struggle, it still beats the alternative, as the abandoned but more experienced lover of "When You're Alone" tells his partner. "There's things that'll knock you down you don't even see coming," he tells her. While he can sympathize with and even forgive her need to light out on her own, he won't be able to simply forget about it if she does. "Now it ain't hard feelings or nothin', sugar," he says. "It's just nobody knows, baby, where love goes / But when it goes it's gone, gone." Here, too, is a kind of toughness: a sober-minded realism about the rules of love that applies to all parties, and an acceptance of what's beyond one's control.

But the great paradox of *Tunnel of Love* is that a man does have some responsibility for handling his feelings, and the most successful men master the most potentially destructive impulse of all: an urge for control. This thirst, and the struggle to contain it, is one of the most important themes of the album, conveyed in a number of songs that unfold like parables.

A case in point is "Cautious Man." The third-person narrator of the song, which unfolds like a short story, describes a protagonist named Bill Horton, who, "When something caught his eye, he'd measure his need / And then very carefully he'd proceed." Horton's fear of commitment makes him seem like an old man and an immature boy simultaneously. Nevertheless, not even he can resist the appeal of love, as he meets, and marries, a young woman. But in the fright of a bad dream, he prepares to flee the fears that love seems to have unleashed. Then, in a moment of clarity, he realizes when he gets to the highway that "he didn't see nothin' but road." He heads back home, brave enough to face the ongoing risks of domesticity.

Other men are not so fortunate. "You play the loving woman / I'll play the faithful man," says the suspicious husband of the hit song "Brilliant Disguise," locked in a struggle for control with his wife in a war of perceptions. By contrast, the barfly husband of another hit, "One Step Up," honestly professes his love for his wife, but can't quite change "the same old act" that leads him to flee home (again). And Bobby, the deadbeat lover and father of "Spare Parts," leaves home for good rather than accept responsibility for his actions. None of these men are able to trust, accept, or sacrifice in ways that would allow them to achieve a fuller sense of manhood.

Taken as a whole, *Tunnel of Love* articulates an understanding of manhood as a form of emotional investment and risk-taking, a willingness to participate in the building of something larger than oneself in a supporting role rooted in the biological fact that women are the first, if not necessarily primary, caregivers in family life. This is not a radical departure from the vision Springsteen learned as a child. But the ends toward which he applies these values are at once broader, deeper, and more inclusive.

Human Touch and *Lucky Town*, released in the aftermath of Springsteen's divorce from Phillips and subsequent marriage to E Street vocalist Patti Scialfa (figure 6.3), build on this new model of manhood. In the case of *Human Touch*, this includes a rejection of traditional machismo. A decade earlier, with "I'm a Rocker," one of Springsteen's characters boasted of having the sexual powers of James Dean or a secret-agent man. But the protagonist of "Real Man" doesn't "need no gun in my fist" to prove his masculinity. Conversely, the reluctant but decisive break that is the subject of "The Long Goodbye" stems from a realization that a man has lived under false pre-

JERSEY GIRL

FIGURE 6.3. Patti Scialfa performs "Lucky Girl," from her 1993 album *Rumble Doll*. Scialfa, who Springsteen had known since she was a teenager and who joined the E Street Band in 1984, became his second wife in 1991. After a string of failed relationships, the bond proved durable, and the couple raised three children. (Screen shot courtesy of Columbia Records)

tenses. "Sure did like that admirin' touch / Guess I liked it a little too much," he explains.

Springsteen's penchant for taking accepted ideas and terminology for manhood and reconfiguring them receives its supreme expression in "Man's Job," a monologue song in which a man in a romantic triangle argues for his worthiness. "Well you can go out with him / Play with all of his toys," he says. "But takin' care of you, darlin', ain't for one of the boys." Yet this character is not content simply to dismiss his lover's choice of a competitor as child's play; he asserts that she's involved in a dangerously reckless game: "Oh, there's somethin' in your soul that he's gonna rob." Which leads to the chorus: "Lovin' you baby, lovin' you darlin', lovin' you woman is a man's man's job."

The progression from "baby" to "darlin'" to "woman" charts a spectrum from dependency to maturity that accentuates the power and appeal of womanhood. Simultaneously, Springsteen reorients the phrase "man's job," which traditionally refers to hard physical labor, toward the arduous task of maintaining and building a relationship. This "man's man's job" obviously contrasts with a *ladies' man's* job—a con job marked by stealth and weakness.

For most of the song, the tone is one of certitude. But then, in a move that gives "Man's Job" much of its drama, the cool, collected veneer of the narrator is shattered at the bridge: "Your hand's on his neck as the music sways / All my illusions slip away." As in any good story, there is a moment of doubt. This man may have worked out a clear argument, but that doesn't mean he's persuaded her—or himself. The point is the nobility of the pursuit, one that clarifies his sense of manhood: "I've got something in my soul, and I wanna give it up," he concludes. "Gettin' up the nerve is a man's man's job." Real strength means acknowledging weakness. Real mastery of one's self allows one to become vulnerable to another. Real freedom lies in the power to make lasting commitments.

In contrast to *Human Touch*, the songs of *Lucky Town* are less centered on paradigmatic romantic situations than on deeply personal ones. This intimacy is obvious, for example, in "If I Should Fall Behind," where a man describes his relationship with his beloved as a partnership, one in which he is as likely as she is to need help: "I'll wait for you / And if I should fall behind, wait for me." What might otherwise be a fairly conventional expression of lifelong commitment is textured by its allusions to hard-earned experience ("you and I know what this world can do"), and the way in which a frank recognition of personal limitations is a condition for marital success. If these are not actually convictions acquired in the aftermath of a failed marriage, they are clearly those of a man who hopes that the lessons of past missteps can help him overcome future ones.

With the wedding song "Book of Dreams," Springsteen brings the accumulated experience that accompanies mature visions of manhood full circle. "Book of Dreams" is a joyful song, but quietly, meditatively so. The happiness has a dappled quality, mixed with sorrows that remain but still somehow leaven the proceedings. "We dance out 'neath the stars' ancient light into the darkening trees," the groom explains, in characteristically chiaroscuro language, savoring a series of wedding rituals. At the same time, however, the song's chorus— "Oh won't you, baby, be in my book of dreams"—has an innocent quality. It sounds like a line that a girl group like the Ronettes might have sung in the early sixties. A wise man, Springsteen seems to be saying, retains the wonder of a child.

Fatherhood

Some people get a chance to change the world, and other people, they get a chance to make sure the world don't fall apart.
—Bruce Springsteen on his father, 1980

Bruce Springsteen has been more open about his relationship with his father than about any other aspect of his life. He's done so not through his songs per se—Springsteen tends to relate experience in figurative or emotional terms rather than literal ones—but rather in his live performances, especially the monologues he uses to introduce songs. In the first half of his career, his father frequently surfaced as a character in these and other stories—as a hectoring critic, as an enraged authority figure, and as an innocent victim of social forces beyond his control.

Commenting on an early postwar photograph of his father in his soldier's uniform, Springsteen once said, "He looked like [actor] John Garfield in this great suit, like he was going to eat the photographer's head off. I couldn't ever remember him looking that defiant or proud when I was growing up. I used to wonder what happened to all that pride, how it turned into so much bitterness."[18] What happened, it would seem, is what had already happened to generations of working-class men before Douglas Springsteen. For a century now, middle- and upper-class American fathers have wrestled with their responsibilities to their children, navigating between their own aspirations, the findings of social scientists, and challenges to their prerogatives by feminists and gender theorists. For many working-class fathers, however, such issues were—and remain—largely beside the point. Tethered to tedious jobs with long hours and little pay, such men were often remote from their children, literally as well as emotionally.

Based on Springsteen's own recollections, Douglas Springsteen was very much a father in this tradition: loving but taciturn, frustrated and frustrating. "My father, he worked in a lot of places, worked in a rug mill for a while, drove a cab for a while, and he was a guard at the jail for a while. I can remember when he used to work down there, he used to always come home real pissed off, drunk, sit in the kitchen," Springsteen related in introducing a cover version of the Animals song "It's My Life." "At night, at about nine o'clock, he used to shut off all the lights, every light in the house. And he used to get real pissed if me or my sister turned any of 'em on. And he'd sit in the kitchen with a six-pack and a cigarette."[19]

The point of this and similar stories was to show how the frustrations of the father would eventually be vented on the son—in some cases, quite literally, as in this story, a spoken introduction to a 1978 version of "Growin' Up" on *Live 1975–85:* "When I was growing up, there were two things that were unpopular in my house. One was me, and the other was my guitar. We had this grate, like the heat was supposed to come through, except it wasn't hooked up to any of the heating ducts; it was just open straight down to the kitchen, and there was a gas stove right underneath it. When I used to start playing, my pop used to turn on the gas jet and try to smoke me out of the room. And I had to go hide on the roof or something." This is meant to be an amusing story, and Springsteen chuckles as he relates it. But a sense of resentment is also quite apparent, resentment that is finally the most salient aspect of the anecdote. But Springsteen's songs themselves are rarely quite this simple, which is one reason why his recordings are finally more complex and interesting artistic productions than his live performances are. Still, a monologue like this may provide a kind of key for listening to a song (in the case of "Growin' Up," by hinting at the sense of conflict that textures the lyrics' generally ebullient spirit).

Such stories notwithstanding, parents are generally absent on Springsteen's first three albums. Those parents who do appear, like the overbearing father of "Rosalita (Come Out Tonight)," are killjoys who in their protectiveness deprive their children of happiness. In this song, Rosalita's father is the more imposing parent, the one who "lower[s] the boom" and refuses to sanction their romance because of her boyfriend's penury. With the help of a recording contract, however, true love conquers all, including the ineffectual (and two-dimensional) parents.

This man is depicted as somebody else's father. When Springsteen characters begin discussing their own fathers, the picture changes dramatically. Gone is the relative detachment that marks a song like "Rosalita," replaced by much more active emotional involvement. Still, the terms of the engagement remain largely negative; loved or hated, fathers are almost always a problem to be confronted, though not solved.

Springsteen began writing a string of father-son songs in the late seventies, a time in his life when he was finally able to gain some perspective on his own troubled relationship with his dad. But he also drew on pop-culture sources to tell his stories. "Adam Raised a Cain," for example, was inspired by the film version of John Steinbeck's *East of Eden* (1955), in which the troubled son Cal Trask, played by James Dean, struggles to deal with the misplaced rectitude of his father, Adam, played by Raymond Massey.[20] Douglas Springsteen lacked the wealth and standing of Adam Trask, and Springsteen himself, while something of a James Dean figure, avoided the fatalism that suffused Dean's characters. But the resulting song captured the stunted strivings that often characterize relationships between fathers and sons: "In the Bible Cain slew Abel, and East of Eden he was cast. / You're born into this life payin' for the sins of somebody else's past." The character singing these lines does so in a voice of barely restrained fury. But having an explanation for his father's bitterness tempers his own. Moreover, this son recognizes a temperamental kinship with his father: "He was standin' in the door, I was standin' in the rain / With the same hot blood burnin' in our veins."

Indeed, even at their most severe, Springsteen's sons never lose the ability to view their fathers with empathy. "Through the mansions of fear / through the mansions of pain / I see my daddy walk through those factory gates in the rain," observes the child narrator of "Factory." He may plausibly worry that he will someday face the same fate, or, more immediately, that he'll be one of those people who's "gonna get hurt tonight" when the men return home from work. But even more than "Adam Raised a Cain," "Factory" suggests the increasing sophistication with which Springsteen portrays the frustrations of fathers on their own terms.

Expressing sympathy for fathers is one thing; wanting to become one is another, something no Springsteen character of the seventies wants to do. "Then I got Mary pregnant / And, man, that was all she wrote," reports the narrator of the "The River." Pregnancy is strictly a trip wire to disaster: prospective fatherhood precipitates a shotgun wedding, a dead-end job, crushing financial burdens, and destroys the love between two people.

If becoming a father is a drag, so, too, is remaining a son. But on "Independence Day," this no longer seems inevitable. Gently but firmly, its protagonist makes a break, and does so in a way that suggests a new maturity in a Springsteen son. "Well Papa go to bed now, it's getting late," he says. He's solicitous, even parental, in his tone, and he recognizes that he and his father have a good deal in common. But he refuses to travel down the same path: "They ain't gonna do to me what I watched them do to you." In the end, independence means leaving town. This is, of course, a standard masculine formulation, whether in a classic western like *Shane* (1953) or a rock song like the Allman Brothers' "Ramblin' Man" (1973). "All men must make their way come Independence Day," concludes the singer, the very title of the song comparing his own break with that of the origins of the nation. But by the early eighties, Springsteen characters are discovering that independence is not always attained by mere physical separation. In fact, it may not even be altogether possible.

Nebraska documents a new sense of skepticism about such autonomy, especially in regard to parent-child relations. The album is haunted by sons who cannot shake off the specter of their fathers. The most obvious example is "My Father's House," in which a son wakes up to awful regret over breaking with his father, only to find that his bid for reconciliation comes too late. The child narrator of "Used Cars" feels the sting of the petty humiliations his father endures and makes his own declaration of (future) independence: "Now mister the day the lottery comes in / I ain't ever gonna ride no used car again." The likelihood of such an event ever coming to pass is uncertain, however, while that of more humiliation is likely. Springsteen's view of fathers, once a vision of contempt and anger, is now one of guilt and shame.

This pall of remorse began to lift in the mid-eighties, but slowly. In "My Hometown," a Springsteen character describes his experiences with his father as well as those with his son, and both relationships appear reasonably healthy. "I'd sit on his lap in that big old Buick and steer as we drove through town," the narrator relates of his father as he repeats the ritual with his own boy. But the overall theme of the song is one of decline, as the vibrant community of the child has become the decaying downtown of the father. However compelling the relationship between father and son may be, Springsteen's purpose here is less to chart a male relationship than to use it as a vehicle for socioeconomic commentary.

A similar investment in parenting is evident in "Seeds," from *Live 1975–85*. Here the father, a displaced oil worker, certainly cares for his children, but his harrowing financial straits deprive him of the ability to do so properly. "Parked in the lumberyard freezin' our asses off / My kids in the backseat got a graveyard cough," he explains. It's not this man's fault that he's living in a family in crisis—that's the point of the song, and Springsteen makes it powerfully—but it's a dysfunctional family nonetheless.

Not until *Tunnel of Love* did a fuller vision of what fatherhood could mean emerge in Springsteen's work. Perhaps his first marriage in 1985 was the catalyst, for it is in "Walk Like a Man," where a son, on his wedding day, addresses his father, that unambiguously positive images of paternal interaction are first described. "All I can think of is being five years old following behind you at the beach / tracing your footprints in the sand," he tells him. The son's memories are not without their shadows ("Well I was young and I didn't know what to do / When I saw your best steps stolen away from you"), and the father's experiences were of limited utility ("I didn't know there'd be so many steps I'd have to learn on my own"). But father has communicated something intangibly valuable to son, something that enlivens his sense of himself as a man.

On *Tunnel of Love*, Springsteen also gives his first positive expression to what becoming a father might mean, in "Valentine's Day": "A friend of mine became a father last night / When we spoke in his voice I could hear the light," he relates. Vicariously, this man zeroes in on the heart of parenthood: a sense of connection. But most importantly, it takes the form of recognizing ties to others, ties that may finally count more than a boy's dream of autonomous freedom.

When Springsteen released "Valentine's Day" in 1987, he had not yet become a father; the first of his three children was born in 1990. Judging from his subsequent music, fatherhood was a watershed experience. When a child is born to a subsequent Springsteen character—in *Lucky Town's* "Living Proof"—the experience is so overwhelming that it takes on religious dimensions: "In his mother's arms it was all the beauty I could take / Like the missing words to some prayer that I could never make." Like the child of "The River," this one has transformative effects; but while that one destroys, this one resurrects. "Living Proof" is all the more significant within the context of fifteen years of indifference or anger about fatherhood on Springsteen's part. Perhaps more than any other song, it portrays a man who has finally grown up.

Ironically, one important manifestation of Springsteen's maturity was a new willingness to deal with fatherhood in ways that do not always reach epiphanic intensity. *Human Touch* closes with Springsteen's version of "Pony Boy," a playful folk song. In a very different vein, the father of "Souls of the Departed" considers murdered children in East Compton, and confronts not-altogether-honorable impulses to insulate his own: "I want to build a wall so high nothing can burn it down / Right here on my own dirty piece of ground."

In some sense, such sentiments bring us back to the issue of class and the ways in which economics shape fatherhood. The fathers in Springsteen's more recent songs, like Springsteen himself, have options that the ravaged fathers of "Seeds"—or fathers like Douglas Springsteen—did not. For these men, the issue is how they will *use* their opportunities to build strong families, not whether they'll *have* such opportunities in the first place. Perhaps a desire for those opportunities, whether realized or not, is one measure of positive masculinity.

Fathering, then, is not simply a matter of biology, and a father-child relationship is not simply a matter of blood kinship. In "The New Timer," a song from *The Ghost of Tom Joad,* an old railroad hobo teaches a needy young man the ropes. When this mentoring father figure is senselessly murdered, the younger man thirsts for revenge. But he also thinks about the son he abandoned for a life on the road. It does not appear that he will return any time soon; although he prays to Jesus for mercy, his heart still lusts for vengeance against the old-timer's murderer. But he seems to know, if not quite feel, what being a man should really be about.

Springsteen's trajectory of fatherhood—of hostility and indifference, followed by engagement and transformation—can be read in a number of ways. The songs discussed here, for example, chart a classic Oedipal sequence of rage, anxiety, and acceptance. But they are also redolent of a much more specific historical development: a new emphasis placed on fathering in the late twentieth century. Here, as in so much else, the women's movement has played an important role. For if feminism has helped women make the psychological (if not economic) shift into the workplace, it may also be helping men make a similar shift into the home.

Old Boys

We're taking this till we're all in the box, boys. Till the wheels come off.
—Bruce Springsteen toasting the members of the
E Street Band, launching a world tour, 2023

Sons, husbands, and fathers have one thing in common with all other humans: they age. *Human Touch* and *Lucky Town* are considered largely forgettable records in Springsteen's canon, but they are documents of his maturation into full adulthood in the early 1990s, a period when his gender identity achieved equilibrium. As he moved into the twenty-first century, Springsteen's meditations on the subject tended to focus less on specific facets of that identity than on the fact that he was growing older.

Springsteen's first sustained engagement with aging came with *Magic* (2007), one of the true gems in his body of work. All the characters narrating its songs are voices of experience of varied kinds. Those of "You'll Be Coming Down" and "Livin' in the Future" have a cynical edge ("You'll be fine as long as your pretty face holds out / Then it's gonna get pretty cold out," reads one verse of the former). By contrast, the narrator of "I'll Work for Your Love" speaks in a voice of earned earnestness couched in religious metaphors: "I'll watch the bones in your back / Like the stations of the cross."

Springsteen's masterpiece on the ambiguities of aging manhood is "Girls in Their Summer Clothes."[21] Fittingly, "Girls" is an act of homage to a great band of Springsteen's youth: the Beach Boys. The song begins with a lush, even caramelized, acoustic arrangement. The lyrics have the feel of a benediction, at least at first, with their invocation of shining streetlights, a summer breeze, and happy couples. And then comes a jarring line: "Tonight I'm going to burn this town down."

Actually, it's the chill of these words that makes the song's true Beach Boy patrimony unmistakable: by conjuring a snake in the sonic garden. Think of the minor-chord ache in Brian Wilson's arrangement of the old folk song "Sloop John B," for example, or the strain of sorrow that runs beneath the loving daydream of "Wouldn't It Be Nice" ("You know, it seems the more we talk about it, / The worse it is to live without it"). And in "God Only Knows" a man dreamily expresses gratitude to a woman by raising the specter of suicide if she were to leave him: "What good would living do me?" Every breath she takes, he'll be watching her.

Like those Beach Boys narrators, Springsteen's narrator here, whose name is Bill, doesn't dwell on notes of unease, dreamily proceeding to the song's chorus. Yet here again there's a discordant note: "The girls in their summer clothes pass me by." An innocuous expression of nostalgia, perhaps—one familiar, at any rate, to virtually every man over the age of about forty—and, one guesses, many women as well, who often become invisible as they age. But it's also more evidence of an unreliable narrator. Unselfconsciously taking in women's looks might have been considered appropriate in 1967, but by 2007—and certainly ever since—subjecting females to this kind of male gaze had become, in the lexicon of our time, toxic. (Puritans of both the seventeenth and twenty-first centuries would deem this man guilty of lechery.) But neither Bill nor Springsteen himself wants us to linger on this, because the words and music—a gently rising crescendo in the drums, like a wave breaking on a beach—re-immerses us in the song's idyllic village setting of bouncing rubber balls, porch lighting, and chiming bells. And then, once again, there's a dissonant note: "Things been a little tight, but I know they're gonna go my way." *He* may know; *we're* not so sure. Actually, on second glance, there are other intimations of unease lurking in the presumably sunny lyrics, including passing mentions of gutters and encroaching darkness. (That chiming? It comes from a local bank, suggesting lurking implications of impersonal exploitation.)

Yet once more we're swept along by the soaring harmonies, organ, and piano fills, which roll into the song's bridge. Bill has made his way to Frankie's Diner, mesmerized by its neon sign, which he compares to a crucifix. A waitress, Shaniqua, comes over and offers him a refill on his coffee, asking him what he's thinking. This is a quintessentially Springsteenian scenario: quotidian moments endowed with almost comic grandeur. Such working-class romanticism was his stock-in-trade decades earlier (recall the Exxon sign illuminating "Jungleland"). But there was often also a spiritual overlay in such imagery, stretching from the roses and crosses of "Thunder Road" to the stations of the cross in "I'll Work for Your Love." Bill's crucifix, stationed over a lost and found, offers a tantalizing promise of redemption—tantalizing, that is, before he proceeds to sabotage it: "She went away, she cut me like a knife / Hello beautiful thing, maybe you could save my life." At the very moment we sympathize with his unwitting rejection by a waitress, he objectifies her in a mash-up of the sacred and the squalid. But the gentle tide refuses to stop rising, pulling us along once more: The girls in their summer clothes will keep passing by, and Bill will keep shadow-dancing with them. We may not approve of his gazing, but we recognize that we're subject to the same forces he is, inhabiting a dappled world of sin, hope, and a receding tide of time that doesn't quite succeed in washing away longing.

By contrast, we get more glimpses of mature love in all its grace and fragility on Springsteen next studio album, *Working on a Dream* (2009). "This Life" and "Kingdom of Days" appear to be affirmations of enduring marriage, as is "Life Itself," with its frank statement of vulnerability: "I can't make it without you." (The album is awash in Beatlesque arrangements, another expression of Springsteen's nostalgia.) *Working on a Dream* also includes an inferior "Girls in Their Summer Clothes" knockoff in the form of "Queen of the Supermarket," which aims for humor in its description of a middle-aged infatuation, but may well vie with "Mary Queen of Arkansas" to be the worst song in the Springsteen canon.

Overall, *Working on a Dream* is one of Springsteen's weaker albums, and it's telling in this regard that it gets a mere two passing mentions in his memoir (most of his albums get entire chapters). There is, however, one standout song that merits exploration here, and that is its opening track, "Outlaw Pete," which has the grandeur of the greatest westerns. (It later became the basis of a children's book.)[22] "Outlaw Pete" is a significant song in Springsteen's canon for a number of reasons, among them the way it considers manhood over the course of a lifetime—and, significantly, because the child who inherits her father's patrimony is female. The title character we meet at the outset of the song—which, clocking in at eight minutes, harkens back to the epic songs of Springsteen's early career—seems like a cartoon figure from an imitation John Ford movie. By the age of six months, we're told, Outlaw Pete had already done three months in jail and "robbed a bank in his diapers and little baby feet." His signature question, "Can you hear me?" seems like a childish, and stereotypically male, demand for attention.

But appearances are deceiving. More specifically, our perception of Outlaw Pete is deceiving. After hearing the seemingly requisite description of a horse-stealing, heart-breaking scoundrel—rendered in an amused voice suggesting that the narrator views Pete as a figure closer to a rakishly charming Jesse James than a hard, frightening Liberty Valance—the story turns on a dime (indicated by the music, which shifts to a repeated phrase of descending notes). Pete gets a vision of his own death that prompts him to settle down with a Navajo woman and their newborn daughter on a reservation. By choosing mature manhood, he gets a new lease on life.

Yet in some sense the story is only getting started. A vindictive law-man named Dan is determined to bring Pete down and precipitates a confrontation. "Pete, you think you've changed but you have not," Dan tells him. This is the existential issue at the heart of the song: to what degree we really do have agency over our fate, a question that still hovers over such issues as the gender wars. In the showdown that follows, Pete is nominally the victor, yet Dan literally gets in a last word in observing before his death that "we cannot undo these things we have done." The question "Can you hear me?" is turned on its head, as Dan speaks to Pete rather than Pete speaking to the world.

Pete, now a fugitive from the law, makes an ambiguous disappearance as the song ends. Is it to be understood from his encounter with Dan that character is destiny? Or is his disappearance an act of abnegation that protects his wife and daughter from the wickedness that surrounds him? It's unclear. Like Alan Ladd in *Shane* or John Wayne in *The Searchers*, Pete catalyzes action that leads to an affirmation of family but also pushes him beyond the frame. An absent father—or, in these cases, an absent father figure—is not necessarily an unde-voted one. And a flawed man may nevertheless do some good.

In any case, by the end of the song "Outlaw Pete" is no longer only, or even primarily, about Pete. The final verses of the song depict Pete's daughter braiding bits of his buckskin chaps into her hair—original sin and grace entwined—with the question "Can you hear me?" now addressed by a child to a parent. She is clearly her father's daughter, which affirms a sense of feminist possibility in terms of both who gets the last word in the song and what she may go on to do. But in suggesting that aspects of our life are hardwired, in part by biology, and thus our possibilities for fashioning our lives are limited, if real, there is also a strong note of conservatism here. Such a recognition may have any number of sources. But one important one is an aging process that cannot but help focusing one's life on its limits, even as it may also prompt a renewed dedication to realizing the art of the possible.

A decade later, in his album *Western Stars* (2019), Springsteen continues in this vein of weathered male wisdom, again rooted in traditional national mythology. It's a sad, wise, but hopeful man who goes to reunite with a flickered flame in "Tucson Train" ("I'll wait all God's creation / Just to show her a man can change," he explains). The movie actor of "Western Stars," who once had a scene with John Wayne, takes Viagra "that promises to bring it all back to you again." But the song ends, as it begins, by affirming survival more than vitality: "I woke up this morning, just glad my boots were on."

It's with *Letter to You* in 2020 that Springsteen truly arrives in old age. The very title and first line of its opening track hint as much: "One Minute You're Here" (followed by "Next minute you're gone"). The rousing "Ghosts" conjures up the spirit of fallen musical comrades, as does "Last Man Standing," a valentine to his early bandmates. The album's concluding track, "I'll See You in My Dreams," includes the assertion that "death is not the end." *Letter to You* also comes full circle in that it includes a rendition of "If I Was the Priest," the song Springsteen performed at his Columbia Records audition for John Hammond almost a half-century earlier. The title track is an expression of his will and testament: "In my letter to you," he sings, are "all the hard things I found out." Those hard things are the product of a lifetime of experience.

"I work to be an ancestor," Springsteen wrote at the end of his 2016 memoir *Born to Run*.[23] It's unlikely he would have thought in such terms as a high-school student in his first rock band a half-century earlier. But as William Wordsworth says in his classic 1802 poem "My Heart Leaps Up," the child is the father of the man.[24] Springsteen now dwells at the edges of shadows. But he's also birthed a living body of work.

♪ So receive me brother
with your faithless kiss ♪

FADE AWAY

FIGURE 7.1. Bruce Springsteen in the video for his Academy Award–winning song "Streets of Philadelphia," from the movie *Philadelphia*, 1994. This towering work of spiritual struggle and engagement depicts a man denying God in the language of faith. (Source: Columbia Records)

CHAPTER 7

God and Bruce Springsteen

I N DECEMBER 1969, while the college dropout Bruce Springsteen was cobbling together an improvised existence in Asbury Park playing area shows with his band, Steel Mill, *Playboy* magazine published "Cross the Border—Close the Gap," an essay by New Jersey native Leslie Fiedler, a literary critic at the State University of New York at Buffalo. Fiedler was staking out a pioneering career as a scholar—he was the first person to apply the term "postmodernism" to literature[1]—by asserting the need to remove false barriers between elite and popular art. In the middle of the piece, Fiedler made an arresting if offhand remark: "To be an American (unlike being English or French or whatever) is precisely to imagine a destiny rather than inherit one."[2] This assertion seemed to come out of nowhere, dropped into the text without any effort to explain or justify it, simply assumed to be clear—and true. And perhaps it was indeed self-evident for the readers of *Playboy*, a publication that was nothing if not a habitat for a certain kind of imagination.

To some extent, the remark is both clear and true. "To imagine a destiny rather than inherit one" is a rather apt way of describing the American Dream. Much of this book has been written under explic-itly "Fiedlerian" premises, attempting to show in any number of ways—whether in terms of upward mobility, a search for community, or gender roles, among other subjects—that Bruce Springsteen has rejected inherited destinies in favor of imagined ones.

But there is another tradition in American life, a deep, broad, and varied one, that has always been skeptical of imagined destinies supplanting inherited ones. The heir of slaves who feels a bond with Africa; the son of Ellis Island immigrants who holds fast to his parents' folkways; the woman who knows in her bones that biology is a form of fate: these are people who cannot believe—or, even if they think they have free will, *do* not believe—that inheritances can be cast aside.

But the most powerful, longstanding source of inherited identity in American life is religion. (This is something that Fiedler, a Jewish scholar, wrote about frequently in his long career.) God was never far from the considerations of most Americans, whether they were among the faithful or not. The bedrock of our national religious heritage is a somewhat idiosyncratic version of English Protestantism, one that took root with notable intensity in seventeenth-century New England and with which all subsequent faiths would have to contend. For all the energy and confidence the Puritans invested in their New World, their doctrine rested on a base of Calvinist predestination: that a person's spiritual fate was sealed from the time of birth—*not* something that could be changed by dint of effort. Puritanism, and the cluster of sects associated with it, specifically rejected the practices of a corrupt Catholicism in which heavenly grace had become a commodity to be bought and sold by priests and politicians in a wayward Europe.

Yet even as these people clutched fiercely to their faith, a belief that true believers might actually hold their destinies in their own hands seeped into New England. It's not hard to understand why. Given the immensity of the hardships they faced—the harsh cold and storms, the blight of disease, the hostility of foreign powers and heathen Indians (a hostility, it should be added, for which they themselves bore a good deal of responsibility)—it's hard to blame them for thinking that their survival was, if not actually a matter of their own will, perhaps at least a sign that they were doing *something* right.

By the mid-eighteenth century, increasing numbers of English set-
tlers were flirting with the Dutch doctrine of Arminianism, which
held that one had some role in achieving one's own salvation. And by
the nineteenth century, American Protestantism was dominated by
the doctrine of perfectionism, which, in marked contrast to older
Calvinist theology, posited the ability of people to effect their own
redemption. Perfectionism was one of the signal characteristics of
the religious revivals that swept the nation at the turn of the century,
and it would soon have secular consequences, notably in the struggle
to abolish slavery, which began as a religious movement and ended as
a political one. Ever since, the perfectionist strain of American Protestantism has, in widely diffused or altered form, influenced a wide
variety of movements, ranging from the agrarian Populism of the
1890s to the Black Lives Matter movement of the 2010s. In this regard,
conservative Christians and woke activists have a lot in common:
both regard the transformation of the world as both possible and necessary, and as a matter of human will.

This is a point that bears some emphasis. By the 2020s, the United
States was experiencing accelerating secularization, with a growing
proportion of its citizens falling into the "Nones" category when it
came to church affiliation, along with fading respect for (much less
fidelity to) matters of religious doctrine. But whether or not one is
inclined to celebrate such a development, the fact remains—despite
the collective enshrinement of choice as the highest of all American
ideals—that traditional notions of Christian faith continue to decisively shape the American moral imagination. It doesn't matter
whether the topic at hand is systemic racism or LGBTQ rights: the
underlying premise remains a core notion of equality rooted in Christianity, whose radical premise was the embodiment of God in human
form. This sacrosanct insistence on the integrity of each soul defined
the country from the moment of its conception: "all men are created
equal," where the possibilities of "equal" always carried with it more
potent implications than the limits of "men." (Indeed, Abigail Adams
was pushing her husband John on this point months before the Declaration of Independence was even signed.)[3] For most Americans,

equality remains *the* measure of morality: that which promotes it is right, and that which ignores or resists it is wrong. This moral imaginary has been central to recent quests for social justice, in which the variant of "equity" rests on an egalitarian premise whose Christian roots run deep in American soil.

In recent decades, the religious foundations of secular life have often been overlooked when they haven't been disparaged. Even as Americans continue to remember and honor the civil rights movement, they forget that its most passionate and effective soldiers, male and female, were anchored in Black churches (the *Reverend* Martin Luther King, Jr.) and mosques (*Minister* Malcolm X). Such people had little interest in relinquishing their collective inheritances, which in fact became the springboards for their soaring hopes.

There is another community in American life in which sacred tradition has long shaped secular hopes and realities: that of Roman Catholicism, which remains a force even as its numbers dwindle. Catholics, too, have maintained a measured distance from the dominant ethos of autonomous individualism at the heart of white, Anglo-Saxon Protestantism. Of course, at some level the Catholic tradition—and the Jewish tradition as well—emphasizes personal agency and responsibility; the ability to distinguish, and choose between, good or evil is at the heart of religious experience. But unlike Protestantism, whose varied theologies rest on the assertion of an individual conscience in the forging of a closer relationship to God, official Catholicism has always insisted on the primacy of the church hierarchy in shaping the entire structure of life on earth. Such a stance was one reason American Protestants were historically suspicious of Catholics' fitness to participate in democratic society, and it was not until the election of John F. Kennedy in 1960 that the issue was apparently resolved—for Protestants, at least. In the years since, the story of American Catholic relations with Rome has been one of dissonance: over a strictly male clergy, as well as contraception, abortion, premarital sex, and homosexuality. The church has severely vitiated its moral authority through its silence and complicity in the sexual abuse of minors by priests, a scandal whose effects remain toxic decades after its first media exposure at the beginning of this century. But even without that towering failure, millions of American Catholics have long resisted many church teachings, some by leaving the church altogether.

Like Judaism, however, Catholicism is a kind of ethnicity that is not shed lightly. Many Catholics uncomfortable with aspects of the catechism or church policy have chosen to become "cafeteria" Catholics, picking and choosing among teachings while retaining a loyalty to core rituals and holidays.[4] Others have renounced Catholicism with a vehemence that belies an ongoing emotional involvement. It was for such people that the phrase "Once a Catholic, always a Catholic" was coined.[5]

Wherever they situate themselves, American Catholics are confronted by a powerful tension between worldly aspiration and otherworldly obligation. It may be no coincidence, then, that some of the most highly charged commentary on the American Dream of worldly success has come from Catholics. It may seem foolish to suggest that the careers of Kate Chopin (born Katherine O'Flaherty), F. Scott Fitzgerald, Margaret Mitchell, Billie Holiday, Eugene O'Neill, Jack Kerouac, Martin Scorsese, Robert Mapplethorpe, and Madonna—to name just a handful of prominent Catholic writers and artists—would have anything in common. But they and many others have circled, often obsessively, around the tension between transcending the limits into which they were born and honoring the obligations, moral and otherwise, of their origins.

Bruce Springsteen is an interesting case in this regard. He has achieved a secularized Protestant dream of grace without the severe trauma that marked the careers of Fitzgerald, Holiday, Mapplethorpe, and others. And yet a strong vein of skepticism, even doubt, about that dream—and the underlying faith that sustains it—has long been a part of his musical vision (figure 7.1). For a man who has experienced an unusual degree of success, he has persistently explored failure in a variety of forms. He's too much of a republican—a political tradition built on Protestant theology—to surrender hope for a better world. But often unwittingly, he has been too much of a Catholic to forget the costs of even imagining an American Dream, never mind pursuing one.

There is, moreover, a peculiarly democratic ethos at the heart of Roman Catholicism. This is something that Frenchman Alexis de Tocqueville shrewdly recognized in his classic study *Democracy in America*, published between 1835 and 1840. "I think the Catholic church has been erroneously regarded as the natural enemy of democracy," de Tocqueville, himself Catholic, wrote. "On doctrinal points the Catholic faith places all human capacities on the same level; it subjects the wise and the ignorant, the man of genius and the vulgar crowd, to the details of the same creed." Acknowledging the undeniably hierarchical institutional structure of the church, de Tocqueville nevertheless asserted that "If Catholicism predisposes the faithful to obedience, it certainly does not prepare them for inequality; but the contrary might be said of Protestantism, which tends to make men independent rather than to render them equal."[6]

At the core of Springsteen's own Catholicism is an "analogical imagination," a term coined by theologian David Tracy to describe a distinctively Catholic way of understanding the world. Analyzing the work of Thomas Aquinas, Martin Luther, and John Calvin, Tracy posits a Protestant "dialectical" imagination that tends to divide spirit and matter, in contrast to a Catholic vision of fundamental unity, or analog. The former is an individualistic sensibility that emphasizes the distance between God and man, while the latter is more communal, emphasizing God's presence in the world.[7]

Catholic sociologist Father Andrew Greeley, who popularized Tracy's ideas (and who sounded the alarm about sexual abuse years before the Church responded),[8] vividly described the difference between the analogic imagination of Protestants and the dialogical imagination of Catholics in pop-music terms. "The church in the Madonna video 'Like a Prayer,' with its stained glass and candles, stands for the Catholic tradition in a way that a church that looks much like a Quaker meetinghouse cannot."[9] Madonna's symbolic vocabulary—one that draws heavily on darkness, rain, and other metaphors that some might consider clichés—is conditioned on a specifically (though not uniquely) Catholic penchant for drawing on collective iconography. Springsteen's similarly obvious affinity for such metaphors, from cars to darkness, has similar ethnic, class, and religious roots—all of which, it should be added, are interrelated.

Such metaphors, and the analogic imagination that animates them, are not simply a curious quirk in Springsteen's musical personality. His attitudes toward Catholicism, like his attitudes toward manhood, can be traced over time, with similarly illuminating results. Doing so vividly illustrates how religion functions less as a set of doctrines or rituals than as a way of thinking, feeling, and living in the world— even when we are unaware of (or avowedly reject) religious doctrine.

Perhaps the most important and striking thing about Springsteen's subtle but powerful Catholic imagination, however, is the way it parallels his politics, aesthetics, and other topics explored in this book. His religious sensibility is the supreme expression of his signal contribution to American culture: his capacity for exploring old ideas and themes, adapting and reinvigorating them, and giving them a new power and relevance in our lives.

Rising Son

Some people pray, some people play music.

—Bruce Springsteen, 1976

On July 8, 1978, Bruce Springsteen and the E Street Band performed in Phoenix, playing for a sold-out crowd at the 10,000-seat Veterans Memorial Coliseum.[10] By this point in his career, Springsteen was well known to audiences on both coasts but largely unfamiliar throughout much of the nation's interior. Phoenix, in fact, was one of the few inland cities where he had a real reputation. Perhaps this is why he added a new element to a story he told as part of his shows at the time. During a musical interlude in "Growin' Up," Springsteen would narrate a monologue about how his parents were worried about his fixation on music, which they felt was no way to make a living. His father thought he should be a lawyer; his mother thought he should become a writer. Eventually, he tells them they'll have to settle for rock and roll, at which point the crowd usually roars.

In Phoenix, however, Springsteen makes a digression. "My mother, she's very Italian, she says, 'This is a big thing, you should go see a priest,'" he explains. So he goes to the rectory and talks with Father Ray, whose very name implies that he will shed some light on the matter. After hearing his dilemma, however, Father Ray concludes, "'This is too big a deal for me. You gotta talk to God.'"

Springsteen has no idea where to find God. So—part of the humor of the story derives from this being described as a logical, even inevitable, step—he asks the E Street Band's saxophonist Clarence Clemons, his can-do sidekick. Clemons, of course, knows just where God is: in a house at the edge of the woods. Springsteen drives over.

Music blasts through the door of the house as Springsteen approaches it. "Clarence sent me," he says, and the door opens to reveal the Lord himself seated behind a drum set. Springsteen explains his dilemma. The Lord replies: "What they [his parents—*all* parents] don't understand is that there was supposed to be an eleventh commandment. Actually, it's Moses's fault. He was so scared after ten, he said this is enough, and went back down the mountain. You shoulda seen it—great show, the burning bush, thunder, lightning. You see, what those guys didn't understand was that there was an eleventh commandment. And all it said was: LET IT ROCK!" With that, Bruce Springsteen receives his confirmation. The show goes on.

Even without the aural and visual cues of a typical rock concert, this anecdote sounds like—indeed, was surely intended to be—an amusing, even silly, story. No one actually believes Springsteen visited God; he's telling a tall tale, not offering a religious parable. But all stories have morals, whether or not those meanings are obvious, conscious, or straightforward.

One of the things that makes this story striking, for example, is the way in which Springsteen takes subtle jabs at his Catholic upbringing. Although Father Ray seems like a decent man, it's Clarence Clemons, not the priest, who helps the troubled youth find God. Once he does,

God informs him that the laws and traditions that have been passed down to him are incomplete, even irrelevant. Far from being the humorless, severe figure of parochial school legend, God has adolescent taste in music and likes a good show (the burning bush, the thunder and lightning, etc.). The rules we inherited, Springsteen tells 10,000 disciples in Phoenix—that mythic bird of resurrection—can be safely ignored.

And yet this story is more religious, and specifically Catholic, than it initially appears. For one thing, it depicts a person genuinely troubled at the prospect of not honoring his father and mother—one of the commandments that Moses *did* bring back from the mountain. The very imagery Springsteen uses to describe God and his actions has an insouciant, even flashy, quality more typical of a Catholic mind than of, say, an abstract Presbyterian one. In fact, it's helpful to go a step further and point out what *doesn't* happen here. This is not a story in which a young man denies the existence of God, or angrily rejects him, or is disappointed by what he finds. Instead, it's a story about a man who seeks—and receives—divine approval for doing what he most wants to do. Which is, in effect, to become a missionary. The happy ending of this story is that the man whose parents fear he does not want to work ends up doing the most important work of all: God's work.

This is not an outcome that anyone, least of all the boy himself, would have predicted. Though Springsteen has a Dutch name, most of his ancestry is Irish and Italian. Adele Springsteen's maiden name was Zerilli, and it appears that her maternal influence played a large role in shaping his musical personality. Springsteen has described his mother as "real smart, real strong, real creative,"[11] and judging from his relatively unfettered, often sexually expressive songs, an Italian strain of Catholicism seems to suffuse his music more than a puritanical Irish one.

In his 2016 memoir *Born to Run*, Springsteen writes of his Catholic heritage with a striking combination of hostility and affection. He grew up next door to a church, and the rhythms of Catholic life, from wedding bells to funerals, were engraved on his imagination. Though

Douglas Springsteen lacked a steady job, Springsteen's parents found the money to send him to Saint Rose of Lima, a parochial school in Freehold. The experience has repeatedly been described as disastrous. "I spent half of my first thirteen years in a trance," Springsteen explained to biographer Dave Marsh. He also (apparently like every single person who has ever recollected a Catholic education) described discipline problems. "In the third grade a nun stuffed me in a garbage can because, she said, that's where I belonged," he recalled. Such experiences were not limited to the classroom. "I also had the distinction of being the only altar boy knocked down by a priest during Mass. The old priest got mad. My mother wanted me to serve Mass, but I didn't know what I was doin' so I was trying to fake it." Throwing in the towel, Springsteen's parents sent him to the public high school in Freehold in the mid-sixties, where his experiences were hardly better, if less costly. Still, the bruises he suffered at the hand of the Church in his childhood were durable: "It left a mean taste in my mouth and estranged me from my religion for good."[12]

And yet his diction here is telling: it remained "my" religion. "In Catholicism I found a land of great and harsh beauty, of fantastic stories, of unimaginable punishment and infinite reward. It was a glorious and pathetic place I was either shaped for or fit right into. It has walked alongside me as a waking dream my whole life." Which is why, notwithstanding the depths of his rejection of the Church in his adolescence, he described himself a half-century later as "still on the team."[13]

Moreover, Springsteen's Catholicism was never far from the surface of his musical imagination. Indeed, it was discernible during his audition for Columbia Records in 1972. Asked by talent scout John Hammond if he had written any songs he would not perform live, Springsteen responded by playing "If I Was the Priest," which described the Virgin Mary running the Holy Grail Saloon, the Holy Spirit managing a burlesque show, and the narrator refusing Sheriff Jesus's request to come up to Dodge City. "When he sang that song, I knew he could only be Catholic," Hammond remembered. The satirical, if not actually contemptuous, thrust of such words—which fuse a specifically American mythology with a more broadly Catholic one—could only come from familiarity.[14]

By the time Springsteen was making his first records, however, his stance toward Catholicism had softened somewhat. He seemed more interested in poking fun at religion than in actively demystifying it. This more playful attitude is evident in "It's So Hard to Be a Saint in the City," the final track of *Greetings from Asbury Park*. "The devil appeared like Jesus through the steam in the street / Showin' me a hand I knew even the cops couldn't beat," goes one typical line. "It's so hard to be a saint when you're just a boy out on the street." Springsteen's Catholic impulses are vividly on display here: an instinctive blurring of good and evil (Jesus as devil); a fusion of matter and spirit (Satan emerging from the mist onto the street); and a view of organized religion as analogous to a police force (which can nevertheless be beaten at its own game). What is most remarkable here, though, is that final line. Directly or indirectly, the singer pleads his case to God; in a kind of mock confessional, he seeks to be excused on the grounds that he's only a boy and can't be expected to have the self-control of a saint. Note, however, that being a saint is merely *hard*, not impossible. The overall feel of the song is rhapsodic, but a nagging guilt tugs, almost unnoticed, at the margins. Even as the boy enjoys himself, he knows all the while that he's not supposed to give in to temptation.

"If I Was the Priest" and "It's So Hard to Be a Saint in the City" notwithstanding, Springsteen rarely engaged with specifically religious issues in his early music. More common in these lyrics are reflexive habits of thought that reveal, perhaps unwittingly, his Catholic background.[15] Such habits are clearly in evidence in "Thunder Road," with its references to "crosses," "praying," "savior," and "redemption." Despite "If I Was the Priest" and "It's So Hard to Be a Saint in the City," Springsteen has no particular interest in confronting religious questions. But religious language and metaphors powerfully shape the narrator's understanding of what romantic love with Mary(!) is about, even when he uses them in a dismissive way.

Conscious or unconscious, hostile or playful, the most salient quality of the young Springsteen's religious character is innocence. With few exceptions, there is no real evil on his early records. Authority figures like clergy and policemen, though hardly respected, are generally depicted as humorless rather than malignant. Small-time criminals pepper these songs, but insofar as any judgment is passed on them, Springsteen is usually approving; the hustlers in songs like "Incident on 57th Street," "Meeting across the River," and "Jungleland" invite identification more than censure.

The notable departure from this generalization, and one that points to the next step in Springsteen's moral development, is "Lost in the Flood," an antiwar precursor to "Born in the U.S.A." "Lost in the Flood" features profane imagery (pregnant nuns, a congregation drinking unholy blood, etc.), but not as a playful joke. Though the "ragamuffin gunner" who this narrator describes would receive a good deal of Springsteen's sympathy and philanthropic support later in his career, the tone here is skeptical, even judgmental. (It seems safe to say that his ongoing opposition to the war and his experiences with the draft did not promote imaginative identification with soldiers at this point in his life.) What "Lost in the Flood" does document, however, is Springsteen's growing penchant for using Old Testament imagery to suggest a harsh or corrupt social order.

This tendency is especially pronounced in *Darkness on the Edge of Town*. Some of these allusions are obvious, almost clichéd, as the very title of "The Promised Land" suggests. But others are more sustained and direct. One such example is "Adam Raised a Cain," in which a young man compares his situation to one in the Book of Genesis: "In the Bible Cain slew Abel, and East of Eden he was cast / You're born into this life payin' for the sins of somebody else's past." The singer's father is an Adam figure, condemned to mortal misery. Bur what may be even more alarming is that he is the father of—is raising—Cain, a man destined for still more misery: "You inherit the sins, you inherit the flames." The song evokes a severe, even vindictive God who makes little allowance for personal aspiration, and a world in which defiance of God's will becomes a way of life. In "Prove It All Night," another song from *Darkness*, sin takes on an almost feral allure. "I've been working real hard trying to get my hands clean," asserts the singer, his voice menacing in its determination. Suspicions that his hands *aren't* clean are confirmed in the final verse when he addresses his paramour: "You hear their voices telling you not to go / They made their choices and they'll never know / What it means to steal, to cheat, to lie." So speaks an avowed sinner. There's no attempt here to excuse or understand stealing, cheating, and lying, the way a liberal Protestant (or an atheist) might. As he moved into maturity, Springsteen's work took on a much tougher yet also more ambiguous moral edge.

New Testament

You don't make up for your sins in church. You do it in the streets. You do it at home. The rest is bullshit and you know it.
  —Charlie (Harvey Keitel), in Martin Scorsese's *Mean Streets* (1974)

In religious terms, *The River* marks a major turning point in Springsteen's career. In the seventies, religion was a matter of metaphor for him, used as a source of playful humor or as a means to describe dilemmas that were perceived as essentially secular, like heterosexual romance in "Thunder Road" or strained parent-child relations in "Adam Raised a Cain." In the eighties, however, it became a subject of increasingly self-conscious exploration in its own right.

One oblique but powerful hint of this emerging sensibility can be glimpsed in the black-and-white image on the back cover of *The River*, shot by longtime Springsteen photographer Frank Stefanko. It depicts cardboard figures of a bride and groom and four bridesmaids (the women wear 3D honeycomb paper dresses) displayed in a store window. The backdrop for these figures includes paper cups, a package of glow-glitter, and other party goods. Cardboard patriotic symbols are also prominent: an eagle, a Liberty Bell, and an unfurled flag (a furled cloth flag stands in the far left of the photo).[16] In another context, such a picture could be used as camp, a mock commentary on shopworn working-class aspirations, especially those of women, or a pathetic illustration of how capitalism packages symbols into disposable commodities. Here, however, the message seems much more empathetic: even the humblest, paper-thin materials can be vessels of meaning and dignity.

On the album itself, Springsteen largely drops the playful mockery that characterized his early work. "I wish God would send me a word / Send me something I'm afraid to lose," says the anguished narrator of "Drive All Night," lamenting a lost love. (The song is used to evocative effect in the 1997 Sylvester Stallone movie *Copland*, directed by James Mangold.) There's no humor or anger here, nor is there subversion or irony in his description of the "fallen angels" who haunt "Drive All Night." But not all of this man's religiosity is cast in negative terms; in fact, one of the more striking aspects of the song is the way ordinary objects are endowed with sacred intensity, as in that back cover. When the narrator of the song sings the chorus—"I swear I would drive all night / just to buy you some shoes"—the ragged, anguished quality of Springsteen's voice forcefully endows a piece of clothing with an almost religious aura.

But the most obvious and important indication of Springsteen's religious evolution on *The River* is his more direct confrontation with the psychological dimensions of sin and human mortality. While the characters of *Darkness* wrestle with burdensome legacies in the struggle to realize their aspirations, many of those on *The River* actually lose the fight. For the characters of the title track, this is an unexpected and uncontrollable event resulting from an unplanned pregnancy and a collapsed economy. In the case of "Hungry Heart," it's part of an ordained (and unpunctuated) order: "We fell in love I knew it had to end." In "Point Blank," the fatal blow is administered by another individual, in this case a former lover.

In early Springsteen songs, characters respond to such adversity with renewed determination. The truly scary songs of *The River* are those, especially on the second half of the album, in which individuals realize that they've come up against something much larger than they can handle. Whereas in "Prove It All Night" sin is an option, a way of asserting one's autonomy in a blandly conformist society, "Stolen Car" depicts an impoverished soul for whom grand theft auto is a compulsion, proof of lost control: "Each night I wait to get caught /

But I never do." Like a character in a Dostoyevsky novel, it seems that this man *wants* to be arrested. Lacking direction, he veers toward a void more frightening than any punishment: "I travel in fear / That in this darkness I will disappear." The muted bass drum that has appeared sporadically through the song becomes incessant during this last verse. It's not loud or obvious, which only increases its ominousness. A dirgelike organ rises after the word "disappear," and one hears a last ripple of piano notes before they fall off, like the last leaves of autumn.

The last song on *The River*, "Wreck on the Highway," suggests the illusory nature of control even for those who are not spiritually ill. The very title of the song, inspired by the Roy Acuff tune of the same name, suggests Springsteen's growing receptiveness to country music, a genre notable for its strong vein of fatalism. In the song, a man driving home from work on a rainy night encounters an accident scene and gets out of his own car to help. He sees blood and glass and hears a pitiful voice ask for help. Eventually, an ambulance comes to take the victim away—a sign of hope—but the narrator remains haunted by the image of a state trooper knocking on a door in the middle of the night to inform a girlfriend or wife about the death of a loved one. Lest there be any doubt, the final verse spells out the implications for his own life: "Sometimes I sit up in the darkness / And watch my baby as she sleeps," he explains. "I just lay there awake in the middle of the night / Thinking 'bout the wreck on the highway."

There's nothing specifically religious about "Wreck on the Highway" (or, for that matter, many of the other tracks on *The River*). An atheist or agnostic can hear and appreciate the message of the song—that life is fleeting and unstable, and that one must attempt to live it in the fullest, most committed way—without drawing a doctrinal moral. At the same time, considered within the context of Springsteen's career as a whole, the song can be heard as part of a larger transition from indifference to broad existential questioning that leads toward deep engagement (and specifically Christian engagement) with them.

Nebraska represents the next step in this process. If the characters of *The River* veer toward a spiritual abyss, those of this album plunge over the edge. Nowhere is this clearer, appropriately enough, than in the title track, whose protagonist (based on Charlie Starkweather, a man who went on a notorious murder rampage in the 1950s) reveals much about the mood of the album. Tried, convicted, and sentenced to death, he is informed that his soul will be hurled into "that great void." Unlike the characters of "Stolen Car" or "Wreck on the Highway," however, he receives this news with an almost unnerving lack of affect. Asked why he has committed such monstrous crimes, he offers an explanation that looms over the album as a whole: "Well sir I guess there's just a meanness in this world."

The disembodied quality of "meanness" is crucial. At the time of its release during the worst recession since the Great Depression, reviewers of *Nebraska* wrote a great deal about the political critique embedded in the album. Far less has been said about the religious foundation of that critique, which rests on a confrontation with the problem—and nature—of evil. While some might project their darkest impulses onto a particular group of people (African Americans, Jews, immigrants) and others single out more socially determined institutional forces (systemic racism, social inequality, economic dislocation), Springsteen posits evil as a force that defies demographic specificity or rational explanation. So when convicted murderer Johnny 99 asks whether you can take a man's life for the thoughts in his head, the question is largely rhetorical: you can, but then you become implicated in the very act you seek to purge.

And the price of sin is costly. This is the message of "My Father's House," Springsteen's most conventionally pious song. An adult son dreams of being lost in the woods with the devil snapping at his heels. He desperately seeks, and finds, his father—only to awaken to a powerful sense of guilt and longing over their broken relationship. Impulsively, he dresses and drives to the father's house, only to learn he no longer lives there. It now stands as an indictment, "Shining 'cross this dark highway where our sins lie unatoned." The imagery here is resolutely simple, even archetypal. Biblical language suffuses the song (most obviously in its very title) but is no longer a mere stand-in for secular concerns as it was in previous Springsteen songs. In a sense, his heritage has finally caught up with him.

Fortunately, that heritage is not unrelievedly grim. Springsteen suggests that there is a flip side to transcendental sin, one he offers in the immediate aftermath of the opening title track. "Everything dies, baby, that's a fact / But maybe everything that dies someday comes back," speculates the narrator of "Atlantic City." The hope here is tempered, but not without a certain plausibility: if sin permeates every action, so, too, may grace. Ironically, it is the very tentativeness of this proposition, asserted amid unmistakable civic corruption, that gives the song its psychological and moral credibility.

Moreover, neither damnation nor grace is wholly independent of individual will. *Nebraska* features a number of songs in which the actions or intentions of particular people can make a difference in each other's lives. In the case of "Johnny 99," such possibilities are defined by their absence: an immoral economic system leaves him with "debts no honest man can pay," and no one steps forward to save him from his damnation. In "Highway Patrolman," by contrast, Joe Roberts repeatedly faces difficult choices in dealing with his wayward brother, Franky. He explains his stance in a pointedly allegorical line, "I catch him when he's strayin', like any brother would / Man turns his back on his family, well he just ain't no good." This does not prevent the prodigal Franky from committing more crimes, and there's no indication that Joe really expects otherwise. But he lets him escape across state lines nonetheless, because he chooses to obey a code of family loyalty.

It's significant that the secular social order of these songs is portrayed as immoral or rigidly indifferent toward human life. Thus, the narrator of "State Trooper" tells the policeman who pulls him over, "License, registration, I ain't got none / But I got a clear conscience 'bout the things that I done." The very skepticism about justice that marks these songs also translates into a reluctance to invest too much credulity in official behavior or explanations. Under certain circumstances, then, a revolt against the status quo is both possible and morally defensible.

But the hopes animating "Atlantic City" or "Highway Patrolman" offer, at best, partial solutions to worldly dilemmas. As often as not, human actors are forced to confront mysteries that are more trying than reassuring. Nor, despite the hopes of some believers (and, perhaps, the assumptions of some nonbelievers), does faith always make matters any easier to understand. It's less a crutch than a challenge.

Springsteen addresses this last point in "Reason to Believe," which closes *Nebraska*. The song is a litany of dead dogs, abandoned lovers, and funerals, each punctuated by an assertion that "at the end of every hard-earned day / People find some reason to believe." Far from the hard-won affirmation that many observers took it to be, "Reason to Believe" is the work of a man more troubled than inspired by the irrational faith of the sufferers he observes.[17] But its very rigor, its refusal to accept simple answers, in itself represents the degree to which a man who started out by poking fun at religion was now fiercely wrestling with it, like Jacob with the angel in the Book of Genesis.

Family Values

Springsteen sings of religious realities—sin, temptation, forgiveness, life, death, hope—in images that come (implicitly perhaps) from his Catholic childhood, images that appeal to the whole person, not just the head, and what will be absorbed by far more Americans than those who listened to the Pope [during a papal visit in 1987].

—Father Andrew Greeley, 1988

Far more than its predecessors, *Tunnel of Love* is an intimate record. Ever since *Born to Run*, Springsteen had been widening his scope to take into account social forces that affected his characters' lives— their family histories, their country, and in the case of *Nebraska*, their faith. Now, in the aftermath of the international hoopla surrounding *Born in the U.S.A.* and *Live 1975–85*, he turned inward. "I was interested in personalizing my music," he explained shortly after the album's release. "It's just a natural thing you want to do. You put something out there, it gets pulled in and taken up, and becomes part of the culture and part of people's lives. And then you have to reinvent yourself."[18]

This reinvention was not simply artistic. In 1985 Springsteen married the model and actress Julianne Phillips and settled down for the first time since his childhood. This was not to be a happy experience, however, and one did not have to be a psychoanalyst or a tabloid newspaper reader to wonder if the marriage was going well, because *Tunnel of Love* conveyed clear signs of distress. Springsteen and Phillips divorced in 1989 amid adultery on his part, news that rippled outward from those tabloids. Again judging from his music, in this case the albums *Human Touch* and *Lucky Town,* Springsteen's subsequent marriage to Patti Scialfa has been far happier—though her own distinguished body of work, notably her 2007 album *Play It As It Lays,* suggests ongoing tensions.

The point here is that the major reorientation in Springsteen's personal life in these years seems to have had direct consequences for his religious sensibility. "I wanted to make a record about what I felt, about really letting another person in your life and trying to be a part of someone else's life," he said in 1988. "That's a frightening thing, something that's always filled with shadows and doubts, and also wonderful and beautiful things."[19] Springsteen is talking about Phillips here, but he could just as easily be talking about the nature of religious experience. Marriage, after all, is a sacrament.

Andrew Greeley put his finger on the spiritual orientation that was taking place. "Religion is more explicitly expressed in *Tunnel of Love* than in any previous Springsteen album. Prayer, heaven, and God are invoked naturally and unselfconsciously as though they are an ordinary part of the singer's life and vocabulary." He adds, "The piety of these songs—and I challenge you to find a better word—is sentient without being sentimental, an Italian-American male piety not unlike that found in some of the films of Martin Scorsese (especially *Mean Streets*). It is, perhaps, not Sunday Mass piety, but it is, if anything, much richer and deeper and more powerful. It is the piety of symbol rather than doctrine."[20]

Actually, in "Walk Like a Man," there *is* an element of Sunday Mass piety. For the first time in a Springsteen song, a church scene is described in a manner he might have actually seen as a child: "By Our

Lady of the Roses, / We lived in the shadow of the elms," he reports, describing his mother's delight whenever she heard wedding bells. More often, however, a state of grace is experienced outside church walls. For the insouciant narrator of "All That Heaven Will Allow," a dance club is a cathedral. In "Valentine's Day," timber wolves, juke-boxes, and cold river bottoms, like wives and children, are reflections of "God's light."

What's especially significant about these songs is the way in which secular popular culture is not simply a symbol of spiritual awareness but an actual means toward achieving it. In "Tunnel of Love," a man involved in a roller-coaster relationship takes his beloved to an amusement park, where many of their dilemmas seem to be dramatically reenacted: "Then the lights go out and it's just the three of us / You, me and all that stuff we're so scared of." At the end of the song, though, the narrator describes what he's learned from riding an actual roller coaster, and does so in language that closely resembles religious teachings. For example, the words of the famous prayer of Saint Francis reads, "God grant me the serenity to accept the things I cannot change, the courage to change the things that I can, and the wisdom to know the difference." Springsteen paraphrases this as "you've got to learn to live with what you can't rise above / If you want to ride on down, down in through this tunnel of love."

The emphasis here on acceptance is especially significant. In his work leading up to *Darkness on the Edge of Town*, Springsteen's focus was almost exclusively on characters who sought to make change on their own terms ("I want the heart / I want the soul / I want control right now," declares the young narrator of "Badlands"). Here, however, a man learns that there are some things you "can't rise above," and that love—in the most specific and transcendental senses of the term—requires a measure of acceptance of things as they are.

These are the "wonderful and beautiful things." But *Tunnel of Love* is filled with—and finally dominated by—"shadows and doubts." The second half of the record in particular portrays people who are wrestling with demons. In "Brilliant Disguise," a husband begins by accusing his wife of infidelity, but as the song proceeds he reveals his own waverings, finally confessing that he, too, wears a mask. This is less a matter of comeuppance than a costly confession. "God have mercy on the man / Who doubts what he's sure of," he concludes. This is meant to be ironic, of course, but like so much else in Springsteen's work, doubt is finally couched in the language of faith, suggesting a powerful sense of struggle.

This sense of struggle often clouds the album's "happy" songs. Bill Horton of "Cautious Man" overcomes the temptation to flee his sleeping wife, returning to her and "the beauty of God's *fallen* light." As the narrator explains, the words "love" and "fear" will always be tattooed on his knuckles. *Tunnel of Love* ends with the epiphanic "Valentine's Day," but the narrator's joy is laced with fear: "I woke up in the darkness scared and breathin' and born anew."

To be scared and breathing, however, is to be vitally alive, and perhaps the most powerful feeling the characters of *Tunnel of Love* project is a strong, even fierce, sense of life itself as a sacramental gift. "Now some may wanna die young, man, / Young and gloriously," notes the singer of "All That Heaven Will Allow. But, he says, "That ain't me." This is less an expression of hostility to larger commitments than a vivid assertion that, even though there may be limits on what is "allowed," love makes mortal life eminently worth living.

This message is communicated most forcefully in "Spare Parts," precisely because the value of life is seriously called into question. "Spare Parts" features a lean, bluesy arrangement and a storyline that unfolds like an Old Testament story (Abraham's near-sacrifice of Isaac and Moses being hidden in the rushes come to mind). Impregnated and abandoned, young Janey gives birth to a son and they move in with her mother. She pines after her lost life, while her lover, down in Texas, vows never to return. Before long, she comes to a crucial crossroads, one that corresponds to the bridge of the song—and, not coincidentally, the entrance of an organ. Tempted to abandon her child at a riverside, Janey veers away from destruction: "She lifted him in her arms and carried him home." Janey takes her wedding dress and engagement ring to a pawnshop for "some good cold cash." Her (literal as well as figurative) immersion in the material world becomes her salvation.

The Springsteen albums that follow *Tunnel of Love* evince a commitment to materialism of a different kind: sexual expression. The very title of *Human Touch* suggests such an emphasis. Nevertheless, the pleasures of the body, like other kinds of worldly creation, are valued not solely in themselves but in the way they open windows to something beyond. This connection between a corporeal state and a spiritual one is spelled out with unusual clarity in *Lucky Town*'s "Leap of Faith": "Now your legs were heaven, your breasts were the altar / Your body was the holy land." While Springsteen has never been a prude, his sexual imagery had never been quite so graphic. Given the stereotype of Catholic priggishness, it's ironic that his more deeply engaged religious heritage appears responsible for this relative openness.

Sexuality is not altogether drained of a sense of sin, however. Adultery looms over "Cross My Heart" (from *Human Touch*) and "The Big Muddy" (from *Lucky Town*). In the latter, Springsteen offers a maxim that captures his basic philosophic stance since at least the time of *Darkness:* "Well you may think the world is black and white / And you're dirty or you're clean," he says. "Better watch out you don't step in those places in between." This is not really advice, however, because neither this character nor the others on these two albums seem to think it is possible to avoid slipping "in between." Thus, to cite another example, the man of "With Every Wish" learns that with fulfillment comes a curse.

The hard ambiguity of everyday life is made explicit in "Souls of the Departed," a latter-day version of "Lost in the Flood." This time, the Persian Gulf War takes the place of Vietnam, and the walls the narrator builds around his home to protect his children take the place of an abandoned shooting victim in the Bronx. Here, however, Springsteen's sense of irony and his self-awareness are sharper. "Now I ply my trade in the land of king dollar / Where you get paid and your silence passes for honor," this character observes. For what it's worth—and this character knows it isn't much—he is *not* silent. What difference that makes is not clear. Hypocrisy is a hardy perennial, but a seed of justice may yet take root.

Yet even in the murkiest terrain lies the possibility for epiphany, as "Living Proof," the most remarkable track on *Human Touch*, makes clear. "Living Proof" is a celebration of the body—in this case, of birth. But like other Springsteen songs, it derives its power from his ability to convey a deep intimacy with the very desecration that characters wish to transcend. His voice here sounds utterly ravaged, never more so than when he says, "You do some sad, sad things, baby, / When it's you you're trying to lose," as if he's reliving the banality of past evil. And yet the gnarled guitars that dominate the song also suggest a kind of flesh-and-blood immediacy, a heightened sense of living in the moment. The birth of this child represents a transfigurative moment, but it is one that is enacted in a material (and still cynical) world, where he compares his family to "a close band of happy thieves." The treasures of the Lord, conferred in mysterious ways, make questions of worldly justice irrelevant. Since no one is ever truly deserving, those treasures should be accepted humbly and with great gratitude.

Conscious or unconscious, sarcastic or sincere, Springsteen's religious imagination has always been marked by a clear tendency to explore spiritual subjects in the most concrete terms, as "Living Proof" makes clear. But in one final layer of development and complexity, he closes *Lucky Town* with "My Beautiful Reward," which moves him into an explicitly mystical dimension: in the final verse, the narrator has been transformed into a soaring bird. "I'm flyin' high over gray fields / My feathers long and black," he explains. Even here, however, an air of realism suffuses the magic; "cold wind," "gray fields," and "black feathers" both ground the imagery and maintain the dappled quality of Springsteen's religious imagination. Such a move seems consonant with the desert landscapes featured in the lyrics booklet of the compact disc. A southern Californian in the early nineties, Springsteen has moved closer to the Latin Catholicism that thrives across the border.

Soul Survivors

That belief in Christ is to some a matter of life and death has been a stumbling block for those who would like to believe it is a matter of no great consequence.

Flannery O'Connor, Wise Blood (1952)

Bruce Springsteen's music has been recorded by a number of other artists and has been used in a number of feature films. But he had never been commissioned to write a song until director Jonathan Demme approached him in 1992 with such a request for *Philadelphia*, a film about a man with AIDS who wrongly loses his position with a law firm. Whether it was his esteem for Demme, a desire to take on new challenges, or a sense of impulsive generosity, Springsteen agreed to see what he could do. The result, of course, was "Streets of Philadelphia," which won multiple Grammy Awards, a 1994 Oscar for Best Original Song, and enjoyed tremendous commercial success as part of the *Philadelphia* soundtrack and as a video that Demme himself directed. Perhaps more than any other record he had ever made, "Streets of Philadelphia" ratified his entrance into the nation's cultural establishment.

Whatever this song may be, however, it is also a profound religious statement. "There was a certain spiritual stillness that I wanted to try and capture," he later told *The Advocate,* an LGBTQ magazine.[21] Springsteen represents an experience outside his own immediate frame of reference—that of a sick, dying, presumably queer man—by drawing on the resources of his Catholic heritage. The way this alchemy of unfamiliar and shared experience resolves itself is perhaps the greatest accomplishment of his career.

"Streets of Philadelphia" depicts a *presumably* queer man; the song, unlike the movie it was written for, never forthrightly states the sexual orientation of its protagonist. By not fixing his sexuality or his disease, Springsteen in effect universalizes this man's situation. To some, this may seem like an evasion. Another artist could have insisted on a specific gay/AIDS setting, especially because there was so much room for denial of both in American society, with dreadful conse-quences, and such a choice would have been legitimate, honorable, and powerful. But not as powerful, one suspects, as the way in which Springsteen chose to write this song, which in quietly inviting identi-fication may be more rhetorically effective.

It begins with percussion, eight measures of a syncopated rhythm that will run through the whole song. This rhythm is reminiscent of the kind of beat heard on hip-hop records: its metronomic quality, produced by a drum machine, calls attention to its very artifice. But while this technique is a source of hip-hop's vitality, the drumming of "Streets of Philadelphia" is notable for its flatness. It sounds, quite lit-erally, like a broken record—or an irregular heartbeat sustained by technological means. The very continuity of this irregularity has a paradoxical effect, though, because it suggests a will to persist, how-ever imperfectly.

The next instrument one hears (Springsteen plays all of them) is an organ. The key is minor, the tone somber. The overwhelming feeling is one of grayness, like very heavy cloud cover. By the time the narra-tor sings the first verse, then, a funereal mood has been firmly estab-lished. In this case, though, it's the music, specifically that organ, that will reveal this man's fate more accurately than his words will. Those words are marked by a potent sense of alienation that operates on a number of levels. First, this man is cut off from himself: "I couldn't tell what I felt / I was unrecognizable to myself." In despair, he addresses a companion: "Oh brother are you gonna leave me wastin' away?" This character could be a family member, a lover, or simply an acquaintance. Our protagonist hasn't given up—he wouldn't ask his question if he had—but he has his doubts. These become clear in the final verse when he tells this "brother" to receive him with his "faith-less kiss," which links his fate with Judas's betrayal of Christ in the synoptic gospels.

This sense of estrangement intensifies, even multiplies, in the bridge of the song. "Ain't no angel gonna greet me," he says flatly. "My clothes don't fit me no more / I walked a thousand miles just to slip this skin." These words are marked by what is now a familiar duality in Springsteen's work. On the one hand is the concreteness of his descriptions. (The mournful way Springsteen sings "clothes" bespeaks yet another kind of alienation: that of separation from the material world of objects.) On the other are habitual invocations of spiritual terms and images, in this case angels. Even the descriptions themselves suggest a kind of internal division. We already know by this point in the song that "friend" is an ambiguous term. Walking a thousand miles to shed a skin suggests simultaneous endurance and exhaustion. Also, while humans walk, it is typically reptiles—specifically, snakes, an icon of evil—who shed their skins. At the same time, shedding a skin is also a symbol of healing and renewal.

The most important form of alienation in the song is spiritual: this man denies a belief in the afterlife. The saving paradox here is that this man denies Christ in the language of faith. The angels, the invocation of Judas, that desire to shed his skin—and through it all, that organ, which brightens noticeably during this bridge—all reveal an almost overwhelming longing for transcendence. At the end of it, that irregular heartbeat stops for the only time in the song. It's as if he's just about to let go.

But not yet. He returns one last time to the earthly side of the cosmic veil, lying awake in the darkness. In a subtle shift, however, he turns his concern outward. In the first verse, he was afraid of being left alone. Now, including his companion in his concerns, he wonders if they will leave *each other* that way. The question is left unanswered as the narrator sings the words "Streets of Philadelphia" for the last time.

But the song is not over; in fact, it goes on for about another minute. The chanting harmonies and drumbeat gradually fade as the organ increasingly dominates the song. The same phrase—the chord progression is one often used for "Amen" during church hymns[22]—is played repeatedly, rising in steps. Finally, the lower notes fall out as the organ notes peak and disappear. He has risen.

"Streets of Philadelphia" is a powerful song in the way it depicts the experience of faith as a mighty struggle—which indeed it must be for any fully realized religious experience. As he moved into the twenty-first century, Springsteen became increasingly comfortable with depicting religious experience in straightforwardly traditional terms. One good example is "Jesus Was an Only Son," from *Devils and Dust*, in which he imagines the death of Christ from Mary's point of view. Throughout *Magic* (as noted in the last chapter), Springsteen invokes classic Catholic imagery on songs like "I'll Work for Your Love" and "Girls in Their Summer Clothes," and the closing track of *Wrecking Ball*, "We Are Alive," couches the martyrdom of a series of characters from American history as an actual resurrection. (See chapter 2 for more on this.)

The keystone of Springsteen's religious vision is *The Rising*, released in 2002 in the aftermath of 9/11. When that fellow motorist shouted "We need you!" from a Sea Bright parking lot in the aftermath of the disaster (see chapter 4), Springsteen was shaken—and moved to act.[23] Amid the attention that accompanied *The Rising*, however, there was one aspect that received virtually no comment in the mass media: the album is a profoundly religious document. This is a matter that deserves some attention, for it sheds a good deal of light on Springsteen—and perhaps more importantly, on Springsteen's audience. The need referred to by that anonymous drive-by fan was spiritual, and one that Springsteen had been fulfilling in a presumably secular way for many years.

On *The Rising*, religion is less an issue or a problem than a vital resource. Nowhere is this more obvious than on the title track, one of the great works of Springsteen's long career (figure 7.2). The song, which proceeds in three stages, opens dramatically with a firefighter ascending a smoke-filled building, groping blindly, with a hose on his back and a cross around his neck. A cascade of sirens has summoned him to the scene, and now he has no idea where he is. At the bridge, there's an inflection of fear in his narrative as he hears voices and sees faces of uncertain reality. By the end of the song, as he describes scenes of his wife Mary (that favored name in the Springsteen lexicon) in their garden and framed photographs of his children dancing, we realize that he is dying, if not actually dead. His "dream of life" becomes an incantation, a choir of voices emerges ever more boldly, and we, the living, are beckoned to join in a chant of resurrection as all souls rise.

STAIRWAY TO HEAVEN

FIGURE 7.2. Still from the video of Springsteen's 2002 "The Rising," which depicts the death—and resurrection—of a firefighter trying to save victims from the attack on the World Trade Center on 9/11. Though Springsteen has rejected many aspects of his Catholic heritage, he has described himself as "still on the team." (Source: Columbia Records)

The plurality of this vision—*we* are beckoned to join the *chorus*—is one of the elements that give "The Rising" distinctively Catholic accents. So is the concreteness of the imagery; the blood of husband and wife mix into a kind of transubstantiation. It is particularly telling in this regard that Springsteen has described "The Rising" as "secular stations of the cross"[24]—which suggests a conscious comparison between his account of the ordeal of this nameless firefighter, who died in the hope that others might live, with the Catholic ritual commemorating the passion of the Christ.

It is also true, however, that *The Rising*, like Springsteen's work generally, is marked by a strongly ecumenical spirit. The gospel sound of "My City of Ruins" has a strong (Black) evangelical flavor, one reminiscent of Springsteen's live shows. The vengeful reference to the bow cut on the plains of Jordan in "Empty Sky"—"I want an eye for an eye"—has a kind of Hebraic starkness to it. But the frame of reference is even wider than that. "I wanted Eastern voices, the presence of Allah," said Springsteen of the album.[25] To that end, a specifically Muslim deity is invoked in the intercultural love song "Worlds Apart." And "Paradise" juxtaposes the thoughts of a suicide bomber contemplating the afterlife with those of a wife mourning the loss of her husband, who died in the attack on the Pentagon. "Mary's Place," a song about a man emerging from mourning, begins with a reference to Buddha, proceeds to an unnamed prophet, and then to eleven angels of mercy, en route to a classic Springsteen rhythm-and-blues rave. In his insistent fusion of joy and sorrow, East and West, life and death, he weaves a musical tapestry that argues for a kind of diverse unity: *e pluribus unum*. This Catholic is catholic.

It's one thing to say, even to show, that a religious sensibility lies at the core of Springsteen's work, as many critics and even theologians have done.[26] It's another to claim that his fans hear him that way. Such an assertion is particularly questionable given the evident appeal of Springsteen's music to those who go to his shows and listen to his music for the sheer pleasure of it, for the *release* from commitment of any kind, religious or otherwise. Such people are wary of attempts to "read too much into" rock and roll, intellectualizing what they regard as an essentially escapist experience. Add to this the bicoastal, secular core of Springsteen's audience, and the attempt to turn Springsteen into some kind of religious figure may seem unlikely, even inappropriate.

And yet there's a real reason to believe that this is precisely the role he plays for at least some of his audience. In his ethnographic study of Springsteen fans, *Tramps Like Us* (1998), musicologist Daniel Cavicchi notes that a major aspect of Springsteen fandom involves what he calls "conversion narratives": stories fans tell of how they discovered his music.[27] Sometimes these conversions are gradual; at other times, there's a Saul-on-the-way-to-Tarsus moment, when a listener is blinded by the light. But the telling of these stories, whether on websites or on ticket lines, has a ritualized quality too widespread to be dismissed as coincidental. There is a similar phenomenon of "pilgrimages," that is, trips people make to significant sites such as Springsteen's home or Asbury Park in an effort to see for themselves the life from which art gets made. Yet another example is the culture of collecting bootlegs or memorabilia, which Cavicchi describes as a quest for "the order found in devotion." Most striking of all is the language fans use. "His songs are my bible," says one. "After a Springsteen concert, you feel like you've been to church," says another. "We talked about a Springsteen show as going to church. You know, 'we're going to go worship tonight,'" says a third.

It's not only ticketholders who report such experiences. The country singer Emmylou Harris, who has recorded a number of Springsteen's songs in her career, once described the experience of singing "My Hometown" with Springsteen in her native Birmingham. Harris found the experience unexpectedly powerful, saying that her whole life flashed before her eyes. "You know, you eat the wafer, *transubstantiation*, is that what it's called?" she asked, referring to the Catholic belief that the wafer of bread blessed during Mass literally becomes the body of Christ. "It was like transubstantiation, it really was. It was like a holy communion. [She laughed.] I know what that's supposed to be about now."[28] An ecumenical spirit tends to characterize a Springsteen performance even when Springsteen isn't doing the performing and the performance isn't on a stage: at an interfaith memorial service in Monmouth County presided over by a rabbi, a chorus responded to a soloist intoning the words of "Into the Fire," repeating its incantations of strength, faith, and hope.[29]

Even in cases that have no obvious religious dimension, one often sees a degree of moral engagement in Springsteen's music that's more than just a matter of mere escapism or the kind of self-affirmation characteristic of New-Age spirituality. One catches vivid glimpses of this in Robert Coles's *Bruce Springsteen's America,* a collection of oral histories in which husbands argue with wives about the meanings of songs, and listeners express puzzlement, even irritation, about what they hear (more than one woman complains about the limitations in Springsteen's depictions of women). Particularly notable in this regard is the Rhode Island policeman who (correctly) notes that Springsteen devotes far more attention to the murderous protagonist of "Johnny 99" than to the victim or his family, and who is clearly troubled by "American Skin"—but doesn't simply dismiss it. Indeed, the police-man carries on an internal monologue with a singer who is telling him things he doesn't particularly want to hear. For people like this man—it's hard to believe he's alone—Springsteen functions as a de facto conscience, a man who provokes and even challenges as well as affirms, in the process allowing his listeners to define the meanings of words such as "right," "good," and "just" in contexts where they might actually mean something.[30]

Springsteen is not alone in generating an audience of listeners eager to decipher each talismanic word; Bob Dylan has engendered a similar hypnotic devotion, and so have Elvis Presley and Taylor Swift. But Springsteen may be unique in the degree to which he seeks to observantly depict the people he speaks for, an identification that could explain an intensity in the bond between artist and audience that may be unmatched in the history of popular music. It's telling in this regard that he does not refer to his body of work in terms of a "career" or even a "calling," but rather by using the more modest term "job"—a prosaic word for a kind of mission that involves a mysteri-ous gift, but one that most of his listeners can readily relate to. "That's part of my job," Springsteen told the *Times* as he reflected on the sig-nificance of the fan who said "We need you!" in that drive-by moment. "It's an honor to find that place in the audience's life."[31]

One of the major points here is that this "place" has been marked by continuity and change. By the early twenty-first century, terms like "Bruce" or "The Boss" were perceived as something akin to brand names that denoted to fans (and even some nonfans) a series of stable qualities: excitement, integrity, intelligence, humor. But it has been over a half-century since Springsteen made his first records, and the scrawny kid with impish charm is now an old man weathered by experience. Perhaps paradoxically, one source of Springsteen's dura-ble appeal is his avowed embrace of change, his willingness to chart the aging process in his songs. This willingness, and his ability to express collective hopes and fears, have made him something of a mediating figure in the lives of listeners who have grown up with them. He has not only kept them company but has helped them to apprehend, frame, and even answer some Big Questions. In short, he has become something like a priest.[32]

"Priest" is not exactly a word that rolls off the keyboard here, and it's one that few people, least of all Springsteen himself, are likely to embrace uncritically. Indeed, a number of writers have complained about the cultlike quality of Springsteen's following.[33] Organized religion of all kinds has fallen into disrepute in many quarters in American life, and priests in particular are looked upon with skepticism even among those with a real commitment to institutional churches. The fact that the vast majority of priests are good people does not really change the perception of not just outsiders but also many Catholics that they are remote, even irrelevant figures: old men ignorant of their parishioners' lives (as any celibate person is likely to be), forced to toe an absurd papal line on issues such as the role of women in the church.

It wasn't always so—or at least it didn't always seem that way. In Hollywood movies, figures such as Spencer Tracy in *Boys Town* (1938) and Karl Malden in *On the Waterfront* (1954) depicted youthful, even virile priests, giving Americans, Catholic and non-Catholic alike, a palpable vision of deeply human people who struggled with their faith and yet were able to point their parishioners in the direction of their best selves. Of course, Tracy and Malden were only playing roles, albeit roles based on real people. But real priests likewise play a role. They serve a ceremonial, mediating function; they are agents, catalysts, instruments of something larger than themselves. As such, they serve a vital purpose. Which may be why there are times when Springsteen on stage resembles a Black Baptist preacher exhorting his congregation to join him in song.

For the truth is that most of us, even those who do not consider themselves religious, still find ourselves with often inchoate longings, longings to be a part of something larger than ourselves, longings to understand the ineffable. These longings seep into the crevices of everyday life. They get filled, to the always partial degree to which such longings ever do, in a variety of ways—in churches, in classrooms, in marriages. These ways are not mutually exclusive, and none of them is wholly complete. One of the most important of these ways, as organized religions of all kinds have long recognized, is by means of art. And art reflects the character of its creators and patrons. In the United States, at least some of that character is democratic. The best American artists honor an egalitarian spirit in the form as well as the content of their art, most obviously in the vast sprawling world of popular culture. And at the center of that world is popular music, a distinctly American contribution to civilization because it rests on a fundamental contradiction: a heritage of slavery and a heritage of freedom. The friction caused by these competing histories generated an African American musical tradition, the bedrock of which—not coincidentally—was religious. On this rock, we have built an unofficial national church.

The Lord of Phoenix was right: Springsteen really was doing God's work.

FIGURE C.1. Springsteen receives the Presidential Medal of Freedom from Barack Obama in 2016. Though no longer a hitmaker, Springsteen remains a touchstone figure of American culture in the twenty-first century. (Source: Pete Souza, The White House)

Conclusion

MILLIONS OF AMERICAN LIVES were shaped in the twentieth century by the medium of radio, though not always shaped in the same way. In its formative years of the 1920s, radio became the primary medium for news and entertainment in American life, an electronic hearth at the center of the nation's households. With the advent of television, radio shifted toward the liminal spaces, where its mobility was especially prized, whether in the form of portable radios (and later boom boxes) or, especially, car radios. Broadcasts of musical recordings had originally been avoided, for technological as well as economic reasons—record companies feared consumers would not buy music they could get free and so refused to license it to radio stations—but beginning in the 1950s it became clear that the two industries were in fact highly symbiotic (much in the way the movie business realized there were great profits to be made in allowing films to be shown on television). And so in the second half of the century, radio became the primary means of transmission of popular music to the public—in effect *creating* a public through the shared experience of listening.

I was one of a great many Americans for whom radio was a lifeline to the outside world. Growing up in a small town, it connected me, through the avenue of popular music, to a shared trans-Atlantic culture. To be sure, I had a particular neighborhood, both literally (metropolitan New York City) and figuratively (my musical home ground was the so-called progressive rock stations that dominated FM radio). But I would sometimes wander the dial, monitoring pop hits on AM radio as well as catching news reports and sporting events.

One precinct where I would occasionally land while searching for songs I liked was an oldies radio station, WCBS-FM. It was there I would hear the music of stars like Elvis Presley, Chuck Berry, and Buddy Holly and girl groups like the Ronettes. This was history for me, and I incorporated it into a musical imaginary that stretched into my own day, which of course included the music of Bruce Springsteen—music that was forged with a highly acute awareness of his forebears.

WCBS is still around, and it's still an oldies station. But the music it plays is what was current when I was a kid—including the music of Springsteen. I reckon it won't be long now before that music gets displaced by songs I barely know, much less like. But that of course assumes that WCBS—that radio broadcasting as I have known it— will be around much longer. (In his 2007 song "Radio Nowhere," Springsteen lamented the less-than-solid state of radio in a digital age: "I was spinnin' 'round a dead dial / Just another lost number in a file.") The adolescents I teach all know what radio is, and a few of them actually listen to it from time to time. But they're far more likely to download podcasts or stream songs than to listen to the radio—or, for that matter, to buy records. In some ways, they're more musically literate than I ever was, able to access Nina Simone or Etta James at the touch of a virtual button. In any case, Springsteen will soon be to them what Bessie Smith or Irving Berlin was for me: vaguely familiar names known more by reputation than sound.

Springsteen himself showed an awareness of such generational evanescence even as a young man. "There's just different people coming down here now," the protagonist of "Independence Day" tells his father, "And they see things in different ways / Soon everything we've known will just be swept away."

It has been a source of comfort and pleasure to be able to revisit this book while Bruce Springsteen is still very much among us. As I write these words, he has embarked on a world tour that is being widely covered in the national media, and set lists and videos from his shows appear regularly on my Twitter feed. ("Twitter? What's a twitter?" a child is likely to ask not long from now.) He's not the hitmaker he once was, but his new album releases receive respectful treatment and he is often invoked as an inspiration by his heirs and invoked by presidents (figure C.1). This book was originally written, and in effect remains, in the present tense. Indeed, its very publication rests on an assumption that a living audience for his work remains.

But that moment is coming to an end. And as I complete this book, I quaintly imagine it sitting on a library shelf to be discovered by an intrepid reader with little knowledge, or even interest, in its subject, but who may yet find it curiously engaging for the very fervency reflected in its prose. Why did people find this Bruce Springsteen person so interesting? How did the preoccupations of his audience coexist with the blind spots and ignorance that people of the past had for the interests and dilemmas of the future? And what lingering relevant light might it shed on the life of that reader?

We'll never know. As a matter of vanity, I hope my work will linger. If so, the most likely and appropriate way it can do so is as an expression of gratitude. Wow, this imagined reader might think—that Springsteen guy really inspired a lot of people. He really seems to have enlarged and enlivened the world.

Yes.

ACKNOWLEDGMENTS

PREVIOUS EDITIONS of this book included an exhaustive list of acknowledgments, which I think would be best abbreviated here so as to focus on expressing gratitude toward the institutions that provided me with the support that allowed me to produce and revise the work.

Its roots date back to my undergraduate years at Tufts University, where I wrote a thesis with little direct, but much indirect, resemblance to this one. My next home was Brown University, where, while writing a little more about Springsteen, I completed my master's and doctoral degrees in American Studies. From there I went to the University of New Hampshire, and then to the Expository Writing and Committee on Degrees in History and Literature programs at Harvard. The original edition was written and published during my time there.

In 2001, I took a job as a high-school teacher at the Ethical Culture Fieldston School in New York. While there, I revised the book, which was published in a second edition in 2005. I remained at Fieldston until 2020, when I moved on to the (new) upper division at Greenwich Country Day School. It was there that this third edition was prepared in 2022–2023.

The final institution I would like to acknowledge here is Rutgers University Press. This is the sixth and final book I have published with the press. I am particularly indebted to editor Peter Mickulas for this one.

A few more personal debts: The spirit and example of my best friend, Gordon Sterling, to whom this volume is dedicated, remain with me years after his passing in 2015. My four children—Jay, Grayson (who helped with illustrations), Ryland, and Nancy, have tolerated my obsessions and absences, literal and figurative. And finally my wife, Lyde Cullen Sizer, associate dean of Sarah Lawrence College (a school where I too have taught over the years and which has been my institutional home away from home since 1994), has been my unshakable companion.

And then there's this Bruce Springsteen fellow. . . .

NOTES

Introduction

1. For an excellent anthology of this body of journalistic critical literature (including reprints of the Knobler and Mitchell pieces), see *Racing in the Street: A Bruce Springsteen Reader*, ed. June Skinner Sawyers (New York: Penguin, 2004).

2. For an ethnographic study of Springsteen's female audience, see Lorraine Mangione and Donna Luff, *Mary Climbs In: The Journeys of Springsteen's Female Fans* (New Brunswick, NJ: Rutgers University Press, 2023).

3. "Summer's Fall: Springsteen in Senescence," in *Long Walk Home: Essays in Honor of Bruce Springsteen*, ed. Jonathan D. Cohen and June Skinner Sawyers (New Brunswick, NJ: Rutgers University Press, 2019), 189–199.

Chapter 1   Republicans and republicans

Section epigraphs: "His attention elicited from me two responses . . . ," Bruce Springsteen, *Born to Run* (New York: Simon & Schuster, 2016), 327; "We may define a republic to be . . . ," Founders Online, https://founders.archives.gov /documents/Madison/01-10-02-0234 (accessed October 30, 2022); "My idea in the early and mid-1980's was to put forth an alternate vision . . . ," Neil Strauss, "Springsteen Looks Back but Keeps Walking On," *New York Times*, May 7, 1995, https://www.nytimes.com/1995/05/07/arts/pop-music-springsteen-looks-back -but-keeps-walking-on.html; "I appropriate to myself very little of the demonstrations of respect . . . ," Abraham Lincoln, "Address to the New Jersey General Assembly," in *Speeches and Writings, 1859–1865*, ed. Don Fehrenbacher (New York: Library of America, 1989), 210.

1. Daniel Cavicchi, *Tramps Like Us: Music and Meaning among Springsteen Fans* (New York: Oxford University Press, 1998). The term is used throughout the text.

2. See, for example, Dave Marsh's review of these shows in *Rolling Stone*, included in *Racing in the Streets: The Bruce Springsteen Reader*, ed. June Skinner Sawyers (New York: Penguin, 2004), 50–51, and Eric Alterman's description of hearing the Bottom Line show of August 15, 1975, in *It Ain't No Sin to Be Glad You're Alive: The Promise of Bruce Springsteen* (Boston: Back Bay, 2001), 73–74.

3. For a brief overview of ties between Sinatra, the Chicago crime family led by Sam Giancana, and John F. Kennedy, connected by Giancana's and Kennedy's trysts with Judith Exner—a subject of folklore in its own right—see J. Randy Taraborelli, *Sinatra: Behind the Legend* (New York: Birch Tree Books, 1997), 221–223.

4. For an earlier rehearsal of the ideas developed at more length here, see Jim Cullen, "Bruce Springsteen's Ambiguous Musical Politics in the Reagan Era," *Popular Music and Society* 16, no. 2 (Summer 1992): 1–22.

5. See for example, the conversation between Springsteen and Obama in the transcripts of their Spotify podcast *Renegades: Born in the U.S.A.* (New York: Crown, 2021).

6. Arnold Sawislak, "Reagan Called 'Amiable Dunce' on New Washington Tape," United Press International, October 10, 1981, https://www.upi.com /Archives/1981/10/10/Reagan-called-amiable-dunce-on-new-Washington-tape /3026371534400.

7. Much of the account that follows draws on Dave Marsh, *Bruce Springsteen: Two Hearts: The Definitive Biography, 1972–2003* (New York: Routledge, 2004), 479–480. The book is a combined and updated edition of two previous Marsh books: *Born to Run: The Bruce Springsteen Story* (New York: Dell, 1979) and *Glory Days: Bruce Springsteen in the 1980s* (New York: Pantheon, 1987).

8. For more context on Will's attendance at the August 25 Springsteen show at the Capitol Theater in Landover, Maryland, see Geoffrey Himes, *Bruce Springsteen's Born in the U.S.A.*, part of Bloomsbury's "33 1/3" series (New York: Bloomsbury, 2005), 107–109.

9. George Will, "Bruce Springsteen's U.S.A.," *Washington Post*, September 13, 1984, https://www.washingtonpost.com/archive/politics/1984/09/13/bruce -springsteens-usa/f6502baa-a8eb-48ad-ba85-7fa848d8833e/.

10. Marsh, *Bruce Springsteen*, 480. For their coverage of Reagan's appearance the previous day, see the September 20 editions of the *New York Times*, *Washington Post*, *Wall Street Journal*, and *Los Angeles Times*.

11. A video copy of Reagan's remarks, archived at the Reagan Library in Simi Valley, California, is available on YouTube, https://www.youtube.com/watch?v

=juiFbHtlVO4 (accessed October 23, 2022). These occur about five minutes into the speech; Springsteen is mentioned about a minute and a half later.

12. This influential analysis was first crystallized by Mary D. Edsall and Thomas Byrne Edsall in *Chain Reaction: The Impact of Race, Rights and Taxes in American Politics* (New York: Norton, 1992).

13. Kurt Loder, "The *Rolling Stone* Interview: Bruce Springsteen on *Born in the U.S.A.*," *Rolling Stone*, December 7, 1984, https://www.rollingstone.com/music/music-news/the-rolling-stone-interview-bruce-springsteen-on-born-in-the-u-s-a-184690/.

14. The literature of republicanism, which, perhaps not entirely coincidentally, flowered in the academy in the very years Springsteen was emerging, is surveyed in Daniel Rodgers, "Republicanism: The Career of a Concept," *Journal of American History* 79, no. 1 (June 1992): 11–38. Rodgers is fairly critical of the way republicanism has been deployed in U.S. historiography, in part because it was applied so widely in ways that stretched, diluted, and even contradicted its meaning. I realize I'm pushing in invoking it here, which I'm trying to do lightly to suggest a cast of mind which, if not necessarily conscious or airtight, nevertheless suffused the collective consciousness in ways that could even inform the pre-political psyche of an ambitious American artist.

15. Thomas Jefferson to John Adams, October 28, 1813, Founders Online, https://founders.archives.gov/documents/Jefferson/03-06-02-0446#:~:text=science%20had%20liberated%20the%20ideas,which%20have%20fallen%20into%20contempt.

16. Thomas Jefferson to Peter Carr, August 10, 1787, Founders Online, https://founders.archives.gov/documents/Jefferson/01-12-02-0021#:~:text=State%20a%20moral%20case%20to,well%20as%20direct%20your%20feelings.

17. John Adams to Benjamin Rush, January 25, 1806, Founders Online, https://founders.archives.gov/documents/Adams/99-02-02-5119.

18. John Adams to Thomas Jefferson, November 15, 1813, Founders Online, https://founders.archives.gov/documents/Jefferson/03-06-02.-0478#RFH92094118131115100_16; Joseph Ellis discussed the two men's ideas regarding natural aristocracy in *Founding Brothers: The Revolutionary Generation* (New York: Knopf, 2000; reprint, New York: Vintage, 2002): 232–237.

19. Thomas Jefferson, Notes on the State of Virginia, Query XIX 1785, https://xroads.virginia.edu/~Hyper/JEFFERSON/ch19.html (accessed October 27, 2022).

20. For more on Springsteen's ancestry, see Peter Ames Carlin, *Bruce* (New York: Touchstone, 2012): 1–6.

21. Steve Appleford, "$5,000 Freeze-Out: Springsteen Fans Feel Betrayed by 'Crazed' Concert Ticket Prices," *Los Angeles Times*, July 29, 2022, https://www.latimes.com/entertainment-arts/music/story/2022-07-29/bruce-springsteen

-concert-ticket-price-ticketmaster. The long-running Springsteen fanzine *Backstreets* suspended publication in 2023 in protest over Springsteen's perceived indifference to his most devoted fans. See "After Ticket Flap, Springsteen's Fan Magazine Shutting Down," *The Hill*, February 7, 2023, https://thehill.com /homenews/ap/ap-technology/ap-after-ticket-flap-springsteens-fan-magazine -shutting-down/.

22. For a good history of the varied manifestations of populism, see Michael Kazin, *The Populist Persuasion: An American History* (New York: Basic Books, 1994; reprint, Ithaca, NY: Cornell University Press, 2017).

23. The American Presidency Project, https://www.presidency.ucsb.edu /documents/address-madison-square-garden-new-york-city-1 (accessed October 25, 2022).

24. Donald Trump, https://www.youtube.com/watch?v=Vpdt7omPoao (accessed February 12, 2023).

25. For Reagan's remarks in Hammonton, September 19, 1984, see https:// www.youtube.com/watch?v=juiFbHtlVO4.

26. For an analysis of Romney's remark, which generated much negative media coverage, see the PolitiFact website, https://www.politifact.com /factchecks/2012/sep/18/mitt-romney/romney-says-47-percent-americans-pay -no-income-tax/ (accessed October 26, 2022).

27. Carlin, 127. On "Roulette" and the MUSE concerts, see Marsh, *Bruce Springsteen*, 213–217, and Carlin, 271–273.

28. Quoted in Marsh, *Bruce Springsteen*, 484.

29. Andrew Carnegie, "Wealth," *North American Review* (June 1889), https:// www.swarthmore.edu/SocSci/rbannis1/AIH19th/Carnegie.html. The best recent biography of Carnegie is David Nasaw's *Andrew Carnegie* (New York: Penguin, 2006).

30. For a good labor-friendly treatment of the Homestead Strike, see Herbert Gutman, *Who Built America? Working People and the Nation's Economy, Culture and Society* (New York: Pantheon, 1992), 132–137.

31. Marsh, *Bruce Springsteen*, 486–487. On Springsteen's setlist for his September 22 show, see the Guitars 101 website, https://www.guitars101.com/threads /bruce-springsteen-e-street-band-civic-arena-pittsburgh-september-21-1984 .697059/ (accessed October 29, 2022).

32. "Closure of the (Mahwah) Ford Motor Plant 36 Years Ago Changed Lives," NorthJersey.com, https://www.northjersey.com/story/news/morris/butler/2016 /04/24/rest-of-the-story-april-24-2017-closure-of-the-mahwah-ford-motor-plant -36-years-ago-changed-lives/94654268/; "Majority from Ford's Mahwah Plant Still Jobless," *New York Times*, April 25, 1982, https://www.nytimes.com/1982/04 /25/nyregion/majority-from-ford-s-mahwah-plant-still-jobless.html.

33. For more on Clay and self-made ideology, see Jim Cullen, "Problems and Promises of the Self-Made Myth," *Hedgehog Review* 15, no. 2 (Summer 2013), https://hedgehogreview.com/issues/the-american-dream/articles/problems -and-promises-of-the-self-made-myth.

34. David Donald, *Lincoln* (New York: Simon & Schuster, 1995), 46.

35. Donald, 52.

36. On the etymology of "boss," see David Roediger, *The Wages of Whiteness: Race and the Making of the American Working Class* (London: Verso, 1991), 54. A new edition of the book appeared in 2007.

37. Springsteen talks candidly about his decision to be, and his comfort with being, a boss in (among other places) *Born to Run*, 149–150.

38. Marsh, *Bruce Springsteen*, 559.

39. Shannon Power, "Bruce Springsteen Reveals What His Granddaughter Isn't Allowed to Call Him," *Newsweek*, November 15, 2022, https://www .newsweek.com/bruce-springsteen-boss-granddaughter-baby-music-1759756.

Chapter 2   democratic Character

Section epigraphs: "The messages of great poets . . . ," Whitman, Preface to *Leaves of Grass*, https://www.poetryfoundation.org/articles/69391/from-preface -to-leaves-of-grass-first-edition#:~:text=The%20messages%20of%20great%20 poets,could%20be%20only%20one%20Supreme%3F (accessed August 17, 2023); "Camerado! I give you my hand! . . . ," Whitman, "Song of the Open Road," https://www.poetryfoundation.org/poems/48859/song-of-the-open-road (accessed August 17, 2023); "Have you heard that it is good . . . ," Whitman, "Song of Myself," https://www.poetryfoundation.org/poems/45477/song-of-myself -1892-version (accessed August 17, 2023); "The nonchalance of boys . . . ," Emerson, "Self-Reliance," in *Selected Essays of Ralph Waldo Emerson*, ed. Robert D. Richardson (New York: Bantam, 1990), 150; "I'll be in the way kids laugh . . . ," Steinbeck, *The Grapes of Wrath* (New York: Viking, 1939; reprint, New York: Penguin, 1976), 537. This line is also spoken by Henry Fonda in the 1940 film version of the novel.

1. These quotations come from "The American Scholar," "Self-Reliance," and "Nature," in *Selected Essays of Ralph Waldo Emerson*, ed. Robert D. Richardson (New York: Bantam, 1990), 87, 155, 53.

2. Emerson, "The Poet," in *Selected Essays*, 212, 221.

3. Quoted in Gay Wilson Allen, *Walt Whitman: A Biography* (New York: Viking, 1981), 400–401.

4. "Song of Myself," https://www.poetryfoundation.org/poems/45477/song -of-myself-1892-version.

5. On Springsteen as monologuist, see Alan Rauch, "Bruce Springsteen and the Dramatic Monologue," *American Studies* 29, no. 1 (Spring 1988): 29–49.

6. Royall Tyler, *The Contrast: A Comedy in Five Acts* (1787; Boston: Houghton Mifflin, 1920).

7. Quoted in Russel Blaine Nye, *Society and Culture in America, 1830–1860* (New York: Harper & Row, 1974), 79.

8. Whitman, poetryfoundation.org: https://www.poetryfoundation.org /articles/69391/from-preface-to-leaves-of-grass-first-edition.

9. Alexis de Tocqueville, *Democracy in America*, Vol. II (1840; New York: Vintage, 1990), 169.

10. Important studies of minstrelsy—a subject of intense academic inquiry— include Robert Toll, *Blacking Up: The Minstrel Show in Nineteenth-Century America* (New York: Oxford University Press, 1977); Eric Lott, *Love and Theft: Blackface Minstrelsy and the American Working Class* (New York: Oxford University Press, 1993); and Yuval Taylor, *Darkest America: Blackface Minstrelsy from Slavery to Hip-Hop* (New York: W. W. Norton, 2012). One movie worth mentioning in this context: Spike Lee's fascinating 2000 feature *Bamboozled*, which imagines a hit blackface television show in the twenty-first century.

11. For more on this, see the best biography on the subject, Ken Emerson's *Doo-Dah! Stephen Foster and the Rise of American Popular Culture* (New York: Simon & Schuster, 1997).

12. On Whitman's passion for popular song, see the chapter on music, oratory, and theater in David S. Reynolds's *Walt Whitman's America: A Cultural Biography* (New York: Knopf, 1995). My own view of the receptivity of Whitman, Emerson, and other nineteenth-century writers to the popular culture of their time has also been influenced by Reynolds's *Beneath the American Renaissance: The Subversive Imagination in the Age of Emerson and Melville* (Cambridge, MA: Harvard University Press, 1988). Although Abraham Lincoln was not nearly as attuned to such culture, Reynolds usefully brings this sensibility to his *Abe: Abraham Lincoln in His Times* (New York: Penguin, 2021).

13. Whitman, https://www.poetryfoundation.org/poems/45477/song-of -myself-1892-version.

14. Tocqueville, *Democracy in America*, 136.

15. Sabrina Tavernese, "Frozen in Place: Americans Are Moving at the Lowest Rate on Record," *New York Times*, November 20, 2019, https://www.nytimes.com /2019/11/20/us/american-workers-moving-states-.html. The trend has not abated in the 2020s: https://www.census.gov/library/stories/2022/03/united-states -migration-continued-decline-from-2020-to-2021.html (accessed March 12, 2023).

16. Mark Twain, *The Adventures of Huckleberry Finn* (1885; New York: Signet, 1959), 119.

17. Mark Twain, "Old Times on the Mississippi," in *Great Short Works of Mark Twain*, ed. Justin Kaplan (New York: Harper & Row, 1967), 1. This essay was first serialized in the *Atlantic Monthly* in 1875; a longer book version was published in 1883.

18. Louis Masur, *Runaway Dream: Born to Run and Bruce Springsteen's American Vision* (New York: Bloomsbury, 2013), 47. Masur notes that Peter Knobler, an early champion of Springsteen who got a preview of the song at Springsteen's Long Branch house, was intrigued to note a poster of Peter Pan leading Wendy out a window over Springsteen's bed.

19. Quoted in Reynolds, *Walt Whitman's America*, 148.

20. On Guthrie at the Forrest Theater, see Joe Klein, *Woody Guthrie: A Life* (New York: Knopf, 1980; reprint, New York: Ballantine, 1986), 145.

21. For more on this point, see Warren French, *Filmguide to 'The Grapes of Wrath'* (Bloomington: University of Indiana Press, 1973), 24–27.

22. See *Past Imperfect: History According to the Movies*, ed. Mark C. Carnes et.al. (New York: Henry Holt, 1995), 226.

23. For Steinbeck's version, see *The Grapes of Wrath*, 537.

24. Klein, *Woody Guthrie: A Life*, 144, 285.

25. Quoted in Tom Schoenberg, "Professor's Research Inspires a Rock Star," *Chronicle of Higher Education* (January 19, 1996): A7.

26. Quoted in Steve Pond, "Bound for Glory," *Live!* (February 1996): 51.

27. Dave Marsh, *Bruce Springsteen on Tour, 1968–2005* (New York: Bloomsbury, 2006), 235.

28. Springsteen, "Chords for Change," *New York Times*, August 5, 2004, https://www.nytimes.com/2004/08/05/opinion/chords-for-change.html.

29. Springsteen, *Born to Run* (New York: Simon & Schuster, 2016), 455–456.

Chapter 3   Realms of Kings

Section epigraphs: "We wanted to play because we wanted to meet girls . . . ," Kurt Loder, "*The Rolling Stone* Interview: Bruce Springsteen," *Rolling Stone*, December 6, 1984: 21, https://www.rollingstone.com/music/music-news/the -rolling-stone-interview-bruce-springsteen-on-born-in-the-u-s-a-184690/; "If you desire negro citizenship, . . ." For the text of this debate, see https://www.nps .gov/liho/learn/historyculture/debate1.htm; "Northern men, northern mothers, northern Christians . . . ," Harriet Beecher Stowe, *Uncle Tom's Cabin, or, Life among the Lowly* (1851; reprint, New York: Bantam, 1981), 442; "What I've come to learn . . . ," Chris Abani, "On Humanity," TED Talk, https://www.ted.com /talks/chris_abani_on_humanity/transcript%3Flanguage%3Den (accessed February 15, 2023); "As Americans, we are all descendants . . . ," Michael Lind,

The Next American Nation: The New Nationalism and the Fourth American Revolution (New York: The Free Press, 1995), 288.

1. The fullest treatment of this well-known "Bruce story" can be found in Dave Marsh, *Born to Run: The Bruce Springsteen Story* (New York: Dell, 1979), 193–194.

2. One example of this can be seen in Presley's 1968 television special, in which he grudgingly pays tribute to newer artists—"the Beatles, the Beards"—while subtly undercutting them at the same time (there were no "Beards," only acts like the Beatles whose hair was to Presley the conspicuous thing about them).

3. Marsh, *Born to Run*, 27; Bruce Springsteen, *Born to Run* (New York: Simon & Schuster, 2016), 38–43.

4. Chuck Berry is listed as the cowriter of "Johnny Bye Bye" on Springsteen's 1998 collection *Tracks*.

5. The following survey of American dream varieties draws on Jim Cullen, *The American Dream: A Short History of an Idea That Shaped a Nation* (New York: Oxford University Press, 2003).

6. The reputed text of the address is widely available; see, for example, https://teachingamericanhistory.org/document/a-model-of-christian-charity-2/ (accessed December 23, 2022).

7. For an e-text version of Thoreau's 1854 text of *Walden*, see https://www.gutenberg.org/files/205/205-h/205-h.htm (accessed December 23, 2022).

8. For a keen reading of Alger's novels in a historical context, see Daniel Rodgers, *The Work Ethic in Industrializing America, 1850–1920*, 2nd ed. (Chicago: University of Chicago Press, 2014); Reverend Wallace's address "The Relation of Wealth to Morals" appears in *Democracy and the Gospel of Wealth*, ed. Gail Kennedy (Boston: D. C. Heath, 1949), 73.

9. F. Scott Fitzgerald, *The Great Gatsby* (New York: Scribner's, 1925; reprint, New York: Collier, 1992), 189.

10. Quoted in Greil Marcus, *Mystery Train: Images of America in Rock 'n' Roll Music*, 3rd ed. (New York: Plume, 1990), 133–134.

11. Parker's officer status was not earned during his stint in the army but was rather an honorary commission he finagled with his carnival connections from Louisiana governor (and country singer) Jimmie Davis. See the first volume of Peter Guralnick's magisterial biography, *Last Train to Memphis: The Rise of Elvis Presley* (Boston: Little, Brown, 1994), 167.

12. Marcus, *Mystery Train*, 125–127.

13. Mikal Gilmore, "Bruce Springsteen," *Rolling Stone*, November 5–December 10, 1987, 26. For an informative history of the rise—and, to some, the fall—of *Rolling Stone*, see Robert Draper, *Rolling Stone Magazine: The Uncensored History* (New York: Doubleday, 1990; reprint, New York: HarperPerennial, 1991). Publisher Jann Wenner—who became a friend of Springsteen's—

gives his version of the story in his memoir *Like a Rolling Stone* (Boston: Little, Brown, 2022).

14. "Battle against Tradition: Martin Luther King Jr.," *New York Times,* March 21, 1956, https://timesmachine.nytimes.com/timesmachine/1956/03/21 /84878577.html?pageNumber=28.

15. Martin Luther King, Jr., "I Have a Dream," in *A Testament of Hope: The Essential Writings of Martin Luther King, Jr.,* ed. James M. Washington (New York: HarperCollins, 1986), 217.

16. Malcolm X, "The Ballot or the Bullet," speech delivered in Cleveland, Ohio, April 3, 1964, https://xroads.virginia.edu/~public/civilrights/a0146.html.

17. Frederick Douglass, "Hope and Despair in These Cowardly Times," an address delivered in Rochester, New York, on April 28, 1861, in *The Real War Will Never Get in the Books: Selections from Writers during the Civil War,* ed. Louis Masur (New York: Oxford University Press, 1992): 101.

18. King, "The Time for Freedom Has Come," in *Testament,* 165. King paraphrased these remarks in "I See the Promised Land" on April 3, 1968; see *Testament,* 286.

19. Morris Dees with Steve Fiffer, *A Season for Justice: The Life and Times of Civil Rights Lawyer Morris Dees* (New York: Scribner's, 1991), 6–49.

20. Michael Cooper, "Officers in the Bronx Fire 41 Shots, and an Unarmed Man Is Killed," *New York Times,* February 5, 1999, https://www.nytimes.com /1999/02/05/nyregion/officers-in-bronx-fire-41-shots-and-an-unarmed-man-is -killed.html. For more background on the development of "American Skin (41 Shots)," see Peter Ames Carlin, *Bruce* (New York: Touchstone, 2012), 401–406.

21. Kenneth Lovett, "Cops to Boss: Go Jump in the River, Dirtbag!" *New York Post,* June 11, 2000, https://nypost.com/2000/06/11/cops-to-boss-go-jump-in-the -river-dirtbag/.

22. Carlin, *Bruce,* 405.

23. Barack Obama and Bruce Springsteen, *Renegades: Born in the U.S.A.* (New York: Crown, 2021), 152.

24. Quoted in Lind, *The Next American Nation,* 380.

25. Frederick Douglass, "The Future of the Colored Race," first published in 1881 and revised in 1892, https://americanliterature.com/author/frederick -douglass/essay/the-future-of-the-colored-race (accessed December 30, 2022).

26. King, "An Address before the National Press Club," in *Testament,* 101.

Chapter 4   Borne in the U.S.A.

Section epigraphs: "I know one of the worst effects of this whole thing . . . ," Clinton quoted in David Maraniss, *First in His Class: The Biography of Bill Clinton*

(New York: Simon & Schuster, 1995; reprint, New York: Touchstone, 1996): 180; "Don't fret too much over this Vietnam thing, Sam . . . ," Bobbie Ann Mason, *In Country* (New York: Harper & Row, 1985; reprint, New York: HarperPerennial, 1993): 57; "And always, they would ask you . . . ," Michael Herr, *Dispatches* (New York: Knopf, 1977; reprint, New York: Vintage, 1991), 206–207; "I think one of the things that shocked people . . . ," "Bruce Springsteen Remembers 9/11 with Emotional 'I'll See You in My Dreams' Performance at 20th Anniversary Memorial," *Billboard*, September 11, 2021, https://www.billboard.com/music /music-news/bruce-springsteen-september-11-memorial-ill-see-you-in-my -dreams-video-9628017.

1. Dave Marsh, *Glory Days: Bruce Springsteen in the 1980s* (New York: Pantheon, 1987), 115–116.

2. Marsh, *Glory Days,* 116.

3. Colin Powell with Joseph E. Persico, *My American Journey* (New York: Random House, 1995; reprint, New York: Ballantine, 1996), 49.

4. Springsteen mentions the trick-or-treaters in both *Songs* (p. 164) and *Born to Run* (p. 314). Marsh discusses the matter on pp. 479–489 of *Glory Days*; the $12 million figure is cited on p. 624. For a discussion of a more spare and haunting rendition of the song, see Jon Pareles, "Hard Times and No Silver Lining," *New York Times*, December 14, 1995, C11, https://www.nytimes.com/1995/12/14 /arts/pop-review-hard-times-and-no-silver-lining.

5. Kurt Loder, "The *Rolling Stone* Interview: Bruce Springsteen," *Rolling Stone*, December 6, 1984: 21, https://www.rollingstone.com/music/music-news /the-rolling-stone-interview-bruce-springsteen-on-born-in-the-u-s-a-184690/.

6. Loder, "The *Rolling Stone* Interview."

7. Marsh, *Glory Days,* 66–77. Muller's quote appears on p. 75.

8. Loder, "The *Rolling Stone* Interview."

9. Loder, "The *Rolling Stone* Interview."

10. Springsteen describes this period—one of a number of depressive episodes— in his memoir *Born to Run* (New York: Simon & Schuster, 2016), 297, 301–310.

11. For more on this point, see the chapter "Reconstructing Dixie" in Jim Cullen, *The Civil War in Popular Culture: A Reusable Past* (Washington, DC: Smithsonian Institution Press, 1995), 108–138.

12. Herr, *Dispatches,* 71.

13. Pat Aufderheide, "Good Soldiers," in *Seeing through Movies,* ed. Mark Crispin Miller (New York: Pantheon, 1990), 81–111.

14. Aufderheide, 111.

15. For more on this, see Erich Schwartzel, *Red Carpet: Hollywood, China, and the Global Battle for Cultural Supremacy* (New York: Penguin, 2022).

16. This tidbit was revealed by Robert Santelli, Executive Director of the Bruce Springsteen Archives & Center for American Music at a 50th-anniversary symposium for *Greetings from Asbury Park*, held at Monmouth University on January 7, 2023.

17. Springsteen, *Born to Run*, 439–444.

18. Springsteen, 443.

19. Springsteen, 442–443; Springsteen, *Songs* (New York: Morrow, 1998; reprint, New York: HarperCollins, 2003), 305–306.

20. Springsteen, *Born to Run*, 442.

21. A. O. Scott, "The Poet Laureate of 9/11," *Slate*, August 6, 2002: https://slate .com/culture/2002/08/bruce-springsteen-the-poet-laureate-of-9-11.html.

22. Mark Twain, https://www.classicshorts.com/stories/phctf.html (accessed January 4, 2023).

Chapter 5   The Good Life

Section epigraphs: "I think that all the great records . . . ," *Springsteen in His Own Words*, ed. John Duffy (London: Omnibus Press, 1997), 38; "When Bruce Springsteen sings . . . ," Pete Townsend quoted in *Springsteen in His Own Words*, 94; "I think that cars today . . . ," Roland Barthes, *Mythologies*, trans. Annette Lavers (1938; New York: Noonday Press, 1972), 88; "Play, we began by saying, lies outside morals . . . ," Johann Huizinga, *Homo Ludens: A Study of the Play-Element in Culture*, trans. R. F. C. Hull (London: Routledge & Kegan Paul, 1949; reprint, Boston: Beacon Press, 1955), 38; "I love those Beach Boy songs . . . ," *Springsteen in His Own Words*, 38; "We refer to the exceptionally talented artist as gifted . . . ," Jackson Lears, *Fables of Abundance: A Cultural History of Advertising in America* (New York: Basic Books, 1994), 7; "Now I see that two of the best days of my life . . . ," quoted in James Henke, "Bruce Springsteen Leaves E Street: The *Rolling Stone* Interview," *Rolling Stone*, August 6, 1992, https://www.rollingstone .com/music/music-news/bruce-springsteen-leaves-e-street-the-rolling-stone -interview-172718/.

1. Quoted in Herbert G. Gutman, *Work, Culture and Society in Industrializing America* (New York: Vintage, 1977).

2. For a piece that traces the emergence of the term "quiet quitting" in the 2020s, see Cal Newport, "The Year in Quiet Quitting," *New Yorker*, December 29, 2022, https://www.newyorker.com/culture/2022-in-review/the-year-in-quiet -quitting.

3. Daniel T. Rodgers, *The Work Ethic in Industrializing America, 1850–1920* (Chicago: University of Chicago Press, 1978), 7.

4. Michal Addady, "Americans Put in Staggeringly Longer Hours Than Europeans Do," *Fortune*, October 18, 2016, https://fortune.com/2016/10/18/americans-work-hours-europeans/.

5. Max Weber, *The Protestant Ethic and the Spirit of Capitalism*, trans. Talcott Parsons (New York: Scribner's, 1930).

6. Robert C. Twombley and Robert H. Moore, "Black Puritan: The Negro in Seventeenth-Century Massachusetts," *William and Mary Quarterly* 24, no. 2 (1967): 235–237, https://doi.org/10.2307/1920837.

7. David R. Roediger, *The Wages of Whiteness: Race and the Making of the American Working Class* (London: Verso, 1991): 24. Roediger's work, like that of virtually all scholars who have investigated this subject since the sixties, is indebted to that of Winthrop Jordan. See Jordan's *White over Black: American Attitudes toward the Negro, 1550–1812* (Chapel Hill: University of North Carolina Press, 1968). Jordan emphasizes the racism at the roots of the very first white/black encounters, but he and others note that the institutionalization of this attitude was a process that took place over a long period of time and was not monolithic.

8. Lawrence W. Levine, "The Folklore of Industrial Society," in *The Unpredictable Past: Explorations in American Cultural History* (New York: Oxford University Press, 1993). See especially p. 295, where Levine explains the position of popular culture relative to folklore. Much of what follows draws from my book *The Art of Democracy: A Concise History of Popular Culture in the United States*, 2nd ed. (New York: Monthly Review Press, 2002).

9. For more on this classic Marxist term, see Russell Berman, *All That Is Solid Melts into Air: The Experience of Modernity* (New York: Penguin, 1988).

10. *Springsteen in His Own Words*, 90.

11. Charles R. Cross, "Reason to Believe," in *Backstreets: Springsteen, the Man and His Music*, ed. Charles R. Cross and the editors of *Backstreets* magazine (New York: Harmony, 1989), 12–15.

12. Quoted in *Springsteen in His Own Words*, 94.

13. George Will, "Bruce Springsteen's U.S.A.," *Washington Post*, September 13, 1984, https://www.washingtonpost.com/archive/politics/1984/09/13/bruce-springsteens-usa/f6502baa-a8eb-48ad-ba85-7fa848d8833e/.

14. For an insightful reading of Berry's automotive imagery, see Warren Belasco, "Motivatin' with Chuck Berry and Frederick Jackson Turner," in *The Automobile and American Culture*, ed. David Lewis and Laurence Goldstein (Ann Arbor: University of Michigan Press, 1983), 279–282.

15. Peter Marsh and Peter Collett, *Driving Passion: The Psychology of the Car* (Boston: Faber & Faber, 1986), 97.

16. Belasco, "Motivatin' with Chuck Berry," 277.

17. *Springsteen in His Own Words*, 58.

18. Dave Marsh, *Born to Run: The Bruce Springsteen Story* (New York: Dell, 1979), 256.

19. Hannah Arendt, *The Human Condition* (Chicago: University of Chicago Press, 1958). See especially Parts III, IV, and V, where Arendt offers a taxonomy of these categories.

20. Arendt, 133.

21. Henke, "Bruce Springsteen Leaves E Street."

22. Barack Obama and Bruce Springsteen, *Renegades: Born in the USA* (New York: Crown, 2021), 13.

23. Springsteen, *Born to Run* (New York: Simon & Schuster, 2016): 498–499.

24. Nick Corasaniti, "Springsteen Reopens Broadway, Ushering in Theater's Return," *New York Times*, June 27, 2021, https://www.nytimes.com/2021/06/27/theater/bruce-springsteen-broadway.html#:~:text=It%20was%20a%20line%20from,particularly%20these%20days%2C%20ous.%E2%80%9D. *Springsteen on Broadway* ran between October of 2017 and December of 2018. As the *Times* story indicates, Springsteen also performed a post-Covid limited run in 2021.

25. Springsteen, *Born to Run*, 470.

26. Andy Greene, "Springsteen Breaks Down His R&B Covers LP—and Responds to Fan Outrage over Ticket Prices," *Rolling Stone*, November 18, 2022, https://www.rollingstone.com/music/music-features/bruce-springsteen-covers-lp-fan-outrage-ticket-prices-1234632658/.

27. You can see it on YouTube: https://www.youtube.com/watch?v=xfJvrH7iQ3c.

28. Jim Cullen, "Springsteen's Early Struggles Reveal How the Record Industry Has Changed," *Washington Post*, January 5, 2023, https://www.washingtonpost.com/made-by-history/2023/01/05/springsteen-greetings-50th-anniversary/.

Chapter 6   Man's Job

Section epigraphs: "The one I love lay sleeping by me . . . ," Walt Whitman, "When I Heard at the Close of the Day," https://www.poetryfoundation.org/poems/50509/when-i-heard-at-the-close-of-the-day (accessed January 16, 2023); "Some people get a chance to change the world . . . ," Springsteen quoted in Dave Marsh, *Glory Days: Bruce Springsteen in the 1980s* (New York: Pantheon, 1987), 87; "We're taking this till we're all in the box, boys . . . ," https://twitter.com/SpringNuts/status/1617700328014745600 (accessed January 24, 2023).

1. Dave Marsh, *Glory Days*, 190–193.

2. Bobbie Ann Mason, *In Country* (New York: Harper & Row, 1985; New York: HarperPerennial, 1993), 97, 190.

3. Merle Ginsburg, "Bruce Springsteen: The Fans," *Rolling Stone*, October 10, 1985, https://www.rollingstone.com/music/music-news/bruce-springsteen-the-fans-55454/,

4. *Springsteen in His Own Words*, ed. John Duffy (London: Omnibus Press, 1997), 92.

5. This account of the Lincoln-Armstrong match relies on David Donald, *Lincoln* (New York: Simon & Schuster, 1995), 40–41; Stephen B. Oates, *With Malice toward None: The Life of Abraham Lincoln* (New York: Harper & Row, 1977; reprint, New York: Mentor, 1978), 20; and Carl Sandburg, *Abraham Lincoln: The Prairie Years and The War Years*, a one-volume edition of the six-volume biography published in 1916 and 1939 (New York: Harcourt Brace, 1954; reprint, New York: Galahad Books, 1993), 25.

6. E. Anthony Rotundo, *American Manhood: Transformations of Masculinity from the Revolution to the Modern Era* (New York: Basic Books, 1993), 31–55.

7. "Random Notes," *Rolling Stone*, January 21, 1982: 28.

8. David Donald, *Lincoln* (New York: Simon & Schuster, 1995), 66.

9. Rotundo, 83–88, 274–279. Donald makes a similar point about men sleeping together, *Lincoln*, 70. For a fuller account of interest—and anxiety—about masculinity at the turn of the century, see Gail Bederman, *Manliness and Civilization: A Cultural History of Gender and Race in the United States, 1880–1917* (Chicago: University of Chicago Press, 1995).

10. For a perceptive reading of the homoerotic strains in Springsteen's performances, see Martha Nell Smith, "Sexual Mobilities in Bruce Springsteen: Performance as Commentary," *South Atlantic Quarterly* 90, no. 4 (Fall 1991): 833–854.

11. David Masciotra, "The Dark History of *The Indian Runner*, Sean Penn's Meditation on American Violence, by Way of Bruce Springsteen," *CrimeReads*, July 30, 2021, https://crimereads.com/indian-runner-springsteen-penn/.

12. For more on this, see Bruce Springsteen, *Born to Run* (New York: Simon & Schuster, 2016), 316.

13. For these prefatory remarks in the performance of "Growin' Up" at Max's Kansas City in 1972, see https://www.youtube.com/watch?v=vrtChmpTkGU (accessed August 20, 2023). For Springsteen's cover of the Carole King classic, see https://www.youtube.com/watch?v=rjE5RalSPoI (accessed January 22, 2023).

14. Smith, "Sexual Mobilities," 842–844.

15. *Springsteen in His Own Words*, 73.

16. For more on the parallels—and contrasts—between Springsteen's and Joel's careers, including their marriages, see Jim Cullen, *Bridge & Tunnel Boys:*

Billy Joel, Bruce Springsteen, and the Metropolitan Sound of the American Century (New Brunswick, NJ: Rutgers University Press, 2024).

17. This point is made by Smith in "Sexual Mobilities," 845.

18. *Springsteen in His Own Words*, 11.

19. Marsh, *Born to Run*, 24.

20. Marsh, *Born to Run*, 209.

21. The analysis that follows is based on Jim Cullen, "Summer's Fall: Springsteen in Senescence," in *Long Walk Home: Essays on Bruce Springsteen*, ed. Jonathan Cohen and June Skinner Sawyers (New Brunswick, NJ: Rutgers University Press, 2019), 195–198.

22. Bruce Springsteen and Frank Caruso (illustrator), *Outlaw Pete* (New York: Simon & Schuster, 2014).

23. Springsteen, *Born to Run*, 503.

24. See Wordsworth, https://poets.org/poem/my-heart-leaps (accessed February 20, 2023).

Chapter 7   God and Bruce Springsteen

Section epigraphs: "Some people pray, some people play music," Dave Marsh, *Born to Run: The Bruce Springsteen Story* (New York: Dell, 1979), 23; "Springsteen sings of religious realities . . . ," Andrew M. Greeley, "Andrew Greeley on the Catholic Imagination of Bruce Springsteen," *America* 158, no. 5 (February 6, 1988): 112, 114, https://www.americamagazine.org/issue/100/catholic -imagination-bruce-springsteen; "That belief in Christ is to some a matter of life and death . . . ," Flannery O'Connor, author's note to the second edition of *Wise Blood* (New York: Harcourt, Brace, 1952; reprint, New York: Noonday Press, 1962). Springsteen read some of O'Connor's short stories after seeing the 1979 film version of *Wise Blood*. See *Glory Days*, 97.

1. Sam Tanenhaus, "Fear and Loathing: How Leslie Fiedler Turned American Criticism on Its Head," *Slate*, February 4, 2003, https://slate.com/news-and -politics/2003/02/remembering-leslie-fiedler.html.

2. Fiedler's *Playboy* piece—notwithstanding its affirmation of erotica as a genre of popular culture, it is still astonishing to consider a work of serious literary criticism showing up in such a publication—was later included in his essay collection *Cross the Border—Close the Gap* (New York: Stein and Day, 1972). I first became aware of this quotation when I read Greil Marcus's *Mystery Train* in the early 1980s. Like Fiedler, Marcus, clearly an intellectual heir of his, has little to say about the remark. Still, its presence in Marcus's book is only one way in which this book is indebted to his.

3. Their famous exchange of March/April 1776, in which Abigail urged John to remember the ladies, and his response that women had a great deal of power already and that such a move would have a fearful (specifically racial) domino effect, is widely available; see https://teachingamericanhistory.org/document /adams-adams-sullivan-letters/ (accessed February 5, 2023).

4. My understanding of this term has been influenced by the work of Catholic sociologist Andrew Greeley. See, for example, *The Communal Catholic: A Personal Manifesto* (New York: Seabury Press, 1976), *The American Catholic: A Social Portrait* (New York: Basic Books, 1977), and *The Catholic Myth: The Behaviors and Beliefs of American Catholics* (New York: Collier, 1990).

5. For a compendium of personal responses to Catholicism, including those of apostates like pornographer Bob Guccione and rock composer Frank Zappa, see Peter Occhiogrosso, *Once a Catholic: Prominent Catholics and Ex-Catholics Discuss the Influence of the Church on Their Lives and Work* (Boston: Houghton Mifflin, 1987).

6. Alexis de Tocqueville, *Democracy in America*, Vol. I (1835; New York: Vintage, 1945), 311.

7. See David Tracy, *The Analogical Imagination: Christian Theology and the Culture of Pluralism* (New York: Crossroad, 1981), especially the final chapter.

8. Peter Steinfels, "Andrew M. Greeley, Priest, Scholar and Scold, Is Dead at 85," *New York Times*, May 30, 2013, https://www.nytimes.com/2013/05/31/us /andrew-m-greeley-outspoken-priest-dies-at-85.html.

9. Greeley, *The Catholic Myth*, 56–57.

10. My information on Springsteen's Phoenix concert and the story he told there comes from Dave Marsh, "Bruce Springsteen Raises Cain," *Rolling Stone*, August 24, 1978, https://www.rollingstone.com/music/music-features/bruce -springsteen-raises-cain-2-179332/. The piece is included in *The Rolling Stone Files: Bruce Springsteen*, ed. Parke Puterbaugh (New York: Hyperion, 1996), 78–83.

11. Dave Marsh, *Glory Days: Bruce Springsteen in the 1980s* (New York: Pantheon, 1987), 87.

12. Bruce Springsteen, *Born to Run* (New York: Simon & Schuster, 2016), 17.

13. Springsteen, *Born to Run*, 17.

14. James T. Fisher has also noted the "mystically concrete sensibility" of "If I Was the Priest." See "Clearing the Streets of the Lost Catholic Generation," *South Atlantic Quarterly* 93, no. 3 (Summer 1994): 616–617. Springsteen wrote another profane song, "Tokyo," in which a soldier asks a chaplain where he can find a "cheap virgin whore," only to receive detailed instructions that evidently come from familiarity. It has never been officially released, but there are live versions online.

15. See, for example, Paul Giles, *American Catholic Arts and Fictions: Culture, Ideology, Aesthetics* (New York: Cambridge University Press, 1992): 70. Giles's book is a superb study of the way Catholicism shapes habits of thought.

16. "A great many flags tend to be waved around in the work of Catholic authors—one thinks of all the icons of national myth in Robert Altman's films—and while this might be attributable to the insecurity of aliens wishing urgently to display their patriotic allegiance, it may also be the case that Catholics have a cultural predilection for seizing upon and investing significance in emblems of communal iconography." See Giles, 156.

17. I was one of a number of people who once saw "Reason to Believe" as an affirmative song. That I now think otherwise is attributable to an interview I conducted with Dave Marsh in March of 1985 and in his own reading of the song in *Glory Days*, 137–139.

18. *Springsteen in His Own Words*, ed. John Duffy (London: Omnibus Press, 1993): 52.

19. *Springsteen in His Own Words*, 53.

20. Greeley, "Catholic Imagination."

21. Judy Wieder, "Bruce Springsteen: The Advocate Interview," *The Advocate*, April 2, 1996: 48. The piece has been reproduced on the "Greasy Lake" Springsteen fan website: https://www.greasylake.org/v6/display_article.php?essential=yes&Id=18&headline=Bruce+Springsteen%3A+The+Advocate+Interview&publication=The+Advocate&concert_date=&release_title= (accessed February 4, 2023).

22. For this observation, I am indebted to Harvard student Aaron Montgomery of Detroit, who noted it when I played the song for a class in November of 1996.

23. Jon Pareles, "His Kind of Heroes, His Kind of Songs," *New York Times*, July 14, 2002, https://www.nytimes.com/2002/07/14/arts/music-his-kind-of-heroes-his-kind-of-songs.html; Springsteen, *Born to Run*, 437–440; Peter Ames Carlin, *Bruce* (New York: Touchstone, 2012): 407–408.

24. Bruce Springsteen, *Songs* (New York: Morrow, 1998; reprint, New York: HarperPerennial, 2003): 306.

25. Springsteen, *Songs*, 305.

26. Among the theologians, Andrew Greeley has been discussed throughout this chapter. For another example, see Jerry H. Gill, "The Gospel According to Bruce," *Theology Today*, April 1988: 87–94.

27. Daniel Cavicchi, *Tramps like Us: Music and Meaning among Springsteen Fans* (New York: Oxford University Press, 1998), 42ff. On pilgrimages, see pp. 170ff. The "devotion" quote can be found on p. 157; quotations from fans come from pp. 186–187. For more deeply personal testimonials about Springsteen's

impact on the lives of his fans, including their spiritual lives, see Lorraine Mangione and Donna Luff, *Mary Climbs In: The Journeys of Bruce Springsteen's Women Fans* (New Brunswick: Rutgers University Press, 2023).

28. "Emmylou Harris in Conversation with Bob Muller," *Backstreets* no. 79 (Spring 2004): 45.

29. Kevin Coyne, "His Hometown," in *Racing in the Street: A Bruce Springsteen Reader*, ed. June Skinner Sawyers (New York: Penguin, 2004): 366.

30. Robert Coles, *Springsteen's America: The People Listening, A Poet Singing* (New York: Random House, 2003), 109–142, 166.

31. Pareles, "His Kind of Heroes."

32. Thomas J. Ferraro has described Springsteen as "a renegade priest for the East Coast working classes." See "Catholic Ethnicity and the Modern Arts," in *The Italian American Heritage: A Companion to Literature and the Arts*, ed. Pellegrino D'Acierno (New York: Routledge, 1998; reprint, New York: Garland, 1999), 347–348. See also Sawyers, ed., *Racing in the Street*, 303–304.

33. See, for example, James Woolcott, "The Hagiography of Bruce Springsteen," included in *Racing in the Street*, 126–129. Sawyers cites a number of other examples.

INDEX

Page numbers in italics refer to photos.

Abani, Chris, 74
"Across the Border," 53
action, compared to work and labor,
    128–129
Acuff, Roy, 183
"Adam Raised a Cain," 115, 124, 157, 158,
    180, 181
Adams, Abigail, 171, 224n3
Adams, John, 15, 16, 171, 224n3
Adams, John Quincy, 35
Adventures of Huckleberry Finn (Twain),
    42, 44
African Americans. *See* Blacks
Agee, James, 52
aging manhood, 141, 143, 161–167
AIDS, 192
"Ain't Got You," 74
Alger, Horatio, 65, 216n8
Allen, Thomas, 55
Allman Brothers, 158
"All Man the Guns," 100
"All That Heaven Will Allow," 188, 189
American Dream, 6, 59–80; and "Born in
    the U.S.A.," 85–86; and Fiedler on
    destiny, 169; and religion, 63–64, 173,
    174; and work ethic, 109

"American Land," 55
"American Skin (41 Shots)," xiv, 77–78,
    199
Amnesty International global tour, xii
amusement parks, 116, 151, 188
analogical imagination, 174–175
And Their Children after Them (Mahari-
    dge), 52
Aniello, Ron, 80
Animals, 156
Apocalypse Now, 95, 101
Appel, Mike, ix–x, xi, 141
Aquinas, Thomas, 174
Arendt, Hannah, 6, 127–128
aristocracy, natural, 14–21, 22, 26, 29
Arminianism, 171
Armstrong, Jack, 136, 137, 222n5
artistic traditions, American: indepen-
    dence in, 32; minstrelsy in, 37–38,
    214n10; simplicity in, 36, 38–39, 40;
    travel and transportation in, 40–43
"Atlantic City," 47, 133, 185
audience of Springsteen, 1–3, 6, 72, 199,
    209n2
Aufderheide, Pat, 96
automobiles. *See* cars

"Baby, Let's Play House," 121

"Backstreets," 147

"Badlands," 72, 188

"Balboa Park," 75

"Ballet or the Bullet" speech, 70

Bangs, Lester, 2

Barthes, Roland, 119

Beach Boys, 51, 119, 122, 122–123, 125, 126, 162

Beatles, 60, 138, 216n2

Berlin, Irving, 45, 103, 204

Berry, Chuck, 60, 71, 121, 121–122, 123, 126, 204, 216n4

Biden, Joe, 56

"Big Muddy, The," 190

Billboard charts, 34, 68, 86, 105

Birth of a Nation, 94

Bittan, Roy, 84

blackface in minstrelsy, 37–38, 214n10

Black Lives Matter, 171

Black Power, 70

Blacks: and American Dream, 68–80; enslaved, 110 (see also slavery); hairstyle of, 89; and minstrelsy, 37–38, 214n10; musical traditions of, 38, 72; and racial themes in Springsteen music, 72–80; and Reagan, 13; and urban riots (1960s), 125; and Vietnam War, 88, 100; and work ethic, 110, 112

"Blinded by the Light," 39

"Blood Brothers," 143

"Blue-Tail Fly," 38, 40

"Bobby Jean," 142

Bogart, Humphrey, 95

Bonds, Gary U.S., 71

"Book of Dreams," 154–155

Boone, Daniel, 41

Born in the U.S.A. (album), 84, 105; and masculinity, 134, 142–143; release of, xi, xii, 12; social issues in, 72–73, 74, 115, 186; tour for, 12, 92, 133, 149

Born in the U.S.A. (Cullen), 5, 7

"Born in the U.S.A.," 82, 83–87, 92, 180; and Reagan, 5, 87; and Vietnam War, 6, 76, 82, 84–85, 100–102; Will column on, 13

Born on the Fourth of July (film), 91, 96

Born to Run, 117; album cover of, 2, 140; and masculinity, 141, 147; release of, x, 11; simplicity in, 34–35; and work ethic, 114–115

"Born to Run," 30, 43, 54, 86; as American love song, 43; and masculinity, 146, 149; and work ethic, 114–115

Born to Run (memoir), xvi, 129, 167, 177

boss, origin of term, 28–29, 213m36

Boss, the, Springsteen name as, 29, 199, 213n37

Bottom Line nightclub, x, 9, 117

Bowie, David, 140

boy-culture values, 137–138, 140, 141, 143, 147

Boy George, 135

"Boys Are Back in Town, The," 140

Boys Town, 200

Brenston, Jackie, 121

Bridge and Tunnel Boys, 5

"Brilliant Disguise," 152, 188–189

Brinkley, Alan, 50

Brinkley, Christie, 150

Brinkley, David, 12

Broadway show, one-man, 130

brotherhood, 136–145

Brown, H. Rap, 70

Brown, James, 118

Bruce Springsteen and the E Street Band / Live in New York City, xiv

Bruce Springsteen Live 1975–85, xii

Bruce Springsteen's America (Coles), 198

Buffalo Springfield, 100

Bush, George H. W., 52

"Bye Bye Johnny," 60–62

"Cadillac Ranch," 123
Calvin, John, 174
Calvinism, 170, 171
"Candy's Room," 116, 148
capitalism, 10, 22, 64–65, 112–113, 115
Carlin, Peter Ames, 4
Carmichael, Stokely, 70
Carnegie, Andrew, 22–23, 65
Carr, Peter, 15
cars, 119–127; and closure of automotive
    plants, 25, 212n32; in "Growin' Up," 33,
    42; in "Thunder Road," 40–41
Carter, Ernest, 71
Carter, Jimmy, 11
Casablanca, 95
Cash, Johnny, 141
Castiles, ix
Catholicism, 162, 170, 172–179, 195, 196, *196*
"Cautious Man," 151–152, 189
Cavicchi, Daniel, 9, 197, 198
Chapman, Tracy, xii
Charlie Daniels Band, 94, 101
Cheyenne Autumn (film), 93
Chopin, Kate, 173
Christgau, Robert, 2
Christianity, 170–201
Cimino, Michael, 96
civil rights movement, 13, 51, 71, 123, 172
Civil War (U.S.), 41, 70, 93–94, 106
Clapton, Eric, 79
Clary, Bill, 136
Clay, Henry, 27
Clemons, Clarence, ix, 71, 140, 176
Cliff, Jimmy, xii
Clifford, Clark, 11
Clinton, Bill, 60, 87, 88
Clinton, Hillary, 56
Cold Mountain (Frazier), 94
Coles, Robert, 198
Columbia Records, xvi, 12, 166, 178
Coming Home, 96

concert performances, 117–119, 130, 131;
    charity donations from, 92; intimacy
    of band members in, 140, 222n10; in
    Phoenix AZ (1978), 175–177; as
    religious experience, 198; ticket prices
    for, 18, 211–212n21; Will attendance at,
    12–13, 118, 210n8; and work ethic, 118
Conrad, Joseph, 95
conservatism, 10, 27
constitutional monarchy, 15
Constitution (U.S.), 17, 70, 71
consumerism, 115
consumption, 113–114, 115
Contrast, The (Tyler), 35
Cooper, James Fenimore, 41–42, 97
Coppola, Francis Ford, 95
Country Joe and the Fish, 100
Coverdale, David, 150
Cox, Courtney, 132, 133
Crecetos, Jim, ix–x
Cross, Charles, 117–118
"Cross My Heart," 190
"Cross the Border–Close the Gap"
    (Fiedler), 169, 223n12
Culture Club, 135

Da 5 Bloods, 100
"Dancing in the Dark," 86, 148–149;
    video for, *132*, 133, 134
"Dancing in the Street," 125
Darkness on the Edge of Town, 2, 74; cars
    in, 124; release of, xi, 140–141; religion
    in, 180–181, 182, 188
"Darkness on the Edge of Town," 141
"Darlington County," 148
Davis, Clive, x
Dead Poets Society, 138
Dean, James, 157
"Death to My Hometown," 27
Declaration of Independence, 17, 64, 70,
    71, 171

Deer Hunter, The, 96, 101
Dees, Morris, 76
Demme, Jonathan, xiii, xiv, *82*, 192
democracy, 14, 15, 174
Democracy in America (de Tocqueville), 36, 174
Democratic Party, 20, 21, 56
democratic republic, 14, 47
Democratic Republicans, 16
democratic tradition and values, 5–6, 31–58; artistic, 33; Guthrie in, 45–51; in "Land of Hope and Dreams," 54; "The River" in, 44; "Thunder Road" in, 35, 43
De Palma, Brian, 100, *132*, 133
depression of Springsteen, 92, 129–130, 218n10
destiny, 169
de Tocqueville, Alexis, 36, 41, 174
Devils and Dust, xv, 6, *82*, 106, 195
"Devils and Dust," 106
Diallo, Amadou, 77, 78
Diner, 138
Dispatches (Herr), 92, 95
"Dixie," 37
"Does This Bus Stop at 82nd Street?," 114
"Do I Love You? (Indeed I do)," 79
Donaldson, Sam, 12
"Don't Worry Baby," 119
Douglas, Stephen A., 67–68
Douglass, Frederick, 70, 78, 79
"Downbound Train," 115
"Drive All Night," 182
Dylan, Bob, 31, 39, 45, 60, 72, 199

East of Eden, 157
Ed Sullivan Show, 60
egalitarianism, 146, 171–172
Emerson, Ralph Waldo, 6, 31–33, 35, 39, 44, 48
Emmett, Dan, 37, 38
"Empty Sky," 105, 197
equality, 146, 171–172

"Erie Canal," 55
E Street Band, 62, 71; and "Born in the U.S.A.," 83, 84; break up of, xiii, 130; chronology of, x, xiii, xiv, xv, xvi; as male fraternity, 140; Morello in, 53; Phoenix AZ performance (1978), 175, 176; and *Rising* album, 105; Scialfa in, 140, 152, *153*; Van Zandt in, 142; Will column on, 12–13
"E Street Shuffle, The," 138

Fables of Abundance (Lears), 127
"Factory," 124, 158
Fairbanks, Douglas, 65
family values, 186–191; and fatherhood, 155–161
fatherhood, 155–161
Federalists, 16
Federici, Danny, ix, 126
"Feel-Like-I'm-Fixing-to-Die," 100
feminism, 145, 161, 166
Fiedler, Leslie, 169, 170, 223n2
"57 Channels (and Nothin' On)," 74
"Fire," 59, 62, 147
Fitzgerald, F. Scott, 65, 173
flags, 86, 94
folk culture, 113
"Follow That Dream," 62
Fonda, Henry, 49, 50
Ford, Henry, 120, 123
Ford, John, 48–51, 52, 164
"For What It's Worth," 100
"For You," 146–147
Foster, Stephen, 36–37, 38, 39
"4th of July, Asbury Park (Sandy)," 116, 147
Frazier, Charles, 94
freedom, travel and cars in, 42, 120, 123
"Freedom," 104
Freehold, NJ, 17, 55
freeholders, 17
Frick, Henry Clay, 23

Frith, Simon, 134
Full Metal Jacket, 96
"Fun Fun Fun," 122
"Fuse, The," 105

Gabriel, Peter, xii
"Galveston Bay," 76–77, 145
Gandhi, Mohandas, 68
Gaye, Marvin, 79
gender: and audience demographics,
    2–3, 209n2; and model of masculinity,
    6–7, 133–167
Generation Z, 109
Ghost of Tom Joad, The, xiv, 52, 53, 106;
    masculinity in, 144–145, 161; socioeco-
    nomic issues in, 74–75
"Ghost of Tom Joad, The," 46, 52–53
"Ghosts," 166
"Girls in Their Summer Clothes," 54–55,
    162–163, 164, 195
Glory, 138
"Glory Days," 142
God. *See* religion
"God Bless America," 43, 51, 103–104
"God Only Knows," 162
Gone with the Wind, 94
Good Morning, Vietnam, 100
"Goodnight Saigon," 101
Graceland home of Presley, 58, 59, 63, 67
Grapes of Wrath, The, 48–51, 53
Grateful Dead, 118
Greatest Hits, xiv, 143
Greeley, Andrew, 174, 186, 187, 225n26
Green Berets, The, 95
Greenwood, Lee, 104
Greetings from Asbury Park, NJ, x, 2, 138,
    146, 1179
"Growin' Up": cars in, 33, 42; masculin-
    ity in, 138, 142, 146, 156; Phoenix
    performance of (1978), 175–176
Guthrie, Woody, 25, 39, 45–51, 52, 54, 72;
    Klein biography of, 46, 55, 91

Hair, 89
hairstyles, 89–90
Halloween trick-or-treaters, 87, 218n4
Hamilton, Alexander, 16
Hammond, John, x, 166, 178
Hammonton, NJ, Reagan campaign
    rally at, 8, 13, 20, 22, 212n25
Hanes, Bart, 88, 91
happiness, pursuit of, 41
"Hard Times Come Again No More,"
    36–37
Harris, Emmylou, 198
"Heartbreak Hotel," 68
Heart of Darkness, 95
Herr, Michael, 92, 95
High Hopes, xvi, 53, 130–131
"Highway 29," 76
"Highway Patrolman," 47, 141–142, 144,
    185
Holiday, Billie, 173
Holly, Buddy, 118, 204
Homestead, PA, 22, 23, 24
Homo Ludens (Huizinga), 119
homosexuality, 139–140, 192
"How Can a Poor Man Stand These
    Times and Live?," 55
Hughes, Sam, 134
Huizinga, Johann, 6, 119
Human Condition, The (Arendt), 128
Human Touch, xiii, 80, 187; and aging,
    161–162; geographic locus of, 74;
    masculinity in, 143, 152, 154, 160,
    161–162; reception of, 130, 161–162;
    religion in, 190, 191; satire of television
    in, 74; sexuality in, 190; and social
    injustice concerns, 51
"Hungry Heart," xi, 2, 12, 40, 41, 45, 54, 182
husbandry, 145–155

Iacocca, Lee, 87
"I Ain't Got No Home," 47
"If I Was the Priest," 166, 178–179, 224n14

"If the South Would Have Won (Woulda Had It Made)," 94
"I Get Around," 122
"I'll See You in My Dreams," 166
"I'll Work for Your Love," 162, 163, 195
"I'm a Rocker," 152
"I'm on Fire," 149
"Incident on 57th Street," 180
In Country (Mason), 87, 134
"Independence Day," 115, 158, 204
Indian Runner, The, 142
individualism, 172, 174
industrialization, 112, 128
"Into the Fire," 54, 104, 198
"It's My Life," 156
"It's So Hard to Be a Saint in the City," 140, 179
"I Wanna Marry You," 139

"Jack of All Trades," 57
Jackson, Alan, 104
Jackson, Andrew, 27, 28
Jackson, Bruce, 118
Jackson, Michael, 11, 134
Jacksonian Democrats, 18, 27
Jagger, Mick, 140
Jailhouse Rock, 61
"Jailhouse Rock," 61, 140
James, Etta, 204
Jefferson, Thomas, 15–16, 17, 41, 64
Jefferson Airplane, 100
"Jersey Girl," 148, 151
"Jesus Was an Only Son," 195
Joel, Billy, 5, 13, 101, 150, 222–223n16
John, Elton, 140
Johnny 99, 141
"Johnny 99," 25–26, 34, 47, 115, 184, 185, 199
"Johnny Bye Bye," 60–62, 216n4
Johnson, Lyndon, 90, 101
Journey to Nowhere (Maharidge), 51–52

Judaism, 172, 173
"Jungleland," 180; gas station sign in, 33, 116, 163; masculinity in, 139

Kennedy, John F., 9, 172, 210n3
Kerouac, Jack, 42, 173
Kerry, John, xv, 55, 56
King, Carole, 123, 146
King, Martin Luther, Jr., 6, 68–71, 73, 79, 172
"Kingdom of Days," 164
Kitaen, Tawny, 150
Klein, Joe, 46, 55, 91
Knights of Labor, 20
Knobler, Peter, 2
Kovic, Ron, 91
Kubrick, Stanley, 96

labor, 128; compared to work and action, 128–129
labor unions, 22–23, 24, 112
Ladd, Alan, 165
Landau, Jon, x, xi, 2, 83–84, 91
"Land of Hope and Dreams," 54, 77
"Last Man Standing," 166
Last of the Mohicans (film), 93
"Last to Die," 55–56
Lauper, Cyndi, 11
Leadbelly, 47
"Leap of Faith," 190
Lears, Jackson, 6, 127
Leaves of Grass (Whitman), 30, 33, 34, 36, 44–45, 143
Lee, Robert E., 94
Lee, Spike, 100
Lee, Tommy, 150
Leibovitz, Annie, 86
leisure, 113, 128
Letter to You, xvi, 131, 166
Let Us Now Praise Famous Men (Agee), 52
Levinson, Barry, 100
"Life during Wartime," 101

"Life Itself," 164
"Like a Prayer," 174
"Like a Rolling Stone," 39
Lil Nas X, 135
Lincoln, Abraham, 27–28, 29; and masculinity, 136–137, 137, 139; plowman capabilities of, 28; as Republican, 22, 68
Lind, Michael, 78
"Line, The," 75
Little Big Man (film), 93
"Little Deuce Couple," 122
Little Richard, 71
Live in Dublin, xv, 37, 55, 93
Live in New York City, 54
Live 1975–85 (album), 47, 186; masculinity in, 143, 147, 148, 156, 159; photo in liner notes for, 118; "River, The" from, 89–90; "Seeds" from, 26–27, 159
"Living Proof," 160, 191
"Livin' in the Future," 162
Locklear, Heather, 150
Loder, Kurt, 14
Lomax, Alan, 48
"Lonesome Day," 105
Longest Day, The, 95
"Long Good-bye, The," 152–153
Long Walk Home, 4
"Long Walk Home," 55
Lopez, Vini, ix
Lorde, 131
Lost Cause, 93, 94
"Lost in the Flood," 180, 190
love: in "Born to Run," 43; in "4th of July, Asbury Park (Sandy)," 116; in "Hungry Heart," 40; and loss, 104, 105, 141, 144; and masculinity, 141, 144, 147; in "River, The," 43
"Lucky Girl," 153
Lucky Town: geographic locus of, 74; "Living Proof" from, 160, 191; masculinity in, 143, 152, 154, 160, 161–162; reception of, 130, 161–162;

release of, xiii, 130; religion in, 160, 187, 190, 191; sexuality in, 190; and social injustice concerns, 51; "Souls of the Departed" from, 102
Luther, Martin, 174

Madison, James, 14, 15, 16, 17
Madonna, 11, 134, 173, 174
Magic, xv, 55, 56, 162, 195
"Magic Bus," 123
Maharidge, Dale, 51–52
Mahwah, NJ, closure of automotive plant in, 25, 212n32
Make America Great Again, 18
Malcolm X, 70, 172
Malden, Karl, 200
Manifest Destiny, 64
"Man's Job," 153–154
Mapplethorpe, Robert, 173
Marcus, Greil, 4, 65–66, 67
marriage: and masculinity, 143, 145–146, 150, 152, 159, 164; to Phillips, xii, xiii, 149–150, 152, 187; and religion, 187, 201; to Scialfa, xiii, 152, 153, 187; and Tunnel of Love, 105, 143, 150, 159, 187; and Working on a Dream, 164
Marsh, Dave, 2, 13, 178
Martha and the Vandellas, 125
"Mary Queen of Arkansas," 164
"Mary's Place," 105, 197
masculinity, 6–7, 133–167; and aging manhood, 141, 143, 161–167; and boy-culture values, 137–138, 140, 141, 143, 147; and brotherhood, 136–145; and fatherhood, 155–161; and husbandry, 145–155; of Lincoln, 136–137, 137, 139; and pack mentality of young males, 139; use of term, 135
Mason, Bobbie Ann, 87, 100, 134
Massey, Raymond, 157
Maverick, 97
"Maybelline," 121–122, 126

Mayfield, Curtis, 54
McCarthy, Joseph, 18
McCartney, Paul, 104
McGovern, George, 21
Mean Streets, 181, 187
"Meeting across the River," 180
Mellencamp, John, 13
Melville, Herman, 42
Mercury, Freddie, 140
meritocracy, 16, 28
Midler, Bette, 104
Milius, John, 95–96
minstrelsy, 37–38, 214n10
Missing in Action, 99
Mitchell, Greg, 2
Mitchell, Margaret, 173
Mondale, Walter, 11
monologue songs, 34
Monroe, James, 16
Morello, Tom, 53, 57
Morrison, Van, 72, 79–80
Motley Crüe, 150
Motown Records, 125, 131
"Mrs. McGrath," 93
Muller, Bob, 91
Musicians United for State Energy
    (MUSE), xi, 21
"My Beautiful Reward," 191
"My Best Was Never Good Enough," 75
"My City of Ruins," xiv, 103, 104, 196
"My Father's House," 159, 184
"My Heart Leaps Up" (Wordsworth), 167
"My Hometown," 72–73, 75, 159, 198
Mythologies (Barthes), 119

National Organization of Women, 139
Nation of Heroes, A, 104
natural aristocracy, 14–21, 22, 26, 29
N'Dour, Youssou, xii
Nebraska, 101; album sleeve of, 133–134;
    "Born in the U.S.A." from, 83–84; cars

in, 124, 148; and economic inequality,
    51, 75; fatherhood in, 158–159; and
    Guthrie, 47, 51; "Highway Patrolman"
    from, 141, 185; "Johnny 99" from, 25–26,
    185; "Open All Night" from, 147–148;
    release of, xi, 12; religion in, 183–186;
    "Used Cars" from, 124, 148, 159
"Nebraska," 47, 184
"New Timer, The," 52, 75, 161
Next American Nation, The (Lind), 78
"Night," 114
"Nightshift," 79
9/11 attack, 102–107; and *Rising* album,
    xiv, 6, 104–106, 195, 196
Nixon, Richard, 60, 90, 101, 109
"No Money Down," 121–122
"No Surrender," 117, 142, 143
"Nothing Man," 104
nuclear power, 21
Nylon Curtain, The, 101

Obama, Barack, xv, 9, 10, 56, 78, 130;
    presenting Presidential Medal of
    Freedom, xvi, 202
O'Brien, Brendan, 104
O'Brien, Tim, 100
O'Connor, Flannery, 192
Offutt, Denton, 136, 137
"Old Dan Tucker," 37
Old Testament imagery, 180, 189
O'Neill, Eugene, 173
"One Minute You're Here," 166
"One Step Up," 152
"Only the Lonely," 34
Only the Strong Survive, xvii, 79–80, 131
On the Road (Kerouac), 42
On the Waterfront, 200
"Open All Night," 115, 147–148
Orbison, Roy, 34, 116
"Out in the Street," 116
"Outlaw Pete," 164–166

"Paradise," 105, 197
Parker, Tom, 66–67, 216n11
patriotism, and Vietnam War, 88, 89, 91
"Pay Me My Money Down," 55
Penn, Sean, 142
"People Get Ready," 54
Persian Gulf War, 102
Peter Pan, 43, 215n18
Philadelphia (film), xiii, 168, 192
philanthropic work of Springsteen, 92
Phillips, Julianne, xii, xiii, 149–150, 152, 187
Phoenix (AZ) concert performance (1978), 175–177
Pickford, Mary, 65
play ethic, 6, 108, 110–131; cars in, 119–127; insight in, 116; music in, 116–117
Play It As It Lays, 187
"Poet, The" (Emerson), 32
"Point Blank," 148, 182
Pointer Sisters, 62, 72, 147
police encounters: in "American Skin," xiv, 77–78, 199; in "Highway Patrol man," 47, 141–142; in "Johnny 99," 25–26, 47, 199; in "State Trooper," 47, 185
"Pony Boy," 160
popular culture, 113–114; Vietnam War represented in, 94–102
populism, 18–19, 20, 21, 25, 171, 212n22
postmodernism, 169
"Powderfinger," 101
Powell, Colin, 85
Presidential Medal of Freedom, xvi, 53, 202
Presley, Elvis Aaron, 59–63, 68, 80; and American Dream, 6, 60, 62, 63, 65–67, 79; audience of, 199; cars in songs of, 121, 123; "Fire" written for, 147; Graceland home of, 58, 59, 63, 67; on oldies radio, 204

"Pretty Boy Floyd," 47
Prince, 11, 86, 134
producerism, of Reagan, 20
Progressive Party, 18
"Promised Land, The," 35, 72, 141, 180
Protestant Ethic and the Spirit of Capitalism (Weber), 108, 109–110
Protestantism, 170, 171, 172, 174; work ethic in, 108, 109–110, 111
"Prove It All Night," 180–181, 182
Puritans, 63–64, 163, 170; and work ethic, 108, 109, 111

Queen, 140
"Queen of the Supermarket," 56, 164

racial issues, 68–80. See also Blacks
"Racing in the Street," 119, 124–127, 146
radio stations, 203–204
"Rainmaker," 56
"Ramblin Man," 158
Rambo movies, 97, 98, 99
"Ramrod," 123–124
"Rave On," 118
Reagan, Ronald, 19–22, 46; and "Born in the U.S.A.," 5, 87; conservatism of, 10; cowboy rhetoric of, 99; Hammonton (NJ) campaign rally, 8, 13, 20, 22, 212n25; re-election campaign (1984), xii, 5, 8, 9–11, 12, 13–14, 19–22, 24, 25, 87; and veterans, 91
"Real Man," 152
"Reason to Believe," 47, 186, 225n17
Reed, Alfred, 55
religion, 7, 169–201; and American Dream, 63–64, 173, 174; and family values, 186–191; imagination in, 174–175; and inherited identity, 170; in Magic, 162, 195; in Nebraska, 183–186; and Phoenix concert (1978), 175–177; and Protestant work ethic, 108,

109–110, 111; in *Rising, The*, 195–196; in
   River, The, 181–183; and secularization
   trend, 171; and slavery, 171; in "Streets
   of Philadelphia," 192–194
Renegades: Born in the U.S.A., xvi
"Reno," 106
republic, concept of, 14–15
republicanism, 5, 15, 18, 135, 211n14;
   compared to Republican Party, 10;
   and Protestantism, 173
Republican Party, 5, 10, 16, 18, 21
Richie, Lionel, 79
Rising, The, 54, 82; and 9/11 attack, xiv, 6,
   104–106, 195, *196*; release of, xiv, 130;
   religion in, 195–196
"Rising, The," 195–196, *196*
River, The, 21; back cover images, 181;
   girls and women in, 124, 139, 148;
   release of, xi, 2, 12; religion in, 181–183;
   tour for, 92
"River, The," 43–44, 115, 182; democratic
   values in, 44, 45; fatherhood in, 158,
   160; live version of, 89–90; wife and
   mother in, 76
"Rocket 88," 121
Rock & Roll Hall of Fame, xiv, xvi
Rockwell, John, x
Rodgers, Jimmie, 25
Rolling Stone, 14, 67, 216–217n13
Rolling Stones, 111, 118, 125, 140
Roman Catholicism, 162, 170, 172–179,
   195, 196, *196*
Romney, Mitt, 20, 212n26
Ronettes, 204
Roosevelt, Franklin Delano, 18, 19, 23
Roosevelt, Theodore, 140
"Rosalita (Come Out Tonight)," 25, 29,
   117, 157
Ross, Diana, 80
Rotundo, E. Anthony, 137, 139
"Roulette," 21
"Royals," 131

Rumble Doll, 153
Rumsfeld, Donald, 56
Russo, Richard, 4
Rust Never Sleeps, 101
Ruth, Babe, 65

same-sex relationships, 139–140, 192
Sancious, David, ix, x, 71
Santelli, Robert, 2
Scialfa, Patti, xiii, 140, 152, 153, 187
Scorsese, Martin, 173, 181, 187
Scott, A. O., 105–106
Season for Justice, A, 76
secularization, 171
"Seeds," 26–27, 159, 161
Seeger, Pete, xv, 48, 55
self-made man phrase, 27, 213n33
"Self-Reliance" (Emerson), 48
September 11 attack, 102–107; and *Rising*
   album, xiv, 6, 104–106, 195, *196*
sexism, 139
sex symbols, *132, 150*
sexual abuse scandal in Catholic
   Church, 172–173, 174
sexuality: and masculinity, 134, 135, 140,
   147, 148, 149; and religion, 190, 192
Shane, 158
Shays, Daniel, 16–17, 18, 26
Shays Rebellion, 16–17
"Shut Out the Light," 86
Simone, Nina, 204
simplicity, 53; in American artistic
   traditions, 36, 38–39, 40; in "Thunder
   Road," 34–35, 40
"Sinaloa Cowboys," 75, 144–145
Sinatra, Frank, 9, 210n3
slavery, 112, 128; abolition movement,
   171; and "Blue-Tail Fly," 38; and "boss"
   term, 28; and Civil War, 93; and
   "Dixie," 37; Douglass on, 70; immobil-
   ity imposed in, 41; and minstrelsy,
   37–38; and natural aristocracy, 16;

Twain on, 44; Whitman on, 44, 45; and work ethic, 110
"Sloop John B," 162
Smith, Bessie, 204
Smith, Martha Nell, 148
Snyder, W. P., 24
social justice concerns, 51, 172
"So Far Away," 123
"Song of Myself" (Whitman), 39, 43, 51
"Song of the Open Road" (Whitman), 40, 43
Songs, xiv
Sony Music, xvi
"Souls of the Departed," 102, 160, 190–191
"South's Gonna Do It Again, The," 94
"Spare Parts," 148, 152, 189–190
Speed, Joshua, 139
"Spirit in the Night," 20, 138, 139
Springsteen, Adele Zerilli, ix, 146, 177
Springsteen, Douglas, ix, xiv, 89, 90, 155, 156, 157, 161, 178
Springsteen, Evan James, xiii
Springsteen, Jessica Rae, xiii
Springsteen, Joosten, 17
Springsteen, Lily Harper, xvii
Springsteen, Pamela, ix
Springsteen, Sam Ryan, xiii, xvii
Springsteen, Virginia, ix
Springsteen on Broadway, xvi
Stallone, Sylvester, 97, *98*, *99*, 182
Statesmen, 137
"State Trooper," 47, 185
Steel Mill, 169
Stefanko, Frank, 181
Steinbeck, John, 6, 48–51, 52, 157
Stephens, Alexander, 93
"Still in Saigon," 101
Sting, xii
"Stolen Car," 182–183, 184
Stone, Oliver, 100
Stowe, Harriet Beecher, 71
"Straight Time," 75, 76, 145

"Street Fightin' Man," 125
"Streets of Philadelphia," xiii; brotherhood in, 144; religion in, 192–194; video for, *168*, 192
Sullivan, John L., 64
Summer, Donna, 72
Sun City, xii
Swift, Taylor, 199

Talking Heads, 101
"Tenth Avenue Freeze-Out," 139
Tharpe, Rosetta, 54
Thin Lizzy, 140
"This Hard Land," 143–144
"This Land is Your Land," 45, 46–47, 51
"This Life," 164
"This Little Girl," 71
"This Train Is Bound for Glory," 54
Thoreau, Henry David, 64, 68
"Thunder Road," 54; cars in, 40–41; as democratic love song, 43; at funeral for 9/11 victim, 103; gender roles in, 146; hope in, 53, 76; play in, 116; religion in, 163, 179, 181; simplicity and frankness in, 34–35, 40
ticket prices, 18, 211–212n21
Titon, Jeff Todd, 3
"Tokyo," 224n14
Tolstoy, Leo, 40
"Tom Joad," 46, 48, 50
Top Gun, 97
"Tougher than the Rest," 150
Townshend, Pete, 117
Tracks, xiv, 86
Tracy, David, 174
Tracy, Spencer, 200
Tramps Like Us (Cavicchi), 197
"Trapped," xii
travel and transportation, 40–43; cars in (*See* cars); freedom in, 42, 120, 123
trick-or-treaters visiting Springsteen home, 87, 218n4

Trump, Donald, 19, 38

Truth, Sojourner, 45

"Tucson Train," 166

Tunnel of Love: "Ain't Got You" from, 74; conceptual focus of, 105; masculinity in, 143, 150–152, 159–160; release of, xii, 186; religion in, 186–190; and social injustice concerns, 51; "Spare Parts" from, 148, 152, 189–190

"Tunnel of Love," 151, 188

Tupac Shakur, 138

Turner, Tina, 11

Twain, Mark, 6, 42, 44, 106

Tyler, Royall, 35

Uncle Tom's Cabin (Stowe), 71

unemployment, 25, 115

United Steelworkers of America, 22, 23

"USA for Africa," xii

"Used Cars," 124, 148, 159

"Valentine's Day," 160, 188, 189

Van Halen, 125

Van Zandt, Steve, ix, xii, 59, 140, 142

Victor Records, 48

Vietnam Veterans against the War, 55

Vietnam Veterans of America, 91, 92

Vietnam War, 6, 14, 76, 82, 87–91, 93; and "Born in the U.S.A.," 6, 76, 82, 84–85, 100–102; cars in era of, 123, 125; in popular culture, 94–102

"Vigilante Man," 47

Vision Shared, A, 47

"Volunteers," 100

voting rights, 70

"Waitin' on a Sunny Day," 105

Waits, Tom, 148

"Walk Like a Man," 159–160, 187–188

Wallace, William, 65

war, 92–102; Civil War (U.S.), 41, 70, 93–94, 106; and 9/11 attack, 102–107;

tradition of victory in, 92–94; Vietnam (*see* Vietnam War); World War II, 51, 88, 89, 94–95

Washington, George, 17, 78

Watergate scandal, 90, 91

Wayne, John, 35, 56, 95, 99, 165, 166

"We Are Alive," 57, 195

"We Are the World," xii

Weber, Max, *108*, 109–110

Weinberg, Becky, 12

Weinberg, Max, 84, 86, 125

Weisen, Ron, 23

We Shall Overcome, xv, 55

Western Stars, xvi, 56, 131, 166

"Western Stars," 166

West Side Story, 139

"We Take Care of Our Own," 130

"When Doves Cry," 86

"When I Heard at the Close of Day" (Whitman), 136

"When You're Alone," 151

"Where Were You (When the World Stopped Turning)?," 104

Whig Party, 18, 27

Whitesnake, 150

Whitman, Walt: on adhesiveness between men, 140; and democratic character, 6, 32–33, 42–43, 54; interest in popular music, 39, 214n12; *Leaves of Grass*, 30, 33, 34, 36, 44–45, 143; "Song of Myself," 39, 43, 51; "Song of the Open Road," 40, 43; "When I Heard at the Close of Day," 136; in Young America movement, 35–36

Who, The, 117, 123

Wild, the Innocent & the E Street Shuffle, The, x, 2, 105, 138–139

Will, George, 12–13, 118, 210n8

Williams, Hank, 72

Williams, Hank, Jr., 94

Williams, Robin, 100

Williamson, Michael, 51–52

"Will You Still Love Me Tomorrow," 146

Wilson, Brian, 162

Wilson, Jackie, 79

Winthrop, John, 63

Wise Blood (O'Connor), 192

"With Every Wish," 190

Wolfe, Tom, 95

women: in audience of Springsteen, 3; and egalitarianism, 146–147; as family caregivers, 152; and husbandry, 145–155; as "little girls," 139; and traditional gender roles, 145–146

Wonder, Stevie, xii

Woodstock festival, 100

Wordsworth, William, 167

work, 128; and capitalism, 22, 64–65, 112–113; and closure of automotive plants, 25, 212n32; compared to labor and action, 128–129

work ethic, 108, 109–112, 135; in live performances, 118; and play ethic, 6, 108, 110–131

working class: and Boss name, 29; and Democratic Party, 56; fathers in, 156; and "Johnny 99," 25; and "My Hometown," 73; in Reagan era, 13–14, 20; Springsteen as representation of, 134; and traditional gender roles, 146; Whitman romanticism of, 33; and work ethic, 114–115; and Working on a Dream, 56; and Wrecking Ball, 57

Working on a Dream, xv, 56, 164; "Outlaw Pete" from, 164–166

"Working on the Highway," 115

"Worlds Apart," 197

World War II, 51, 88, 89, 94–95

"Wouldn't It Be Nice," 162

Wrecking Ball, xv, 27, 54, 56–57, 130, 195

"Wreck on the Highway," 183, 184

Wright, Richard, 75

"You Can Look (But You Better Not Touch)," 115

"You'll Be Coming Down," 162

Young, Neil, 101

Young America movement, 35–36

"Youngstown," 52

"You're Missing," 104, 105

Zerilli, Adele (later Springsteen), ix, 146, 177

ABOUT THE AUTHOR

JIM CULLEN teaches history at Greenwich Country Day School in Greenwich, Connecticut. He is the author or editor of twenty books, among them *The American Dream: A Short History of an Idea That Shaped a Nation* and *Bridge & Tunnel Boys: Billy Joel, Bruce Springsteen, and the Metropolitan Sound of the American Century*. His essays and reviews have appeared in the *Washington Post,* CNN.com, *USA Today, Rolling Stone*, and the *American Historical Review*, among other publications. A father of four, Jim lives with his wife, historian Lyde Cullen Sizer, in Hastings-on-Hudson, New York.